A QUIET HAVEN

A QUIET HAVEN

Quakers, Moral Treatment, and Asylum Reform

Charles L. Cherry

Rutherford • Madison • Teaneck
Fairleigh Dickinson University Press
London and Toronto: Associated University Presses

Associated University Presses
440 Forsgate Drive
Cranbury, NJ 08512

Associated University Presses
25 Sicilian Avenue
London WC1A 2QH, England

Associated University Presses
P.O. Box 488, Port Credit
Mississauga, Ontario
Canada L5G 4M2

The paper used in this publication meets the requirements of the American National Standard for Permanence of Paper for Printed Library materials Z39.48–1984.

Library of Congress Cataloging-in-Publication Data

Cherry, Charles L., 1942–
    A quiet haven : Quakers, moral treatment, and asylum reform /
Charles L. Cherry.
        p.   cm.
    Bibliography: p.
    Includes index.
    ISBN 0-8386-3341-2 (alk. paper)
    1. Psychiatry—Moral and ethical aspects—History—18th century.
2. Psychiatry—Moral and ethical aspects—History—19th century.
3. Society of Friends—Charities.   4. Psychiatric hospitals—
England—History.   5. Psychiatric hospitals—United States—
History.   I. Title.
RC438.C47   1989
616.89′0088286—dc19   88-48019
                                                            CIP
                                                            Rev.

PRINTED IN THE UNITED STATES OF AMERICA

For Caroline

CONTENTS

ACKNOWLEDGMENTS

I am grateful to a number of individuals for assistance with a project that became a pleasant, if sometimes frustrating, diversion from my duties as an academic administrator. First, to the late Richard Hunter for his friendship and encouragement, and to Barbara Curtis for her enthusiastic guidance through Quaker bibliography; to Edwin Bronner and his able staff of the Quaker Collection of Haverford College Library, especially Elisabeth Potts Brown, Diana Alten, Eva Myer, and Sheilah Hallowell; to Villanova University for financial and logistical support, especially to Rev. Lawrence Gallen, O.S.A., Kay Lawless, Nora Ferry, Loretta Stango, and Gina D'Ascanio; to the English-Speaking Union for a Cooper-Wood Memorial Fund travel grant enabling me to visit York Retreat; to Haverford College for a T. Wistar Brown Fellowship in Quaker Studies for 1982–83; to the Lilly Foundation for a summer grant at the University of Pennsylvania to attend a seminar on "Technology and Society"; to John Gillespie, for his courtesy and assistance with my research at York Retreat; to Bill and Margaret Sessions, knowledgeable York Friends and publishers, for their research assistance and kindness to me and my family during our stay in York.

A number of library and hospital staffs were most helpful: Villanova University's Falvey Memorial Library, especially Andrew Zand; the University of Pennsylvania Library; the College of Physicians Medical Library, especially Ellen Gartrell; the Library of the Religious Society of Friends at Friends House, London, especially Malcolm Thomas; Swarthmore College Library; the University of York's Borthwick Institute of Historical Research, especially D. M. Smith; Archives of Friends Hospital, especially the current and former directors of the Hospital—James M. Delaplane and William P. Camp; David Arnold, Director of Development at Friends Hospital, and his associates Allison Staib and Judy Kelius; Priscilla M. Tainter of The Sheppard and Enoch Pratt Hospital.

I owe debts as well to a number of individuals: to Gerald Grob, Norman Dain, Russell Maulitz, Andrew Scull, and Rosemary Stevens for their early guidance; for their readings and recommendations to George Murphy, Patricia D'Antonio, Sheilah Marshall, John Immerwahr, Michael Hones, and Hugh Ormsby-Lennon; for research assistance to Sterling Delano, Joseph McGowan, Robert Wilkinson, Karen Soisson, Ronni Rosenberg, Michael Keenehan, Anne Gallagher, Robert A. Clark, and Mark Finnane; to Morris Gorlin for his criticism of my work on Morgan Hinchman and to Frank Fox for materials on Warder Cresson; to Edward Teitelman for his loan of building committee materials on Friends Hospital. For permission to use unpublished materials I owe thanks to Catherine Higgins of Bryn Mawr College; to Thomas Hodgkin of Warwickshire for permission to quote from Thomas Hodgkin's papers on microfilm at Friends House, London; to the Library Committee of London Yearly Meeting of the Religious Society of Friends for permission to quote from the Southern Retreat records; to the University of York's Borthwick Institute of Historical Research for permission to quote from York Retreat and Tuke papers; to the editors of *Medical History* and *Quaker History* for permission to use materials published earlier in those journals.

I thank my children, Helen and Greg, for their patience and for allowing me to use the computer.

The dedication is to my wife who, in editing as in life, makes all things new.

A QUIET HAVEN

1
QUAKERS AND ASYLUM REFORM

Thesis

Born in a period of religious anarchy, when sects were spawned on marginal differences of rite or rule, Quakerism not only survived but prospered, so that by 1661 its estimated strength was around forty thousand members. Its survival was the result of a strong corporate meeting structure and an equally strong support system among individual members. Religious aberrations were controlled by a loving system of restraint as Quakers, while remaining religious enthusiasts, sought social legitimacy. This tradition of internal discipline, loving restraint, and sensitivity to public mores operated as well when Quakers became involved in institutional care of the mentally ill. The theoretical framework for their care of the "distracted" emanated from a dynamic amalgam of Quaker theology, Scottish and Associationist philosophy, contemporary theories of faculty psychology, and common sense, but the institutional use of "moral treatment" was a more explicit outgrowth of the support systems already mentioned. The use of this therapeutic approach, its influence, and eventual disfavor are best seen in the care provided at York Retreat and Frankford Asylum (now Friends Hospital); the establishment of such Quaker-influenced institutions as McLean Asylum for the Insane, New York Hospital's Bloomingdale Asylum, the Hartford Retreat, and Sheppard-Pratt Hospital; and a detailed discussion of events such as the proposed Southern Retreat and the Hinchman case.

I attempt to structure a context in which to examine Quakers and the treatment of the mentally ill from 1652 to 1850. I do so from a sociohistorical/religious point of view, keeping in mind Vieda Skultans' remarks:

Psychiatry deals with people and it is, therefore, inevitably influenced by the values, beliefs and attitudes important at a particular period. Thus the investigation of ideas about madness is no longer a straightforward historical narrative but acquires a socio-historical dimension. As an ideal, this is

highly commendable, in practice it may not be possible to document all
aspects of society. Nevertheless, the goals are worth pursuing. (1975, 145)

My study should be seen as another reminder that knowledge is not
easily divisible.

The important events leading up to the eighteenth- and nineteenth-
century reform movements in the care of the insane have been ably
documented. I provide but a cursory overview of them in this introduction. My more important task is to identify some of the major
critical attitudes toward the history of reform and more particularly
toward the Quaker reform movement. I do so by way of framing my
central thesis and its more detailed development in the later chapters.

Background

The sufferings of three figures were important to the eighteenth-
century reform movement in the care of the insane. The first was
George III, that troubled monarch whose mental instability, perhaps
caused by porphyria, drew the attention of the public to a problem
that far too often had been consigned to the attic, jail, and private
madhouse. The second was James Norris, an insane American whose
alive but emaciated body was discovered chained in Bethlem Hospital
in June 1814. A sketch of this pathetic figure etched by George
Cruikshank was exhibited by Edward Wakefield to the Select Committee of the House of Commons on Madhouses in 1815, causing the
appropriate reactions of pity and horror that helped reinvigorate
reform movements and parliamentary investigations. The third was
Hannah Mills, a young Quaker woman who died on 30 April 1790
under mysterious circumstances at York Asylum and whose case motivated William Tuke and other York Friends to establish York Retreat.

The interest in asylum reform inspired by these figures, complemented by the accompanying publications and investigations, showed
that in fact when it came to medical care of the insane, the medical
emperors had few clothes. Particularly damning were the statements
before the 1815 parliamentary committee of asylum physicians such as
John Haslam and Thomas Monro. Their testimony showed how
meager was the theoretical knowledge of insanity and how ineffectual
and inconsistent the methods of treatment. Small wonder then that
the successful approach to the treatment of the insane developed by
the Quakers at York Retreat, as reported by Samuel Tuke in his
influential *Description of the Retreat* (1813) and favorably reviewed by
the popular Sydney Smith in *Edinburgh Review,* would meet with such

a positive response from politician and layman alike. T\
approach seemed to provide a satisfying, successful solu
complex issue. Small wonder too that by contrast with the
press afforded the majority of traditional asylums and their at
physicians, the role of the Tukes and Friends as enlightened ar.   ..ɔ
would lead to imitative efforts in England and the United States, to a
heightened sense of optimism as to the reform of asylum care and the
successful use of treatment, and to the apotheosis of William Tuke in
the history of psychiatry as a noble figure who in concert with Philippe Pinel helped foment a positive revolution of benevolent care of
the insane.

However, the appraisal of Tuke and the efforts of the Quakers at
York Retreat has not always been consistently positive. Critical studies
of moral treatment as conceived and practiced by Friends fall, like the
general history of psychiatry, into three related approaches.

The first is that of the critic who perceives the history of psychiatry
as a movement toward the truth, not as the history of science with its
victory over a disease through an evolving understanding, grounded
in research, of the particular ailment and its treatment, but rather as a
humanistic identification of a pattern of figures (like Tuke) who
through quasi-scientific or simple humanitarian efforts seem to mark
advances in the treatment of the insane. Persons such as Pinel and
Tuke thus come to be placed in the pantheon of those who somehow
rise above the confusion of their age to establish new, more con-
structive patterns of treatment and care of the insane. Gregory
Zilboorg's *A History of Medical Psychology*—with its discussion of the
"great men who devoted their lives to psychiatry and who made
creative contributions to the welfare of the mentally sick" (1941,
409)—and *The History of Psychiatry* by Alexander and Selesnick
(1966) are two examples of this approach to the history of psychiatry.

The second approach is a more iconoclastic appraisal of the past that
attacks the "great men" view, if not by debunking heroes at least by
casting a cold eye on their achievements. Michel Foucault's work
(1965) is important in this respect and has drawn numerous followers
and imitators, attracted no doubt by the brilliance of his dense prose
and the belligerence of his Marxist critique. At its best, as in Foucault's
work and the sociological studies of Scull (1979 and 1981) and
Goffman (1961), there is a creative corrective to a distorted, romantic
sense of the past. One is also grateful for the assertive scholarship and
creativity of such gadflys as R. D. Laing, Thomas Szasz, and David
Rothman, who though they may indulge in debates with the establishment remain stimulating and positive.

The third, less controversial approach involves such figures as the

remarkable mother-son team of Ida Macalpine and Richard Hunter,
Keith Thomas, Michael MacDonald, and others who have been more
concerned with establishing accurate records and proper contexts and
ultimately see the history of psychiatry as "a record of perennial
problems, recurrent ideas, disputes and treatments, trailing in the
wake of medicine and exhibiting paradoxically—as medicine did of
old—a mixture of as many false facts as false theories" (Hunter and
Macalpine 1963, ix) but who embrace even contemporary confusion
as an important part of this history. Walter Pagel, discussing his own
historiography of science in his recent study of Joan Baptista Van
Helmont, notes the following:

> An attempt has been made to resituate [Van Helmont's scientific and
> medical discoveries] in their original context and background, which were
> neither modern, nor scientific, nor medical. The savant is presented as an
> integrated whole in his own personal view of God, the world, and man—
> "idiocentrically"—by contrast with a selection of what strikes us as relevant
> and meaningful today—"nostricentrically." It demands an effort at con-
> verting oneself into a contemporary of the savant. (1982, ix)

Contextual history is essential, not least because psychiatry, as a less
rigorous, less predictable discipline than formal medicine, has been
more directly influenced by social, philosophical, legal, and religious
pressures. Thus it demands an interdisciplinary approach.

The fact that when it came to care of the insane, Quakers seemed to
succeed where many others had presumably failed and that their
approach appeared a radical contrast to then current theory—an approach that was not wholly without precedent or in its ultimate efforts
not without failure—has raised a number of questions in historians'
minds. Why and how did Quakers come to develop the theory of
moral treatment? By what process did they arrive at a rejection of
medical therapeutics? To what specific factors can their success be
attributed? What were the liabilities of their approach? While the
three scholarly approaches are not mutually exclusive, at this point in
contemporary scholarship the most provocative answers to these questions have been found not in the reassuring but sometimes treacly
historians of the "great men" school but in those with more iconoclastic instincts. The most important of these writers are Michel
Foucault and Andrew Scull.

Foucault

In *Madness and Civilization: A History of Insanity in the Age of Reason*
(1965), a work that is often profoundly exciting and yet sometimes

more brilliant than useful, Michel Foucault likens the incarceration of the mentally ill beginning in the seventeenth century to the ships of fools of an earlier time; both were a way for society to isolate and exclude what it feared or spurned. The madperson no longer was an eschatological figure like Bosch's demons, but more domesticated and accessible and for this reason all the more threatening and fearsome. That is, people began to see that madness could strike anyone, for no clear reason.

Beginning in France around 1656 with the founding of the Hôpital Général, a number of institutions arose that were designed to rid the streets of idle poor, prostitutes, vagabonds, and the insane. These institutions became a semijudicial "third order of repression" (40) beyond the police and courts. Civil law joined with a sort of moral imperative to demand that the idle work and that liberty be traded for a modicum of bed and board. Sequestering a potentially unruly and licentious horde of the lower orders was also a way of providing social protection against riots and agitations, just as isolating lepers had once been a way of preventing the spread of the disease. In a fallen world, it was everyone's duty to work; not to do so was a form of sin subject to punishment and moral correction. Alluding again to the exclusion of lepers, Foucault says: "The old rites of excommunication were re-vived, but in the world of production and commerce" (57). The mad were included with the poor and beggars because there was a clear sense that they had personal responsibility for their illness and thus their sloth.

The neoclassical period, unlike the Renaissance, was ashamed of unreason and felt the need to hide it in the silence of an institution. The mad were often exhibited for profit, but they appeared behind bars rather than as a part of everyday existence having symbolic value, as was the case in the Renaissance. Madness was not merely a bestial element; the madperson was a beast—devoid of any humanity and to be treated as such in the institutions. Thus caretakers of the mad resorted not to medicine but to harsh discipline and brutal treatment in order, says Foucault, not "to raise the bestial to the human, but to restore man to what was purely animal within him" (75). The notion of madperson as beast was not used as in the medieval iconography or bestiary to represent a visage of evil; the madperson was simply a beast, an unnatural order-threatening entity capable of cracking or destroying the links in the great chain of being.

The medical practice of the time, based on principles of solids and fluids, was quickly seen as useless in dealing with madness; orthodox belief and scientific process cried out for clear mind-body correlations, but these were not evident. Foucault notes that some madness could be explained in a more unitary fashion, as is the case with imagination.

is imagination is not madness but a possible step toward it. Imagation assaults reason with a battery of images both fantastic and unreal; madness begins beyond imagination when the mind seizes these images and affirms them as real and true. Instead of simply evaluating the image, the mad surrender to it; in such madness the mind is limited to the locus of appearance that the image defines. In the seventeenth and eighteenth centuries the mad were seen not so much as victims of illusion but the responsible creators of that illusion and thus the cause of their own error. They caused their own unreason or nonbeing.

In discussing the eighteenth-century relationship between doctors and patients, particularly with respect to methods of treatment, Foucault notes that society moved from the use of medicine as a moral therapy to remove sin and error to a simple physical therapy used to regulate and punish. Medicine existed not to restore the patient to some external truth but to produce a series of internal effects of a mechanical and psychological nature. The cures attempted joined together physical intervention with psychological appeal, yet the two "complement each other, but never interpenetrate" (178). In the neoclassical period one could only separate physical and moral treatment when "fear is no longer used as a method of arresting movement, but as a punishment . . . in short, when the nineteenth century, by inventing its famous 'moral methods,' . . . brought madness and its cure to the domain of guilt" (182). Psychology and moral treatment did not exist until the practitioner began to establish a discourse with unreason.

Having established these theoretical foci, Foucault concludes his book with a direct attack on two monuments of humanitarian treatment of the mentally ill—Tuke and Pinel. He theorizes that Tuke and the Quakers, by coercing the patients at York Retreat to follow established norms of religious conduct and sanity, manipulated the patients' fear, and this conduct was, for its depth and subtlety, more profoundly brutal than physical mistreatment. Quakers attempted by discourse with unreason to create an internalized sense of guilt that would restore patients to sanity and proper religious decorum. Tuke "substituted for the free terror of madness the stifling anguish of responsibility; fear no longer reigned on the other side of the prison gates, but now raged under the seals of conscience" (247). Thus the mad, driven by guilt, sought self-esteem by the return to reason, a process facilitated by the regularity and restorative value of work and the depersonalized "tea parties" in which the mad were pressured to conceal any individual propensities in order to integrate themselves into the whole community. Madness became externalized, subject to observation in a world of judgment, silent until given a means of discourse in the later development of psychoanalysis. For Foucault "the absence of constraint in the nineteenth-century asylum is not unreason liberated but madness long since mastered [by authority]" (252). In the "family" atmosphere, the insane became children dominated by adult authority figures. The great battle of reason and unreason was reduced to a family squabble.

Pinel's asylums also became an instrument of moral uniformity. While showers had been used in medicine of the neoclassical period in an attempt to relax the nervous system or to shock the mad back to sense, according to Foucault Pinel utilized them as a means of repression and punishment, forcing the patient to internalize the sense of authority controlling her life and creating a sense of remorse. Foucault also notes that in Pinel's asylum patients were ostracized and isolated for three offenses against established values: religious fanaticism, theft, and resistance to work. Pinel and Tuke also introduced the medical figure not as a scientist but as a kind of family head who creates a moral and social order as a way of leading patients to mental health. Foucault concludes that Pinel and Tuke, in their attempts to liberate the insane, merely created a "gigantic moral imprisonment" (278).

Foucault's work is a densely metaphorical, far-ranging treatise that has stimulated a number of analyses of post-Enlightenment efforts to deal with the confinement of the insane, the criminal, and the poor. As the "most audacious and learned challenge to the medical Whig tradition," Foucault's book has had a widespread influence, even though many of its historical points are questionable.[1] In attempting to undermine the sense of Enlightenment achievement in the eighteenth century, Foucault provides a useful tonic to the "great men" theories and an insightful effort to get at the "deepest meanings of madness and the underlying structures of knowledge within a given period" (Midelfort 1980, 259). He raises important questions and challenges traditional assumptions. Was the separation of deviants in institutions part of a conspiracy of professionals and bureaucrats to seize power over the infirm so that they could be reformed by a mixed regimen of medicine and manipulation, or was it more simply a case of humanitarian optimism that, although ultimately doomed to failure, was nonetheless sincere? Was the end of confinement to be control or protection from worse fates outside the asylum doors? Were doctors selfishly advancing the notion of confinement or merely responding to societal need? Were the humanitarian values espoused by such reformers as Pinel and Tuke real achievements or merely subtle manipulative controls? Was the eighteenth-century Enlightenment a legitimate social and intellectual achievement or merely a sham? Foucault is clear in his answers to these questions, as can be seen in his comments regarding the Quakers. In their desire to inculcate in their patients a "need for esteem" the Quakers according to Foucault denied the imaginative instincts of their patients and straightjacketed them in a bourgeois value system.

Scull

In another important and related work—*Museums of Madness: The Social Organization of Insanity in Nineteenth-Century England* (1979)—Andrew Scull examines the attempt by the medical profession in England to determine who was mad and who should be confined and from the mid-eighteenth to mid-nineteenth century to identify a deviant population of the insane among England's masses and confine them in bureaucratically organized state-supported institutions. Scull shares much of Foucault's scepticism and argues that these reform efforts were not simply "a triumphant and unproblematic expression of humanitarian concern" (15) but were closely related to capitalism as a social phenomenon.

As Scull rightly indicates, one must look not simply at the social intentions of reformers, who always perceive their work to be beneficial: whether confining or freeing the mentally ill from institutions, leveling whole neighborhoods of row homes to make way for high-rise public housing, or busing large numbers of students in the name of social engineering. One must cautiously look beyond the rhetoric to the reality. So too with the notion that with the decline of traditional religion and the growth of a healthy scientific skepticism came advances in secular understanding and the treatment of medical problems, including mental illness. Scull is clearly on firm ground in dismissing this idea. As can be seen later in an overview of medicine and mental illness in the eighteenth century, few real breakthroughs were achieved, and the usual "cures" ranged from the curious to the outrageous.

Scull notes that the sense of moral outrage about the treatment of the insane came about because of a changed view of the insane. The person afflicted with madness was perceived as essentially lacking in order and discipline but was nonetheless seen as a human rather than a mere brute. Gradually people like John Ferriar at Manchester Lunatic Asylum and Edward Long Fox at Brislington House established alternative modes for treatment of the insane that were in strong contrast to the more traditional brutalizing approach. York Retreat became the national model for "moral treatment" of the insane, that is, for a more humane, restrained approach to mental illness; but Scull, influenced by Foucault, talks of this effort as one of transforming the lunatic "into something approximating the bourgeois ideal of the rational individual" through the "internalization of moral standards" (69). By analogy, Scull argues that concurrently the heads of industry perceived that in order for people to function effectively in factory situations they needed to internalize new attitudes and work skills. Thus Tuke, accustomed to mercantile success through hard work and self-discipline, attempted to inculcate a similar value system to achieve the recovery to reason of his patients.

Tuke's system of classifying patients by the degree of reason they displayed and withholding privileges accordingly was a way of managing patients just as much as the use of whips and chains. As Scull notes, it is a "cruel irony [that] . . . the same central feature of moral treatment which gave it its appeal as a humanitarian reform and which allowed its transformation into a repressive instrument for controlling large numbers of people" (121) was popularized by the success of York Retreat. Moral treatment weakened physicians' arguments for the hegemony of medicine in the treatment of mad people. Yet the Quakers continued to use the medical terminology of "mental illness," "patient," and "treatment"; they failed to develop their own terminology and a clear methodology and theoretical construct for moral treatment. In fact, Tuke argued that this should not be done. As a result, the doctors eventually recaptured power. As Scull points out, the Friends' refusal to reduce moral treatment to a set of procedures was praiseworthy, but it eventually weakened this approach; they "delayed the rise of an occupational group claiming training in the new therapy" (159). Also, the medical people wisely argued that the instrument of the inviolable soul is the brain, and its diseases are the source of all mental illness. Since its source is somatic (even though this fact could not be clearly demonstrated), a medical approach is best to treat it.

The strongest aspects of Scull's book are his analysis of exactly how the medical profession managed to recapture control of the treatment of mental illness from the enlightened amateurs with their moral treatment, and how the explosive growth of the asylums in England led to the mere warehousing of patients. His work is less firmly grounded when he moves to a more abstract level of argument, discussing Quaker intentions in dealing with the mentally ill, and arguing that the emphasis at York Retreat on the search for self-esteem

and the dignity of labor betokened the subtle imposition of a bourgeois value system that had as its ultimate end the development of an
effective, efficient system for remodeling individuals to the workplace.

Scull is not simply an iconoclast, nor is he by any means damning
the Friends for their efforts. He rightly notes that despite noble
intentions, the results of the revolution inspired by York Retreat were
far from satisfactory. He is not merely being polemical, as he later
charges Szasz and Rothman, when he portrays asylum inmates as
being "caught up in some largely arbitrary scapegoating processes"
(256). His book is a useful corrective to a blinkered appraisal of a
humanitarian revolution as totally positive. York Retreat was in fact a
bit of an anomaly—a wholesome, well-intentioned experiment that
was successful in part because of the scale of the effort, its setting, the
coherent intentions, and religious homogeneity of its prime movers.
What Scull fails to take into consideration is the religious background
and tradition both of Quaker philosophy and Quaker benevolence. It
is these factors, I believe, more than any abstract social manipulation,
that inspired Friends to establish York Retreat and made them sensitive to the concept of mental illness. The roots of that concern are to
be found in Quaker history and in contemporary attitudes toward
reason and imagination.

The thrust of my book is fourfold. First, to examine how a traditional identification of Quakers with religious enthusiasm made them
sensitive to the issue of mental illness and how such a social identification persisted into the eighteenth century and beyond. Second, how
within the context of eighteenth-century medical theory, the Quaker
approach to mental illness and the entire mind-body dilemma was
inspired by their sense of the "Inner Light," that is, by religio-
philosophical considerations more than the socioeconomic factors
suggested by Foucault and Scull. Third, I hope to show that the
establishment of York Retreat was, in part, a desire for religious
exclusivity born out of the Quakers' traditional sense of separateness
from English society, with the entire approach of moral treatment
hearkening back to the dissenting tradition of George Fox and early
Quaker leaders. Finally, I will examine the direct influence of York
Retreat on American care of the insane, in particular the establishment
and development of Friends Hospital, the first nonprofit mental hospital in the United States. In doing so, I will look at the concept of
moral treatment and how one of its offshoots, the idea of moral
insanity, become problematic in the American setting.

Ultimately, my book should be seen as a corrective to a rigid
identification of Friends with this or that social or economic movement; such identifications may make sense, but not if the basic reli-

gious tenets inspiring Quaker involvement in matters of social action are overlooked or deemphasized. The Quakers should be perceived in context, not just as reformers in an alien field but in terms of their history in British and American society and their distinctiveness as close-knit dissenters who somehow survived the religious imbroglios of the seventeenth century. Just as the historian of a period must take into account regional differences—that, for example, attitudes toward the insane in sixteenth-century Germany differed substantially from those in France—so too must the historian of ideas resist the temptation to lump Quakers too quickly with their fellow citizens and attribute to them similar motives and beliefs. A group as different as the Quakers, with their own distinctive beliefs, speech, and dress, remained anomalies in an eighteenth-century England that was relatively homogeneous both politically and religiously. Yet the impact of Friends on that society (and in America) not only in terms of commercial success but, more importantly, of social change with regard to slave, asylum, and prison reform, was substantial. This book deals with part of that history and the motivation for it.

2

QUAKERS AND ENTHUSIASM

This chapter aims to show how Friends were consistently attacked for their religious enthusiasm, how they were sensitive to and responded to such attacks, and, by implication, how such sensitivity would ultimately shape their approach to mental illnes. My purpose is not to give the early history of a religious sect but to show how that history would incline Quakers toward a fruitful and influential concern for mental illness. It is in the seventeenth century where the roots of Quaker concern for the mentally ill are to be found.

George Fox and the Mentally Ill

Francis Bugg, the vigilant ex-Quaker who wrote a series of anti-Quaker books and pamphlets at the end of the seventeenth century, traced the origins of Quakerism to the imprisonment of John Fretwell in 1650 by Justice Bennet at Derby for disturbing public worship (Bugg 1696, 4). Bugg saw the seeds of disorder and anarchy (or "quaking") that would mark this religious movement. A more common date for the genesis of Quakerism is 1652, when George Fox had a vision on Pendle Hill—a dramatic but not quite accurate supposition, since by 1646–48 there were meetings of Friends in Nottingham, Clawson, Eaton, and Leicestershire (Barbour 1964, 36).

One cannot question, however, the rapid growth of Quakerism. Five hundred Friends were convinced before 1652; five-thousand by 1654, twenty-thousand by 1657 (Barbour 1964, 182). From 1650 to 1700, Friends published 3,750 titles by 650 authors, including eighty-two women (Barbour and Roberts 1973, 14). *Early Quaker Letters from the Swarthmore MSS to 1660* (Nuttall 1952), a repository of letters sent to Fox and Margaret Fell, indicates that Quakers were quickly and well organized and counted among their leaders a number of strong, disciplined figures, none more so than George Fox, who was the prime mover in the organization and growth of the Society of

Friends. Braithwaite (1955, 274) may say that Dewsbury was the "wisest and sweetest of Friends," Barbour (1964, 38) may call James Nayler the "best writer on theology among early Friends," Ellwood (Crump 1900, 13) may admire Burrough as a "scholar," but it was Fox, as first among equals, who shouldered the major burdens of shaping a disparate group of independent religious spirits into a sect, who in his constant imprisonment and foreign travel provided a model of patient endurance and commitment, who was driven to do God's work far from the comforts of Swarthmore Hall, and who set the tone and direction of Quakerism until his death. Certainly Emerson's sense of Quakerism as the lengthened shadow of George Fox rings true; it is to Fox that one may look for the personal and theological character of this burgeoning religious body in the seventeenth century. More than anyone else, he took a potentially splintered collection of individuals in a religiously chaotic period and shaped it into a movement that not only endured but grew so that by 1661 it numbered around forty-thousand members.

Since early Quakerism cannot be discussed separately from the personality of George Fox, and since what has accrued around Fox's personality touches so directly upon the central concerns of this book—questions of madness and enthusiasm, medical treatment and miracles, religion and magic—I must spend some time on this central figure. Inevitably this means considering Fox's *Journal*. This work, written in 1675, was not published until 1694, so that the official version homogenized by Thomas Ellwood, Fox's literary executor according to the Quaker custom of peer review of publications, is revealing both for what is omitted and what remains. As Nuttall says, despite the deletions, Fox still manages to "speak through" (1961, 50).

Quaker concern for the mentally ill dates back to George Fox's activities described in his *Journal* (1694) where he encountered and healed several individuals who were "distracted" or "moping" or "troubled." The first mention of such encounters in the *Journal* occurred in 1649 at Skegby at the home of Elizabeth Hooton, Fox's first convert. It concerned a woman "possessed two and thirty years" who had been bothering Friends at a meeting. Fox expressed concern over such intrusions:

> At that time our meetings were disturbed by wild people, and both they and the professors and priests said that we were false prophets and deceivers, and that there was witchcraft amongst us. The poor woman would make such a noise in roaring, and sometimes lying upon her belly upon the ground with her spirit and roaring and voice, that it would set all Friends in a heat and sweat. And I said, "All Friends, keep to your own, lest that

which is in her get into you," and so she affrightened the world from our meetings.

Then they said if that were cast out of her while she were with us, and were made well, then they would say that we were of God. This said the world, and I had said before that she should be set free.[1]

Friends then prayed with her and she was healed:

She rose up, and her countenance changed and became white; and before it was wan and earthly; and she sat down at my thigh as I was sitting and lifted up her hands and said, "Ten Thousand praise the Lord," and did not know where she was, and so she was well; and we kept her about a fortnight in the sight of the world and she was wrought and did things, and then we sent her away to her friends. And then the world's professors, priests, and teachers never could call us any more false prophets, deceivers, or witches after, but it did a great deal of good in the country among people in relation to the Truth, and to the stopping the mouths of the world and their slanderous aspersions. (1975, 43)

These remarks support the contention of Howard Collier (1944, 280–88) and Henry Cadbury (1948, 19–32) that many Friends, as former Seekers, equated miracles with inspiration and that early Quaker leaders tried to accommodate such views by attempting various cures. Although Fox characterized many such efforts as "mad whimsey," the testimony of the *Journal* and certainly of the reconstructed "Book of Miracles" suggests possession on his part of remarkable healing powers and his belief that the display of such powers would not hurt his growing religious movement. Thus in the case cited above of the woman at Skegby, Fox perhaps saw miracles as a way of legitimizing Quakerism among its enemies.

Other Friends disagreed. "The Book of Miracles," a fragmentary record of the more than 150 "miracles" or cures associated with Fox, was suppressed during his lifetime. Friends such as Penington, Barclay, and Ellwood, concerned that talk of miracles might too closely ally Friends with fanatical sects and Roman Catholics, decided not to disseminate the "Book" and even excised accounts of miracles appearing in the original manuscript of the *Journal*. Barclay was especially forceful on this point:

Some rash and unwise Protestants have sometimes said that if we really have the direct call that we lay claim to, we ought to confirm it by miracles. . . . We do not need miracles, because we preach no new gospel, but only what has already been confirmed by the numerous miracles of Christ and his Apostles. We offer nothing which we are not ready and able to confirm with the testimony of the same scriptures which are already acknowledged to be true by both Catholics and Protestants. (Freiday 1967, 189–190)

Barclay goes on to say that many early prophets, including John the Baptist, performed no miracles but clearly had a divine mission to prepare the way of the Lord.

This is an early instance of a problem that continued to plague the Quakers. Born out of the religious turmoil of the seventeenth century, which saw an enormous growth in splinter sects, Quakers always had to steer a delicate line between being perceived as fanatical enthusiasts and rigid if secret papists. With their doctrine of the Inner Light and innate tolerance for eccentricity, Quakers were particularly accessible to a variety of enthusiasts with unstable minds as well as tattered theological cloth. Fox wished to treat them with compassion while attempting to cure them. For this reason a number of the miracles dealt with mentally unstable people. The *Journal* contains accounts involving seven individuals, six women and one man, while Cadbury notes that in the "Book of Miracles" fourteen cases are indexed under "distracted," two under "moping," and one each under "possessed" and "troubled" (1948, 69–70). More instances may be found of cases in which the person is simply referred to as "sick."

Fox appears to have used no means other than prayer and the force of his personality to help people dispel their "vain imaginations." A typical instance, occurring also in 1649, took place at Mansfield-Woodhouse, where Fox came upon a "distracted woman under a doctor's hand with her hair loose all about her ears." Though he had her bound and held down the doctor was unable to succeed in bleeding her. Fox then tried his own approach:

> And I desired them to unbind her and let her alone, for they could not touch the spirit in her, by which she was tormented. So they did unbind her; and I was moved to speak to her in the name of the Lord to bid her be quiet and still, and she was so. The Lord's power settled her mind, and she mended and afterwards received the Truth, and continued in it to her death. And the Lord's name was honoured, to whom the glory of all his works belongs. (1975, 43–44)

Thus Fox, anticipating the Tukes, used kindness to exorcise the "demons" plaguing the woman. I have discovered no instance where he used medicine of any kind in working with the mentally ill.

I mention this because of Fox's own interest in becoming a doctor. He says in the *Journal* that "physicians were out of the wisdom of God by which the creatures were made, and so knew not the virtues of the creatures, because they were out of the Word of wisdom by which they were made" (28). I interpret this not as a condemnation of doctors but an assertion that increased faith would bring them increased knowledge. Fox once said: "I was at a stand in my mind whether I should practice physic for the good of mankind, seeing the nature and virtue of the creatures were so opened to me by the Lord" (1975, 27). He owned a copy of Nicholas Culpeper's *The English Physitian Enlarged* (Cadbury, 1948, 51); at the same time he distrusted much of the physic practiced by contemporary physicians and tended to rely more on herbal medicines and natural healing. Lady Penn and Robert Barclay's wife shared this penchant.

It is safe to assume that at first Fox took cases as they came and did not construct any theoretical approach to dealing with the mentally ill. Gradually, however, he saw the need for a more formalized approach to care of the insane. In a 1669 epistle (no. 264), he urged Friends to "have and provide a house for those that are distempered," a charge later amplified:

> That friends do seek some place convenient in or about ye City wherein they may put any person that may be distracted or troubled in mind, that so they may not be put among the world's people or run about the streets.[2]

In 1673 there is a record of "John Goodson offering to take a large house for distempered and discomposed persons." Goodson, a surgeon, apparently set up the house in a "quiet locality of Bartholomew Close," but beyond this there is no record. Auguste Jorns suggests that it was soon given up, prompting the placement of the Quaker mentally ill in asylums run by non-Quakers.[3] The problems associated with Friends being under the care of non-Friends led to the establishment of York Retreat.

Fox had good reason to have particular empathy for the mentally disturbed or depressed, having himself experienced problems. Early in the *Journal* he spoke about the dark night of the soul—a condition that recurs throughout a number of Quaker and non-Quaker journals dealing with religious development. At Barnet, when he was twenty, he felt a "strong temptation to despair" (1975, 4) and continued in this state so "dried up with sorrow, grief, and troubles" (6), he said, that the doctors were unable to perform therapeutic bleedings. Plagued by bad dreams and finding no consolation from priests, Fox continued in despair for three years until 1674, when from the depths he heard a voice saying, "There is one, even Jesus Christ, that can speak to thy condition" (1975, 11). So armed with hope and faith, he set out to convert others.

Anton Boisen sees this period in Fox's life as ultimately healthy; the illness was a successful effort of psychological reorganization in which the "entire personality, to its bottommost depths, is aroused and its forces marshaled to meet the danger of personal failure and isolation" (1936, 59). Boisen characterizes the upheaval experienced by Fox in his early twenties as "catatonic dementia praecox" and sees in this period characteristics exhibited throughout Fox's ministry: identification of himself as a "unique spokesman of the Lord"; cosmic identification; passage through the crucible of darkness and death to a new birth into the light; receiver of direct revelations from God; obedience to "openings." Boisen is struck by the fact that like other religious leaders, Fox overcame potentially disruptive disturbances and became not a madman but a forceful, prophetic leader. William James was similarly struck by Fox's skirting a fine line between sanity and pathological behavior. Had Fox not experienced an integration of personality through religion, James suggests, he would have suffered a breakdown (1902, 3–26; 475–509).

Thus Fox had particular sensitivity to those troubled in mind. Beyond the need to perform miracles to increase the number of followers, especially among Seekers, he had a genuine desire to release men and women from the barriers of unreason caused by mental breakdowns. Also, his own sometimes eccentric conduct might have attracted similarly affected individuals. For the man with old leather breeches and shaggy locks certainly had tinges of excess, both in word and deed; his walking barefoot while decrying the sinners of Lichfield is an early and famous example of such conduct.

Many writers defend this behavior. Charles Morgan notes that "the hopelessly sane men are the bores" (Trueblood 1968, 36). Howard Brinton categorizes such early Quaker vigor as "ethical mysticism"— not a retreat from the world but a dynamic embracing of it. He says that Quakerism is an interesting if contradictory fusion of Hebrew prophetic activism and Greek mysticism, with Fox and Friends closer to the Hebrew mode (Brinton 1973, 40). Geoffrey Nuttall affirms that such enthusiasm counters mere notional assent and reminds us of the experience of religion. Nuttall alludes to Richard Baxter's *Five Disputations* (1659): "It's better that men should be disorderly saved, and that the Church be disorderly preserved, than orderly destroyed" (Nuttall 1961, 42).

Still, Quakerism remained vulnerable to the charge of madness or at least serious disorder. Richard Blome's *The Fanatick History* (1660), for instance, lists a variety of examples of aberrant Quaker conduct. The subtitle of his work is revealing:

> an Exact Relation and Account of the Old Anabaptists, and New Quakers. Being the summe of all that hath been yet discovered about their most

Blasphemous Opinion, Dangerous Practices, and Malitious Endevours to subvert all Civil Government both in Church and State. Together with their Mad Mimick Pranks, and their ridiculous actions and gestures, enough to amaze any sober Christian. Which may prove the Death and Burial of the Fanatick Doctrine.

The dedication of this work to Charles II asks the king to restrain the Quakers. Whole chapters are devoted to John Gilpin's and John Toldberry's accounts of their demonic possession caused by contact with Quaker preachers. Another chapter deals with a favorite target of anti-Quaker writers, James Nayler. Chapter 5 lists forty-five specific instances of Friends going naked, bothering the worship of others, drugging people to attend Quaker meetings, possessing people, leading people to copulate with the devil, assaulting Ministers, and claiming to perform miracles.

The Nayler Episode

Fox certainly was aware of the dangers of inspiration. The Quaker appeal to direct experience rather than external authority may, as Digby Baltzell notes, have been related to the mid-seventeenth-century empiricism of the New Philosophy (1979, 21), but the dangers of such a subjective approach were certainly not lost on Fox. In the *Journal* he consistently warns against "vain imagination" and counsels Friends to "let your moderation and temperance, and patience be known to all men" (Fox, 1911, 28). He would concur with Catherine Phillips's 1798 admonition to young people "to guard their own mind, lest they admit of any pleasing imagination and stamp it with the awful name of revelation" (Brinton, 1972, 28).

No incident better encapsulates Fox's particular sensitivities about Quakers being identified with religious extremism or the association of orthodox Quakerism with antic behavior than the James Nayler episode of October 1656. At that time Nayler was led into Bristol on horseback by Hannah Stranger and Martha Simmonds holding the bridle and chanting, "Holy, holy, holy, Hosannah," while surrounded by cheering followers. Arrested for blasphemy, Nayler was eventually convicted by Parliament and sentenced to prison after being publicly whipped and having a hole bored through his tongue.

This incident is significant for a number of reasons. First, Nayler was an important Quaker leader, second in many respects only to Fox. A former lay preacher in a Puritan regiment, Nayler was a dynamic preacher, the best Quaker theologian before Barclay and yet a man of sweet, simple character; Brayshaw says that he had "a spirit of wonderful beauty" (1933, 135). Thus the example he set was very important. Fox had censured him several times for religious excesses and for keeping company with Martha Simmonds, whom Fox perceived as a negative influence. In fact, when arrested, Nayler had in his possession a letter from Fox chastising Nayler for some of his failings.

Second, there were serious political ramifications of his action. At a terribly unsettled time, his deeds were upsetting to many. Some, like Christopher Hill, see his persecution as a turning point in the history of both Quakerism and the Interregnum. Parliament was eager to end the period of religious toleration and excesses; Nayler's torture was thus a warning to others and a clear signal that Cromwell was open to challenge. Parliament's ability to strike at Nayler was a blow as well against Cromwell and was seen as a weakening of the Puritan movement, indeed of all separatist sects.

Third, the Nayler incident had a profoundly disturbing effect on Quakerism, helping, as Hill claims, "to restore a sense of sin to the Quaker movement" (1972, 200). It brought to a head concerns expressed earlier by many sensitive Friends about fellow members who would "walk out" and become "disorderly." For instance, Richard Farnsworth, formerly a Seeker who was "next to Fox, the chief leader in the North of the new movement" (Braithwaite 1955, 59) perhaps had such aberrations in mind when earlier on 8 June 1653 he wrote to Margaret Fell and others: ". . . take heed of getting above the cross, and so you run astray from the Lord, speaking beyond your line or measure. . . . Take heed of running into extremes in anything, let your moderation be known to all men, for the lord is at hand, and behold the Judge standeth at the door" (Nuttall 1952, no. 25). Also, George Bishop, a Bristol Friend, reported with some relish to Margaret Fell that Bristol Quakers had disowned Nayler. Bishop even regarded the event as an effective lancing of a potentially infectious boil:

> So that as the wisdom of the Lord hath ordered it, seeing this was to come forth, it is best that at first it should come out here, and in such a manner, before it had either scattered here, or defined other parts. For now it is manifest, and a Testimony from the living presence of the Lord is gone and given against it in the hearts of all, and the letters of Friends saves the truth, and this work of Darkness is cut off, and confounded and all Friends in all parts preserved, whose simplicity is not beguiled, but witnesseth against those works of Darkness. (Nuttall 1952, no. 188; Barbour and Roberts 1973, 484)

After Nayler's immoderate acts became public, a host of concerns were expressed in the letters sent to Swarthmore Hall. In November

1656, Arthur Cotten wrote to George Fox from Plymouth, "that about James Nayler hath drawn out the minds of many Friends in many places" (Nuttall 1952, no. 334). Gervase Benson refers to troubles to Friends caused by Nayler (no. 336). William Caton, who with William Ames was the founder of Dutch Quakerism, wrote to Margaret Fell in January 1656–57, saying that in Holland "strange reports concerning James Nayler is gone over so that many stumbling blocks is laid in the Way" (no. 356).

Thomas Salthouse, in January after the incident, writes that "this business about James Nayler hath made a great tumult in the minds of many weak Friends" (no. 357, 30 January 1656–57). Even as far away as Barbados the reports of James Nayler's antics caused problems (no. 381, Henry Fell to Margaret Fell, 14 April 1657). The followers of James Nayler caused disturbances in Meetings and even motivated some to try miracles themselves. For instance, Thomas William wrote Margaret Fell in February 1657 (no. 368) about Mrs. Pearson, who said that she would imitate the prophets by raising William Pool from the dead. Fox's marginal comment on this pronouncement was "mad whimsey."

Nayler was eventually released from prison on 8 September 1659 and was reconciled with Fox in January of the following year. Yet Quakerism would never be the same. Quakers ceased to indulge in miracles or even discuss them, the individualist appeal to the Inner Light was deemphasized, organization and discipline received more emphasis, human sinfulness as opposed to perfectibility was given more attention, and most Friends stopped going naked as a sign. All of these impulses were discussed in Barclay's important *The Anarchy of the Ranters* (1676) in which he "theologized the Quakers' return to sin" (Hill 1972, 204). Nuttall claims that after 1660 Quakerism degenerated into a "shallow humanism" (Nuttall n.d. 20) led by Fox, but Hill takes a more balanced approach: "It is as pointless to condemn this as a sell-out as to praise its realism; it was simply the consequences of the organized survival of a group which had failed to turn the world upside down" (1972, 205).

Of course, the shift was not immediate. Quakers did not suddenly join nor were they welcomed into the English mainstream. They faced a series of repressive laws through the latter part of the seventeenth century designed both to punish them and prevent their advancement in the world. The Second Conventicle Art of 1669, for example, called by Andrew Marvell "the quintessence of arbitrary malice,"[4] renewed and reinforced the First Conventicle Act of 1664, which provided punishment for anyone over sixteen attending worship in other than approved liturgy, at which there were five or more beyond the household. If found guilty, one would be fined with the money going in thirds to the king, the poor, and the informer. *The History of the Life of Thomas Ellwood* provides an account of such informers and of Ellwood's perjury case against them.[5]

These acts[6] complemented the Corporation Act of 1661, which made it illegal to collect more than twenty signatures on any petition. The Act of Settlement of 1662 gave justices of the peace authority to displace squatters, discourage emigration of labor, and enclose lands; the Act of Uniformity required that by August 1662 all parish ministers use the Book of Common Prayer weekly; the Corporation and Test Acts barred nonconformist laymen from all offices in government, military and universities; the Oath of Praemunire and Oaths of Abjuration and Allegiance of 1655 and 1660 required the swearing of fealty to the king and antipathy for the pope and could not be taken by Friends since they opposed all oaths. Such a battery of legal and social constraints tended to erode religious and civil liberties of Quakers in particular and all dissenting groups in general. However, because of their steadfast adherence to principle Quakers suffered the most. Barbour estimates that 450 Friends died in prison during this period, 15,000 were jailed, and 243 were sentenced to penal colonies, though only a few dozen were actually transported (1964, 70).

The Toleration Act of 1689 removed a number of these restrictions and direct punishments, but Friends nevertheless moved into a more quietistic period in which they gradually embraced the Protestant ethic and began to replace with a more parochial concern for internal discipline and order the radical perception of themselves as reviving early Christianity. Yet Quakers were still perceived as religious enthusiasts and were still attacked into the eighteenth century, though in a less acerbic, personal way, for what their opponents saw as heightened eccentricity and religious extremism. With some exceptions, the strain of anti-Quaker writings (over a roughly 150-year period) is consistent but shifted from a litany of personal abuse and paranoid invective in the mid-seventeenth century to a still suspicious but considerably modulated note of criticism. This change in part reflected the transition from a frenetic age of religious and political revolt to a more settled, urbane time. It reflected as well a blunting of Quaker religious feeling and their gradual absorption into the religious and commercial mainstream.

1655–70 Attacks

Joseph Smith's *Bibliotheca Anti-Quakeriana* (1873), though by no means complete, contains hundreds of references to attacks on Friends and their responses. Fox's *Great Mistery of the Great Whore Unfolded,* published in 1659, seven years after his Pendle Hill experience, clearly indicates both the range of contemporary attacks on Quakerism and the time and energy taken by Fox and his coreligionists to refute them. Barbour notes that of the 150 authors who wrote against Quakerism between 1653 and 1660, only six went without an answer (1964, 53). The *Great Mistery* alone contains in its over six hundred pages answers to charges in 106 books, pamphlets, personal statements and group attacks, ranging from an answer to Samuel Eaton's "The Quaker Confuted" to Thomas Hodges's "A Scripture Catechism." The spectrum of criticism clearly testifies to Quakerism's growing strength and its implied threat to other religious sects.

Mid-seventeenth-century attacks tended to be more virulent and personal, the ad hominem assaults relating to the supposedly "rude" uncultivated background of Friends, Fox's robust physique, the Quakers' political manipulations, and their Papist tendencies. There was particular emphasis on the relation of enthusiasm and madness. Richard Sherlock in *The Quakers Wilde Questions* (1654) contrasted the decorum of formal worship to the ecstatic private visions of Quakers. He charged Friends with using the liberty of conscience "to become vain in their imaginations" in order to indulge subjective views rather than worship that which is "decent, reverend, uniform and orderly" (iii). Such idiosyncratic beliefs produce a variety of sects and "strange, wilde, and fanatic opinions." He argued the need for "unity and order" in worship.

There was a common alliance of pride with ignorance. In a companion publication, *A Discourse of the Holy Spirit,* Sherlock speaks of men "whose ignorance accompanyed with excessive pride of heart, which makes their ignorance the greater, that through pride, they will not know, or acknowledge it upon this ground." The Devil knows how "to insinuate his Lyes and Errors into mindes unsettled" (1654, 96). Quakers infect Christ's Church with their pretensions to divine inspiration and defame the sanctuary by acts of "spiritual fornication." Quakers "enshrine and idolize their owne fond, vain, and lying imaginations" (1654, 112). Quakers were particularly sensitive to assaults on their notion of the Inner Light. Sherlock said that Friends were "led by their own ghost only, following their own private Will and desires, imaginations and opinions, as their only guide and dictator" (1654, 111). Presbyterians called the Inner Light "Jack-in-the-Lantern and Will-o-the-Wisp." The roots of such attacks from Puritans and Church of England members alike stemmed from the Quakers' apparent neglect of Scripture in asserting their religious beliefs. This left them prey to charges of a prideful personal inspiration, a charge that would form the basis of many neoclassical attacks in the eighteenth century.

John Gilpin's *The Quakers Shaken* is important if only because it became a touchstone piece throughout the latter half of the seventeenth century for its attacks on Quakerism. A convert to Quakerism in May 1653, Gilpin went through a period of crying and quaking, sensed a "new birth," and believed himself beaten and penetrated by the "spirit of God." Later, in rejecting Quakers, he saw such ecstasy as insane "imagination" aroused by Quaker preaching. His work is a vivid and powerful account of demonic possession and identifies aberrant conduct and demonic possession with Quakerism.[7]

Such identifications of Quakers as foes of both personal and social order were seen throughout this early period. The anonymous *Semper Idem: or a parallel betwixt the Ancient and Modern Phanatics* (1661) used Fox's own words to identify him with treasonous rebels like Sir John Oldcastle and Sir Roger Acton, Lollards who rebelled against Henry V. Richard Baxter said in *The Quakers Catechism* (1655) that Quakers used "Grumblestool Rhetorick" to subvert both state and church. He spoke of their "horrible Pride" and their alliance with Papists to undermine the sufficiency of Scripture. Calling them "so wilde a Generation," Baxter preferred separatists and Anabaptists over Quakers.

Ralph Farmer's *The Great Mysteries of Godliness and Ungodliness* (1655) stressed that Quakers were "much given to *Enthusiasms, and immediate Calls, and Revelations,* and apt to entertain fantastick dreams and fancies" (24). Farmer equated them to Ranters. Christopher Atkinson made a similar charge (with mention of Gilpin) in his *The Sword of the Lord Drawn and Furbish'd Against the Man of Sin* (1654). Farmer dwelt on the Nayler incident in his *Satan Inthron'd in his Chair of Pestilence* (1657). William Prynne's *The Quakers Unmasked* (1655) uncovered Quaker involvement in a "Romish" plot to overthrow the nation. With a rhetorical flourish in the subtitle, he said Quakers are but the "Spawn of Romish Frogs, Jesuits and Franciscan Friars; sent from Rome to seduce the intoxicated Giddy-headed English Nation." Again Quakers are lumped together with Ranters as well as Anabaptists, Independents, Seekers, Dippers, Anti-Trinitarians, Anti-Scripturists. Prynne said that Quakers share in common with Catholics:

> *their pretended extraordinary sudden extravagant Agonies, Trances, Quakings, Shakings, Raptures, Visions, Apparitions, Conflicts with Satan, Revelations, Illuminations instructions in new divine Mysteries and seraphicall Divinity, whereof they pretend they were wholly ignorant before, being illiterate persons.* . . . (1655, 6)

In this early period of attack, from 1655 to 1667, Quakers endured a number of personal tirades against their supposed humble roots, radical politics, alliance with Rome, subversion of the state, and demonic disorder.[8] Contemporary enemies to Quakerism wished especially, as in the case of Farmer, Atkinson, and Prynne, to stain them with the tarbrush of Ranterism. Ranters were true anarchists who blurred the dualism between good and evil to argue for the subjective determination of actions rather than socially based standards and controls. Their expression, "All is ours," connoted a vague pantheism that blurred the distinction between good and evil and permitted them to do anything pleasing to the flesh. The Blasphemy Act of August 1650 was specifically aimed against Ranters' subjective morality with its potential for civil disorder (Hill 1972, 167). For Ranters, feeling it was right made it right; thus they "afforded no test by which the individual could distinguish between the voice of the Spirit and the voice of his own will." The Quakers, however, saw themselves as "children of the Light" who "insisted that there could be no guidance of the Spirit apart from a walking in the light." This, Braithwaite contends, was an "antidote to Ranterism" (1955, 37). If so, it was a painfully thin one and seemed to leave the same dilemma of subjectivism.

While the early Quaker movement may have been "far closer to the Ranters in spirit than its leaders later like to recall" (Hill 1972, 187), Quakers managed through a system of communal restraint and their credal commitment (such as it was) to the concept of the Inner Light to avoid the moral and social anarchy to which the Ranters were especially prone. Yet the dangers and temptations of subjective morality and the religious imagination continued to plague Friends, and the fear of such impulses and warnings of their dangers are a constant theme throughout the century.

William Penn somewhat blithely defended Quakers as turners of the world upside down, not in a political sense "but in no other than that wherein Paul was so charged, viz. to bring things back to their primitive and right order again" (1694). Fox, ever hesitant to move against "leadings" of the spirit not obviously selfish or heretical, eventually relied on the consolidation of the faithful into monthly and quarterly meetings as a means of preserving order and communal restraint on those who might embarrass the group. Ellwood says Fox established such a structure for "better ordering the affairs of the Church . . . and exercising a true gospel-discipline for a due dealing with any that might walk disorderly under our name" (Crump 1900, 257).

In Epistle no. 32 to Friends, Fox says that minds should not go out from the Spirit of God into their own notions for there "lodgeth the enchantor and sorcerer" (1831, 38). Yet what standards would Quakers use to prevent excess? Fox was confident of his own ability to distinguish truths directed by the Inner Light from mere sentiments of the earthly will: "To speak of truth when ye are moved, it is a cross to the will; if ye live in the truth which ye speak ye live in the cross of your own wills" (1831, 38). Yet as Braithwaite notes, such moments of true religious devotion can still admit human imperfections (1955, 147). When Friends left the cross and confused the spirit with moral notions, they got into trouble. Francis Bugg in *The Pilgrim's Progress from Quakerism to Christianity* (1698) said that while a Friend he was told "to wait in the Light, out of ourselves, out of our thoughts, out of our Willings and Runnings, in that which is invisible, and then we should receive the hidden Manna. . ." (4). Quakers saw that people could mistakenly allow "will-works" to substitute self for the power of the Inner Light; the Light is not reason, or ego, or conscience—not man's spirit, but God's. No matter if one accepts the Light as Christ, Spirit, or a mystical shining—Quakers used these concepts inter-changeably—one can be misled into misinterpreting conscious or subsconscious impulses as leadings of the Spirit. Thus Friends de-veloped tests to separate true inspiration from subjective, potentially hurtful impulses. These included moral purity, waiting in silence, and self-consistency of the Spirit through biblical role models and com-parisons of conduct. Regarding silence, Fox said: "if you sitt still in the patience which overcomes in the power of God, there will be no flyinge" (Barbour 1964, 120). Thus with their "high doctrine of spiritual guidance" (Braithwaite 1955, 148), early Quakers tended to overlook religious excesses.

Later Friends were not as tolerant. Robert Barclay, as a second generation Friend (his "convincement" came in 1666) and as the major Quaker theologian, desired to make more respectable a faith that seemed often too individualistic, even solipsistic. He assumed a less tolerant, firmer stance suitable for the final quarter of the seven-teenth century. As a "rational evangelical" (Trueblood 1968, 240), Barclay saw experience as primary but argued for reason as a guard and check; he saw a Cartesian need for both intuition and deduction. For instance, Barclay saw silence as merely a preparatory discipline; without messages ("iron sharpening iron") silence can become not spiritual depth but wasted time. Barclay sought order as well as liberty in religious worship. In *Truth Triumphant* he said: ". . . some are so great pretenders to inward motions, and revelations of the spirit, that there are no extravagances so wild, which they will not cloak with it; and so much are they for everyone's following their own mind, as can admit of no Christian Fellowship and Community, nor of that good order and Discipline, which the Church of Christ never was nor can be without" (Trueblood 1968, 48). Barclay walked a fine line. Like Fox, he saw the Inner Light as transcending the natural order, and he distinguished "true reason" from "natural reason."[9] The latter, because it is corrupt, may at times prevent a person from using the "true reason" of the Inner Light and may even lead one to establish false gods of his/her own. Yet he saw equal danger in a generalized mysticism, like that espoused by Henry More and the Cambridge Platonists. For Barclay, inward revelation is primary, but it does not and should not contradict Scripture or reason.

Barclay's strongest statement on religious order and discipline is *The Anarchy of the Ranters* (1676), in which he attempted to disassociate Quakers from Ranters. In 1661 John Perrot proclaimed a leading of the Inner Light directing that men should not remove their hats in prayer unless speaking and that Friends should forsake the customary handshake. Like Wilkinson and Story some time later, he also opposed having fixed times and places for worship, arguing that the Spirit should lead. These seemingly minor cavils precipitated great divisiveness over the question of the degree and extent of authority that should be imposed on Friends and their religious practices. Gradually Fox and many other Quaker "elders" argued that the intervention of man's will here on earth was necessary for God's work and witness. Should external authority or internal spirit dictate? This was the nub of the debate. While Friends managed to avoid strong statements of creed or dogma, they nonetheless had to contend with this issue of authority versus freedom. Barclay clarified the problem and established a firm position for one side of it. His was an heroic, if ultimately unsuccessful, attempt to establish standards by way of testing the truth of one's leading.

He addressed three main questions: 1) What kind of order and government is needed in the Church? 2) What is the source of this authority and how far may it extend? 3) Is it in any way similar to the authority of the Church of Rome or other "antichristian" assemblies? He argued that Scripture and the works of the early Apostles, when led by the Spirit, are appropriate guides and tests of one's leadings. He flirted with the idea of these becoming independent external authorities replacing one's sense of religious intuition; while he never said so explicitly, the implication was there. Such a rhetorical balance of opposing concepts fell apart in the nineteenth century as the Gurneyites and Hicksites separated over such questions. Barclay wanted to show that Quakers were neither Papists nor Ranters. For him, the religious life must have both freedom and order. Heresy is extremism because it lacks some of the wholeness and balance of life; truth rests in the avoidance of extremes.

Friends also had problems in making the distinction between reason and imagination (with imagination taken here as a form of grace). They walked a precarious line regarding the function of reason. They certainly concurred with Abraham von Frankenberg's *A Warning Against the Deceit of Setting Up Man's Reason as Judge in Spiritual Matters* (1677), in which he attacked the "Idol Reason," which overrules the promptings of simple faith and the Light of obedience of Christ. Man is corrupted by the Fall and needs God's Light to overcome falsehood. Early Friends called the devil "the Old Reasoner" (Frost 1973, 128) and believed reason was irrelevant to faith and could not enable the corrupted to achieve salvation; only the work of the Holy Spirit could do this. Yet such disparagement of reason began to weaken with Barclay's strong theologizing and with William Penn's influence. As a Whig and a scholar, Penn was in some ways closer to the Cambridge Platonists and his fellow members of the Royal Society than his fellow Quakers. He said that "the understanding can never be convinced nor properly submitted but by such arguments as are rational, persuasive, and suitable to its own nature." He also affirmed that "Reason, like the sun, is common to all, and tis for want of examining all by the same light and measure that we are not all of the same mind. . . ."[10]

A similar change took place with regard to the nature of conscience. For early Friends conscience was an agent of the Light, but it gradually became a more autonomous faculty, one that could move judges in favor of Quakerism without making them Quaker. It could be an active faculty leading people to embrace essential political, moral, and social reforms. It was no longer a passive instrument of God's Light, but a self-directed "privilege which men are born with" (Penn 1670, 19).

1670–1706 Attacks

Eighteenth-century abhorrence of emotion and enthusiasm had its roots in the religious chaos of the seventeenth century, and in the years 1670 to 1706 anticipations of anti-Quaker themes emerged that would be developed later in the eighteenth century. This period saw a diminution of personal animosity but a continued concentration on the Quakers' lack of order and external standards. Francis Bugg was perhaps the most energetic, prolific critic of Friends during this time. In his *Battering Rams Against New Rome* (1690), *Quakerism Drooping and its Cause Sinking* (1703), *A Quaker Catechism* (1706), and the later *The Quakers Present Principles Farther Expos'd to Publick View* (1711), Bugg attacked Quakers as unchristian with a contempt for Scripture as external authority, a contempt of ordinance, a denial of Jesus Christ as the Son of God, and an adherence to antimonarchical principles. He also cited them as political pragmatists and proud hypocrites allied with the Roman Church:

> Thy Elder Sisters' tripple Crown,
> Whose Pride doth not exceed
> The Pride of thee, which doth abound,
> Exceeding her indeed.
>
> (1690, 27)

Even such a balanced critic as Benjamin Coole, while believing Quakers closer to apostolic truth than any other sect, expressed concern about the "madness" created when their "hot Zeal Transports them beyond either the Bonds of Religion or Reason" (1712, 88). In their defense, he said that this excess was the result of a few zealots who may be found in any faith.

Earlier critics did not make such generous allowances. There were several reverberations of previous attacks. For instance, in *The Sad Effects of Cruelty Detected* (1675) several Westminster Friends reacted to a pamphlet charging Quakers with being "Morose, Sullen, Reserved and Melancholy." This pamphlet had singled out a woman driven mad by her adherence to Quakers' "Uncertain Light and Private Spirit," and who by attendance at Meeting was exposed to "strange Chimera as to her Fancy" and "driven to Strange Rapture." In fact, said the authors, the poor woman was beaten and reviled by her husband and through such oppression was driven to madness. Physical abuse, not Quaker religion, was the source of her difficulties. The epigraph to their pamphlet was: "Oppression maketh a Wise Man Mad." And Edmund Elys, commenting on a pamphlet written by John Elliot, said that Elliot's Quaker book was written at the "Instigation of the DEVIL" (1695, n.p.).

More settled and subtle attacks, however, anticipated later charges in the eighteenth century. Quakers were still identified with a leaning toward enthusiasm, but the attacks became slightly more philosophical. The most famous of these, indeed one of the most noteworthy anti-Quaker works, was Charles Leslie's *The Snake in the Grass.* (1697). Leslie first defined enthusiasm as "False Pretence to Revelation," then proceeded to distinguish divine from diabolical enthusiasm. In the former the Holy Scriptures acted as a "monitor" to control any excess. Such an enthusiasm, mediated through the Scriptures, filled the believer with humility and was tantamount to genius. Diabolical enthusiasm, or immediate inspiration, filled the follower with pride. He called Fox and Lodowick Muggleton "twin-Enthusiasts, both born in the Year 1650." Fox, he said, saw the Inner Light not as inspiration sent from God but as the essential God; Christ was not in heaven but in the heart. The Inner Light was not natural reason or conscience but Christ. For Fox, as in the next century for William Blake, all deities resided in the human breast and thus made one divine. Leslie called this pride and said such thinking led Quakers not to subscribe to church, state, or scriptural authority: "In short, *Enthusiasts* have no *Principles,* They have no *Rule* but their own *Fansie* (which is strongest in *Mad-Men*) and this they mistake for *Inspiration*" (1697, 95). Later Leslie compared the madness of Fox and Muggleton. The ground in each instance was "Despair," so much so that Fox could not be bled; his blood was dried up with grief. In this despair he became inspired by thoughts of religion and became possessed with "whatever Roving *Imagination* (which is strongest in Mad-Men), took place in his Head" (1697, 332).[11]

Henry Hallywell (1673) had earlier also identified the source of Fox's difficulties as melancholy; indeed the Quakers, says Hallywell, may well be the most "Melancholic Sect that ever came into the World." This melancholy accounts for the false persuasion in them of being inspired. Hallywell then went on to provide a remarkably specific analysis of the physical basis of Quaker problems:

> When therefore the Melancholic and Hypochondriacal Humor (which is extraordinarily predominant in them) mixing with the Blood and Spirits is somewhat refined in the Heart, and being warmed there, ascends copiously into the Brain, if affects the mind with varieties of Imaginations, and intoxicates and makes the man as it were drunk for the present, till by stretching his Voice, and the Earnestness and Motions of his body, it becomes in some degree evaporated. And all that time that his brains are turgid and full of this Humor, he is wonderful eloquent and bewitchingly talking. . . . Whereas all this is only an effect of his Melancholic Temper, the *Hypochondria* rising into the Region of the Brain: which is ordinary in Poets and Orators. . . . (n.p.)

Fox and George Whitehead spent much time defending Quakers and the notion of the Inner Light against such attacks. In *Something In Answer to Lodowick Muggleton* (1667), and more particularly in his *Great Mistery* (1659), Fox said the Inner Light was essential to perceive God. In *Enthusiasm Above Atheism* (1674) Whitehead answered the charges made in a work entitled *The Danger of Enthusiasm Discovered,* which attacked the Quakers' "Wild Notion of men's being guided by the Internal Teachings of the Spirit, without Outward

Teaching" and for "Enthusiastical Fancies" (1674, 11). Whitehead, in defending internal illumination, argued that to deny the true God, who is Light, was atheism; thus to deny his Light in man was to deny the true God.

At the same time, it is easy to understand why so many of the attacks on Quakers would focus on the question of madness. Any opponent is less formidable if she is made to appear irresponsible or at least slightly ridiculous. A good caricaturist understands the advantages of exaggeration over invective—far better to make your opponent appear less than human or somewhat animalistic. Quakers encouraged such attacks by the kind of conduct ascribed to them or admitted by them. It did little good for Fox in his *Journal* to warn Friends of "vain imagination" and, especially after the Nayler episode, to counsel Friends to "let your moderation, and temperance, and patience be known to all men" (1975, 281). The non-Quaker public formed its image of Quakers from the number of notorious and often outrageous, eccentric acts that came to be identified as peculiarly Quaker: from William Simpson, who wore a sackcloth for three years during the days of Oliver Cromwell's Parliament; from Nayler, who had himself proclaimed savior and formed his own cult; from Gilpin's claims of possession while under Quaker influence; from James Milner, who prophesied that 1 December 1652 would be the day of judgment and that 2 December would be the first day of the new creation marked by a sheet descending from heaven with a sheep in it (Braithwaite 1955, 147–149); or from Fox himself decrying the sinners of Lichfield. The sometimes crudely literal reenactments of the Bible by Quakers—going naked, for instance, in imitation of Isaiah— seemed to confirm the validity of the charges of madness asserted by Quaker critics.

These more radical activities of early Friends continued to influence public imagination. Blome's *The Fanatick History* (1660), with its compelling compilation of incidents taken from Friends' own accounts or contemporary testimony as to the bizarre behavior of various individuals, is a work whose influence lingered long after its publication date; Penn and Whitehead addressed its argument in their *Serious Apology*, published in 1671. While aware of the danger of Quakers being labeled mad or disorderly, the authors hesitated to criticize or disassociate themselves from earlier Friends. Rather, they attacked Gilpin as a drunkard under the sway of Presbyterian priests like Jenner and Taylor, who published *The Quakers Shaken* (1653) in Gilpin's name. They said that these priests, not Quakers, were the cause of Gilpin's "vain Imaginations, Dreams, and Fancies against the Power of God" (1671, 14). Quaking did take place at religious meetings, but it was a sign of spiritual possession, not "Antick Motions agitated by the Devil"; Quakers were not the "off-spring of Satan's inspired Enthusiasts" (1671, 16). Regarding nakedness, they said that it can be a "true sign" to the Presbyterian priests of their spiritual nakedness, and they maintained that community witness in England and Ireland was the best defense of Quakerism. Penn and Whitehead admitted that miracles, visions, and revelations had been experienced by Quakers, but they did "utterly renounce and deny" that the only evidence of inspiration was miracles, as charged by Jenner and Taylor. Their defense is worth reciting:

> I know the *monstrous Conceits,* that some have of our meaning by *Revelation,* fancying we understand *Whimsical Raptures, Strange and Prodigious Trances;* but such imagine evil of things they know not: *We disclaim any share or interest in those Vain Whimsies and idle Intoxications;* professing our Revelation *to be a solid and necessary Discovery from the Lord, of those things that do import and concern our daily conditions, in reference to the Honour which is due to him,* and Care owing to our own Souls (1671, 87–88).

Rather than miracles, they concluded, Quakers use *"Truth, Reason, Equity, Holiness, and Recompence of the Christian Religion"* (88).

The Toleration Act of 1689 restored to Quakers many of their religious and civil liberties, but they continued to maintain a quiet posture in order not to draw attention to themselves. For instance, the yearly meeting epistle for 1690, signed by Benjamin Bealing, cautioned Friends "to beware of all airy discourses, disputes and controversies about the kingdoms of this world; that all might walk wisely and circumspectly . . . ; to our Grief, we have heard too much complaint and reflections, occasioned by some who have not observed a true Bridle to their tongues, but have been too busy, loose and airy, in discourses of that Nature" (40). The older generation of Friends began to die off, leaving behind a leadership that was perhaps more conservative, certainly more bureaucratic, perhaps even more sensitive to Friends showing any hint of disorder or internal discord to the world. Fox died in 1691, outliving such Quaker leaders as Francis Howgill, Ellis Hookes, Richard Hubberthorne, James Nayler, John Stubbs, Isaac Penington, Christopher Taylor, Thomas Taylor, Edward Burrough, Robert Barclay, John Audland, Richard Farnsworth, and Samuel Fisher. Surviving him were his wife, Margaret Fell (d. 1702), and William Penn. Penn did not die until 1718, but his financial problems and increasingly bad health seriously undermined his involvement in Quaker affairs. George Whitehead (d. 1713) and Thomas Ellwood (d. 1723) continued as important leaders, functioning primarily as clerks or "weighty Friends" responsible for yearly

meeting epistles and other organizational matters. The result, according to Toynbee, was that by becoming too prosperous and part of the
ruling majority Friends ultimately lost an opportunity to be "an
interior proletariat" (Brinton 1973, 22). They moved away from
being a small group of dedicated persons maintaining a strict discipline, though such a change would not take place for a number of
years.

1707–1823 Attacks

While Quakers moved into a period of quietism, the attacks did not
abate. Perhaps because of their commercial success; perhaps because
of their singular mannerisms of dress, speech, and conduct, which
Knox calls their "eccentric rigorism" (1950, 147); perhaps because of
their theology stressing personal divinity and religious fervor; perhaps
because of their simple survival from the welter of radical religious
movements that had scarred the moral and physical landscape of
England and Europe—whatever the specific reason, Quakers continued to endure insults and verbal attacks. Throughout the eighteenth and even into the early nineteenth century there was a
particular animus directed against Friends; they in fact became a
favorite target of literary satirists. As a leader of the Quakers, Fox was
singled out for attack. Jonathan Swift may well have had Fox in mind
when he said that "the Two Principal Qualifications of a Phanatic
Preacher are, his Inward Light, and his Head full of Maggots, and the
Two different Fates of his Writings are, to be burnt or Worm eaten"
(1958, 62). Macaulay in his *History of England* (n.d) said that Fox had
"an intellect in the most unhappy of all states, that is to say, too much
disordered for liberty, and not sufficiently disordered for Bedlam"
(4:132). Knox maintained that these early Quakers reproduced the
exhibitionism of the Adamites and Turlupins, suggesting that psychological abberations go "hand in hand with a simplified theology"
(1950, 104).

The attacks on Quakers near the start of the eighteenth century,
however, dwelt on the question of religious enthusiasm. A host of
writers attacked enthusiasm through the period, often identifying it
with madness. Shaftesbury, in his "A Letter Concerning Enthusiasm"
(1714, 1:1–55), mildly rebuked the religious excesses of the French
Protestants newly arrived in England. He was concerned about an
"Imagination so inflam'd, as in the moment to have burnt up every
Particle of Judgment and Reason." He made the conventional distinction between inspiration and enthusiasm; one is a "real feeling of the

Divine Presence," the other a false one. But the passions aroused are the same and result in similar transports of the mind. He moved into physiology: "Something there will be of Extravagance and Fury, when the Ideas or Images receiv'd are too big for the narrow human Vessel to contain" (53). Such delusions "come arm'd with the specious Pretext of moral Certainty, and *Matter of Fact*" (44). In this cosmopolitan, deistic piece, Shaftesbury recommended "Good Humour" as the appropriate counter to enthusiasm.

A less civil, indeed scatological attack on enthusiasts took place in Swift's *A Tale of A Tub* (1710).[12] He equated enthusiastic preachers to the Aeolists, both inspired with subterranean vapours that "overshadow the Brain" producing conceptions that smack of "Madness or Phrenzy," and generally issuing forth in nauseous "Fistula." He took particular aim at "Female Priests" or "Quakers who suffer their Women to preach and pray" (1958, 157), likening them to the tenders of the oracles: "It is true indeed, that these were frequently managed and directed by *Female* Officers, whose Organs were understood to be better disposed for the Admission of those Oracular *Gusts,* as entering and passing up thro' a Receptacle of greater Capacity, and causing also a Pruriency by the Way, such as with due Management, hath been refined from a Carnal, into a Spiritual Extasie" (165). The brain, Swift affirmed, when in "its natural Position and State of Serenity" does not prompt anyone with a thought of drawing the masses to

> his own *Power,* his *Reasons* or his *Visions.* . . . But when a Man's Fancy gets *astride* on his Reason, when Imagination is at Cuffs with the Senses, and common Understanding, as well as common Sense, is Kickt out of Doors; the first Proselyte he makes, is Himself, and when that is once compass'd, the Difficulty is not so great in bringing over others; A strong Delusion always operating from *without,* as vigorously as from *within.* (171)

In *The Spectator* no. 201 for Saturday, 20 October 1711 (1965, 2:287–90), Joseph Addison distilled into brief compass the pervasive eighteenth-century fear of religious excess—a concern all the more real and urgent for a writer as close as Addison to the sectarian turmoil and broils of England's seventeenth century. He first applauded devotion as occasioning sublime ideas, warming the soul, and separating us even more than the faculty of reason from the animal world. He saw the act of devotion itself as an affirmation of the "Supreme Being" as its first Author through the "Natural Light of Reason."

Unless checked by reason, however, Addison explained, devotion may degenerate into enthusiasm or superstition. The former, a more serious failing, may "disorder the Mind, unless its Heats are tempered with Caution and Prudence," for we must "guard our selves in all Parts of Life against the Influence of Passion, Imagination, and Constitution." Excessive devotion leads to self-delusion when products of fancy are mistaken for divine inspiration. Addison's remarks anticipated these lines by Alexander Pope:

> For virtues' self may too much Zeal be had;
> The worst of Mad-men is a Saint turn'd mad.
>
> (Evans 1752, title page)

Or, as Locke described the circular logic of the Enthusiasts: *"It is a Revelation, because they firmly believe it, and they believe it, because it is a Revelation"* (1975, 702).[13]

Addison displayed special distaste for Catholics because of their superstition and for some of the Protestant sects because of their enthusiasm. The second trait was a more serious danger: "Enthusiasm has something in it of Madness, Superstition of Folly." Addison praised a "strong steady masculine Piety," but disavowed enthusiasm and superstition as weaknesses of human reason "that expose us to the Scorn and Derision of Infidels, and sink us even below the Beasts that perish." A vice that would propel a human being so low on the chain of being was indeed a heinous one, and that Addison would attack it with such vigor and vitriol revealed something about his fears and those of his contemporaries. The thousand nameless fears that haunt human beings coalesced, as it were, into a century's fear of madness. No deformity makes one less human, no flaw more occasions a dreaded ostracism from the polite, civil coffeehouse society sought in the eighteenth century. Addison was the son of an Anglican clergyman, with knowledge through older relatives of the religious chaos of the seventeenth century; he had direct experience of the Irish problem during his tenure from 1708 to 1710 as secretary of the Irish government under Lord Wharton. In his almost radical defense of reason and a concomitant lack of tolerance for both ambiguity and eccentricity, he was consistently a man of his age.

Johnson, Swift, Steele, Pope, Sterne, Fielding, Butler—these and others were equally strong in attacking any deviations from what they saw as proper norms of conduct. They cried out insecurely, like Johnson in *Rasselas,* against the "uncertain continuance of reason" (1958, 595).[14] Reason became a talisman against unreason in the search for control and mastery over disorder. Like Coleridge's powerful subterranean river in Kubla Khan's garden, the disorder was always there, ready to erupt and cause individual and communal chaos.

Any number of sects could have been singled out for their enthusiastic eccentricities, including the Ranters, the Fifth Monarchy Men, the Muggletonians, the Camisards, and later, the Methodists. But beyond the obvious Catholic target, no religious group was more open to abuse than the Quakers. For instance, Addison's coauthor of *The Spectator,* Richard Steele, in issue no. 396 for 4 June 1712, spoke of "the Fraternity of the People call'd Quakers" who have "that Overflow of Light which shines within 'em so powerfully, that it dazzles their Eyes, and dances 'em into a thousand Vagaries of Error and Enthusiasm" (Addison, 1965 3 : 484). In Theophilius Evans's *The History of Modern Enthusiasm* (1752), the criticism was more social than religious. He called Fox a "Mechanic" with little learning and his followers a "conceited, senseless, most ignorant, and blasphemous crew, destitute of common Modesty" (74–77). Without Scripture as religious ballast and an appropriate limit to their religious fervor, the Quakers were prone to enthusiastic excess. John Lewis wrote a sober pamphlet in 1759 defending Quakers against Evans's attacks. Lewis, citing Penn, said that the Inner Light was a true spiritual force; it was not an effect of melancholy or enthusiasm or the suggestion of an evil spirit. Lewis also referred to Barclay: "We distinguish betwixt a Revelation of a new Gospel, and new Doctrines, and a new Revelation of the good old Gospel and Doctrines; the last we plead for, but the first we utterly deny" (5). And, ironically, he quoted John Locke's statement that God will assist us: "He will give us *his spirit* to help us to do what and how we should" (16).

While the attacks became more moderate and subtle, they continued throughout the century. In 1793, Edward Ryan attacked Quakers in *The History of the Effects of Religion on Mankind,* saying their "violent enthusiasm" caused them to disrupt public worship and suggested an association with the Hermhutters of Germany and the Convulsionists of the Low Countries whose "faith was not a rational conviction of the truth of the Scriptures, but a medley of ill-grounded imaginations and raptures of the soul" (2 : 150).

Most writers on enthusiasm quoted Addison with pleasure and took John Locke as a guide, especially his 1695 work on *The Reasonableness of Christianity,* where with vigorous attacks on enthusiasm and fanaticism, he developed a religious approach that was more strongly Apollonian than Dionysian.[15] Benjamin Coole, in *Religion and Reason United* (1712), pleaded for a union of heart and mind to overcome religious squabbles.[16] Thomas Green's *A Dissertation on Enthusiasm* (1755) made specific use of Locke to say one must be careful "not to entertain any proposition with greater assurance than the proofs it is built upon will warrant." He said that people often mistake madness for inspiration, and thus "one of the greatest calamities that attends human life, appears as one of the greatest blessings." Perhaps with Quakers in mind, Green said that with their rejection of reason, enthusiasts were a threat to the moral order and boasted a faith built not upon a gospel but "on their own ill-grounded imaginations and pretended inward feelings . . ." (71). Further, enthusiasts often were melancholy individuals with a gloomy countenance. Quoting Henry More's *Enthusiasmus Triumphatus* (1656), in which More claimed that true religious experience was never irrational, Green said that physical quaking resulted from "the fervor of spirits and heat of imagination, which persons of a melancholy complextion are liable to" (1755, 103). Like Hallywell, Green provided a physical explanation of enthusiasm:

> strong fancy impregnated by heated melancholy, for this sometimes warms the brain to a degree that makes it very active and imaginative, full of odd thoughts and unexpected suggestions, which will be often taken for the immediate actings of the Holy Spirit: And those thoughts by the help of pride and self-love, may work so much upon the heightened affections, and they upon the body so far, as to call it sometimes into a kind of *raptures* and *extasies;* where every dream will be taken for a *prophesy,* and every image of the fancy for a vision. (56)

Thus the enthusiast identified the passions of a "heated imagination" with divine promptings; fanaticism heated the mind without purifying it.

Worthy of special mention for the zest and rhetorical flourish of its attacks is John Dove's *An Essay on Inspiration* (1756).[17] While the attacks were conventional, the language was not. He said that Quaker enthusiasm "out-does the extravagancies of Don Quixote." It was a "spiritual mange," a "poison that destroys the very texture of the blood and rots the bones; and when it spreads in society, it licks up the very sources of virtue, destroys the very seeds of humanity, and spreads a bane worse than ten thousand plagues; for it diffuses a moral contamination into the consciences of all that breathe in its baneful atmosphere" (94, 109). Dove said that the entire Quaker "system (if they have any)" was "fit only to be thrown to the bittern and the hobgoblins" (107). Throughout his arguments, Dove relied strongly on Lockean empiricism: "If men would here take Mr. Locke's advice, and first settle the limits of their understandings, and determine what objects lay beyond, and what within their reach; they would not venture at things too high for them" (102).

Other eighteenth-century works concentrated on doctrinal disputes and criticism rather than ad hominem attacks or suggestions of madness. Thomas Bennet's *A Confutation of Quakerism* (1733) and Patrick Smith's *A Preservative Against Quakerism* (1740) conceded that Quakers had matured from their Ranter and Familist roots. Both books were designed to convince rather than provoke and dealt with more directly theological matters such as baptism, infallibility, the trinity, tithes, the Body of Christ, and immediate revelation. Several works avoided general attacks on Quakers while still lodging a variety of assaults on James Nayler. These included Aikin's *Memoirs of Religious Impostors* (1823) and D. Hughson's *The Life of James Nayler, A Frantic Enthusiast* (1814). The second work in fact made a clear distinction between this "miserable visionary" and "that worthy class of men" called Quakers (1).

As can be seen, even into the nineteenth century Quakers were not immune from conventional attacks. The phrase "mad Quaker," for example, endured even up to Sydney Smith's benign use of it in his 1814 discussion in the *Edinburgh Review* of Samuel Tuke's *Description of the Retreat*. He noted that "a mad Quaker belongs to a small and rich sect; and is, therefore, of greater importance than any other mad person of the same degree in life" (197). Yet he maintained that Quakers were "a charitable and humane people" (198). Less sympathetic was Francis Jeffrey's 1807 review of Thomas Clarkson's *A Portraiture of Quakerism*. He attacked the book and Quakers for their spiritless faith and their hypocritical absorption in trade. He says that Fox was "exceedingly insane" and that Quaker doctrines were "too high-flown for our humble apprehension" (85, 102).

Summary

Religious enthusiasm and its relationship to madness was an important theme into the nineteenth century. Quakers feared being branded as mad enthusiasts and thus somehow dismissed or at least taken less seriously as a religious movement. The more personal, vindictive attacks on early Friends reflected the manners and harsh rhetoric of a society turned upside down by religious chaos and bespoke a bitter respect for the gains made by Quaker ministers; the Quakers' harshest critics tended to be ministers of other faiths whose losses were Quaker gains. Later attacks, however, reveal more about a predominant world view and shed light on the eventual establishment of York Retreat. The neoclassical age—born out of Lockean empiricism, reflecting a cosmos modeled on the great chain of being, promoting satire with its implied moral and social standards—was not a suitable environment for the nurturing of Quakerism. In a period where order/disorder—

not good/evil—was the major dualism, one can comprehend society's fear of enthusiasts and how, in light of seventeenth-century history, religious excess would be identified with social and political chaos. The fact that Fox and Friends committed apparently irrational acts did not make them antirational, but their implied deviation from social norms left them open to attack and identified them in many minds with the kind of religious enthusiasm that led to social disorder.

In the various anti-Quaker writings and the Quaker responses, one can see a consistent split between reason and imagination, order and disorder, piety and enthusiasm. Many Quaker opponents followed seventeenth-century empirical philosophy, identifying imagination as the faculty that collects impressions from the senses and presents them to the mind as images or ideas without the monitor of reason. Madness could result if reason were overwhelmed by unbridled images; this could lead to the destruction of minds, souls, and possibly social order. Quaker interest in and sympathy for the insane, compounded by their own melancholy demeanor, frequently produced guilt by association. Quakerism became synonymous with madness and made Quakers defensive.

As a result perhaps of these external attacks, Quakers began to embody such tensions in themselves. A faith that cut itself off from the world yet in its commercial ventures clearly was of the world; a sect with strongly enthusiastic roots yet hypersensitive to external attacks for that very reason; a people committed to the spiritually vibrant concept of the Inner Light yet of a homogeneous, sober demeanor; a group composing the radical vanguard on a variety of social fronts yet adopting a conservative lifestyle; a people believing that there is that of God in everyone yet ready all too quickly to ostracize members for deviance from social and religious norms. With so many anomalies to resolve, it is not farfetched to see these tensions as the cause of the melancholy that recent Quaker psychologists have identified as characteristic of some Friends.[18] Such a past might also account for Quaker receptivity to and interest in efforts to help the mentally ill.

I have argued that what enabled the Quakers to survive seventeenth-century religious divisiveness and intense persecution was a combination of Fox's and Fell's organizational skills—especially the establishment of the Meeting structure and constant attendance upon such Meetings—and a strong communal corrective to those Friends who would "run out" or exhibit "hurry of the mind." The analogy of the extended family with relatives taking care of their own is not unwarranted. As will be seen in a later chapter, this communal control was replaced by an institutional one, but the family concept still remained important.

3
EIGHTEENTH-CENTURY INTELLECTUAL BACKGROUND

Introduction

It is a comfortable notion to regard York Retreat as offering a radically more humane approach to the mentally ill than the "beat and bleed" therapeutics used by its predecessors. It is tempting to use such terms as "progress" or "improvement" when contrasting York Retreat with the numerous private and public asylums that were its progenitors. As will be discussed later, the therapies developed at the Retreat—that is, "moral treatment," or a regimen of fresh air, nutritious food, and kindness—were certainly as effective if not more so than the conventional treatments that often exacerbated the physical and mental torment of patients. Yet it is unwise and historically invalid to overlook or dismiss the science and philosophy of care antedating York Retreat. While York Retreat arose in part as a response to an incident, it flowered because it built on rather than rejected the treatment then current. This treatment resulted from a confluence of social, philosophical, and medical factors as well as from different assumptions about the individuals being treated and the methods of treatment.

Social Factors

Ideas about insanity cannot be fully understood without analyzing the society that produced those ideas; this means a forthright examination of the science current during this period.[1] Thomas Kuhn's *The Structure of Scientific Revolutions* (1962) warns against assuming a pride of historical position from which one regards with amusement what passed for science in former times. Such earlier beliefs, though perhaps absurdly wrong by today's standards, were no less scientific in their day. To use Kuhn's terminology, they provided a thesis against which another paradigm would react to contribute a wholly different way of looking at the same problem. By "paradigm" Kuhn means "universally recognized scientific achievements that for a time provide model problems and solutions to a community of practitioners" (x). Still controversial, though used by a variety of disciplines as a theoretical linchpin, Kuhn's book is valuable if only because it demonstrates forcefully the social dimension of scientific knowledge. It is an important buttress to the notion of showing science's "historical integrity" (3). Thus Kuhn does not see science as a progress toward truth but accepts older science on its own terms and substitutes "evolution-from-what-we-know for evolution-toward-what-we-wish-to-know" (170).

To achieve an overview of the "science" of psychiatry in the eighteenth century—an amalgam of inherited magic, Galenic/humoral therapy, theological ideas of possession, class analysis, and empirical philosophy—it is necessary to identify the influential events and philosophical changes that occurred during the period from around the fifteenth century to 1813, the publication date of Samuel Tuke's *Description of the Retreat*. A significant pattern during this period was the increasing control of the medical profession over the treatment of the insane, and to track this development is to detect a number of influential trends:

1. Medieval healing was in the hands of the clergy both because of the theological dimension of illness and because what passed then for the English medical profession—physicians, surgeons, apothecaries—proved ineffectual, even harmful. Sprenger and Kraemer's *Malleus Maleficarum* (1487), in showing how the devil was a causative agent of melancholia and manic conduct, encouraged the torment and death of numerous sick individuals branded as witches or warlocks (Zilboorg 1941, 144–74). Eventually the New Science began to replace the superstitition and anthropomorphism that dominated medical care, but not until England experienced a transition phase of practitioners employing in their armamentarium of aids an intriguing blend of astrology, magic, religion, and folk medicine.

2. Many of the enthusiasts and divines such as Fox and Wesley were identified with amateur or folk medicine and faith healing. Wealthier, more conservative classes eschewed such healers and leaned to more traditional therapeutics and professionals. In this sense, the work of York Retreat, with inspired care undertaken by concerned laypersons, was a hearkening back to the dissenting tradition and went against the move toward the professionalization of treatment for the mentally ill.

3. The new epistemology of Locke and Hobbes led to a closer

examination of the processes of the mind and the interrelationships of the faculties. It was combined with a deistic notion of the banished god and an increasing emphasis on social decorum as a prerequisite for order and harmony. The closer one examined human nature, the more complex and confusing but less mysterious things became. There was a sense that answers could be found in the context of known science, and the need to look for supernatural explanations diminished.

4. By the eighteenth century the growing institutionalization of mad people required the bureaucratization of treatment. The sheer scale of the problem called for larger institutions of care and an increasing degree of specialization among those charged with providing treatment, even though these efforts resulted in no higher rates of cure. The dilemma faced by the physician/psychiatrist in earlier ages, perhaps in any age, was ably summarized by John Stuart Mill: "The tendency has always been strong to believe that whatever received a name must be an entity or being, having an independent existence of its own. And if no real entity answering to the name could be found, men did not for that reason suppose that none existed, but imagined that it was something peculiarly abstruse and mysterious" (Gould 1981, 320). The result was a mélange of hints, assertions, prejudices, guesses that passed for quasi-scientific theorizing, and a dogmatic commitment to theories born out of an insecure tolerance for ambiguity.

Only in the eighteenth century did mental illness become a subject for objective medical research. Until then, it was perceived either as a god-centered phenomenon—that is, an aberration sparked by a kind of divine frenzy or demonic possession—or as a failure of the will to control the passions. Only with the decline of traditional religion, combined with the Enlightenment idea that planning and scientific advancements could cure social ills, did mental illness become a subject open to rational investigation. The idea developed that the roots of the problem were in society's structure rather than in the individual's moral failings. Thus a person became mentally ill not as a punishment from god but because of poor surroundings or failure of individual faculties. Reason faltered not because it was corrupted by the Fall but because of any one of a host of possible physical and philosophical explanations.

MIDDLE AGES-RENAISSANCE

These changes merit close examination. During the Middle Ages and Renaissance, for instance, interest in insanity grew. The proposed causes of insanity were numerous, ranging from physical illness to myriad conditions in the natural world, from floods and fires to star-crossed fate. While arguing that physical illness and stress could cause insanity, writers of the day also emphasized supernatural causes, both divine and diabolical. Penelope B. R. Doob's *Nebuchadnezzar's Children: Conventions of Madness in Middle English Literature* (1974) traces theories of how God drove sinners to suicide, from Nebuchadnezzar to Judas. Healers frequently sought to break the hold of malevolent spirits on patients and to restore a sense of natural order to mind and body. Even the dissecter of melancholy, Robert Burton, balked at listing the various causes of the ailment, merely saying in *The Anatomy of Melancholy* (1621) that the causes are "as divers as the infirmities themselves" and that it would be a Herculean task to ferret out all of them (1927, 116).

Treatments were equally diverse, generally based on a blend of classical science and medieval cosmology. Especially important was humoral physiology as developed by Hippocrates, Aristotle, and Galen, with its effort to achieve balance of blood, phlegm, yellow and black bile though purgings and bloodlettings. This was the basic medical principle guiding the efforts of physicians of both mind and body (usually the same individuals). Faculty psychology made use of the theory of humors and integrated it with additional knowledge passed down by Aristotle and Plato concerning the nature of the soul and human faculties. The faculty psychology of the period, especially as articulated by Robert Burton, asserted that one has three souls: rational, sensitive, and vegetative. The rational soul, allied with the angels, controls the will and the understanding; the vegetal soul controls the powers of growth, nutrition, and generation; the sensitive soul shares with the beasts the corporeal agencies of knowledge (imagination, memory, common sense, the senses) and the passions. The sensitive soul has five outward senses to present images to the three inward senses of common sense, memory, and imagination. The common sense arranges external impressions into accessible images for the memory or the imagination; the imagination presents these images to the understanding, which by using its judgment corrects these images from appearance to reality (for example, realizing that the sun in fact is not sinking into the sea). Passions are also important, providing the rational soul with the energy needed to implement the decisions of the will.

The full integration of all faculties into a harmonious interdependent order constitutes sound mental health. The greatest threats to this balance were seen to arise from physical disorders, such as an imbalance in the humors or blows to the head, but also from the disorder of the faculties, especially the passions and imagination. While Platonic and Christian traditions emphasized the separation of soul and body, such a division was honored more in theory than practice, and practitioners often adopted an Aristotelian-Galenic sense of interaction between the two. Disorder in one can provoke disorder in the other. Fear and despair can lead to insanity and suicide, just as physical pain from fevers or childbirth can drive humans mad. Imagination as a conjurer of images provides for dramatic interplay and the potential for insanity unless controlled by the reason, which directs will and judgment. Imagination can also sometimes trick the reason into approving the passions.

In the Renaissance view, the failure of the understanding to control the passions results in evil. Pre-Lockean and pre-Hobbesian faculty psychology dealt not with order/disorder but with the moral battleground exemplified by Milton's Adam in the Garden of Eden. In book 5 of *Paradise Lost,* Milton expresses the popular faculty psychology of his day:

> But know that in the Soul
> Are many lesser Faculties that serve
> Reason as chief; among these Fancy next
> Her office holds; of all external things,
> Which the five watchful Senses represent,
> She forms Imagination, Aery shapes,
> Which Reason joining or disjoining, frames
> All what we affirm or what deny, and call
> Our knowledge or opinion; then retires
> Into her private Cell when Nature rests.
> Oft in her absence mimic Fancy wakes
> To imitate her; but misjoining shapes
> Wild work produces oft, and most in dreams,
> Ill matching words and deeds long past or late.
>
> (1667, 100–113)

When not governed by reason, such as during sleep, the imagination conjures frightening and fantastic shapes. Reason is God's viceroy, and like any foreign governor is subject to assault either from outside force or the potential for disorder within all of us. For the besieged sufferer of the Renaissance, treatment came from the efforts of licensed and unlicensed physicians, surgeons, apothecaries, and midwives, augmented, especially among the poor, by a gallimaufry of quacks, herbalists, and astrologers. Treatment of the insane ranged from dunkings and masses to exorcise evil spirits to the application of various salves and potions, such as putting into ale "bishopwort, lupins, betony, the southern (or Italian) fennel, nepte (catmint), water, agrimony, cockle, marche" (Hack Tuke 1882, 4). But all too frequently, the therapeutics amounted only to whippings or to Sir Toby's prescription in *Twelfth Night* for Malvolio of having him "in a dark room and bound" (3.4). Reginald Scot's insight in his *Discovery of Witchcraft* (1584) seems profoundly contemporary: "Alas, I am sorry and ashamed to see how many die who being said to be bewitched, only seek for magical cures, whom wholesome diet and good medicines would have recovered . . ." (Hack Tuke 1882, 35). In fact, not until 1736 were the English laws against witchcraft abolished, and in 1722 at Sutherlandshire the last judicial murder of a witch occurred in the British Isles.

Throughout the sixteenth and into the seventeenth centuries, the clergyman became the basic psychotherapist, as doctors became the butt of fearsome jokes and steadily sank into disrepute. Lodowick Muggleton summarized prevailing sentiment when he pronounced that doctors of physic were the "greatest cheats . . . in the world. If there were never a doctor of physic in the world, people would live longer and live better in health" (Thomas 1971, 14). The profusion of medical approaches was not simply the result of the failure of the medical profession to have a consistent nosology and therapeutic approach but reflected an attempt by the doctors and cleric/physicians to reconcile magic, religion, and science. Such an attempted reconciliation, or at least a sense of urgency about attempting to do so, was to bedevil the medical practitioner throughout the seventeenth and eighteenth centuries. Philosophical debates about the mind-body relationship became central to the formulation of an acceptable orthodox approach to mental illness.

Keith Thomas's *Religion and the Decline of Magic* (1971) and Michael MacDonald's *Mystical Bedlam; Madness, Anxiety, and Healing in Seventeenth-Century England* (1982) provide solid summaries of many of the changes taking place during this period. MacDonald indicates that before the English Revolution the medical profession made little headway in establishing itself as the sole group qualified to deal with the sick; he notes that the treatment of sick people continued to be characterized by "professional eclecticism and therapeutic pluralism" (1982, 9). Sensitive to the conditions addressed in Pope Adrian's supposed remark about doctors covering up their mistakes with earth, lay people were generally cynical about the medical profession and turned increasingly to clerics for assistance with both physical and mental ills. While certainly not unsympathetic to medical approaches, such dissenters as George Fox, John Wesley, and George Whitfield used religious convictions and the power of their own personalities (plus electricity, in Wesley's case) to cast out devils and cure, or at least calm, mad people. However, even though it used therapies that were often disagreeable and ineffective, the medical profession gradually reasserted its preeminence in treating illness. As Thomas notes, by the end of the seventeenth century a "loose hierarchy of prestige" had been established among mental healers, and at the top of the chain were the "humanistic physicians" who regarded madness and melancholy as natural rather than supernatural disorders.

The doctors won the debate for essentially political and social reasons. Because dissenters like Fox and Whitfield were perceived as threats to public order, the upper classes sanctioned the physician as the primary source for treatment of the insane. Also, law and medicine increasingly provided more reliable sources of income than the often precarious vocation of priesthood or clergy. As MacDonald indicates, the dominance of medical therapies over psychological healing can also be seen in the therapies practiced at the proliferating number of private madhouses and public asylums. The often successful approaches to psychological healing practiced by Napier—one of the seventeenth century's major magicians—and many of his colleagues were discredited because of their association with religious radicalism and superstition. MacDonald says:

> The traditional fusion of natural and supernatural beliefs about disease and misfortune was discredited; the eclectic methods of psychological healing that had been grounded upon it were stigmatized as base ignorance and quackery. The formation of an elite culture compounded of rational religion, neoclassicism, and natural philosophy created an atmosphere in which Richard Napier's fame could not long survive. (1982, 231)

As will be seen later, the sympathetic, nonviolent methods of curing practiced by Friends at York Retreat, resembling as they did the methods employed by Fox and other dissenters, would because of religious and class associations come under similar suspicion and challenge by the medical profession.

The elements comprising this more rational revolution in care from the seventeenth to the eighteenth century were many and diffuse, with the seeds for change found in the seventeenth century. Certainly, a key element in the change was the dominant empirical tradition and associationist psychology. These ideas can be traced to the father of associationism, Thomas Hobbes, who in his *Leviathan* (1651) postulated the existence of a "trayn of thoughts" based in the senses, which can associate themselves without conscious control: "All Fancies are

Motions within us, reliques of these made in the Sense" (Hunter and Macalpine 1969, 135). Thoughts may come unbidden and without harmony, "as the sound which a Lute out of tune would yield to any man; or in tune, to one that could not play" (136). Hobbes's work, written during the English Civil War and later popularized and disseminated by Locke, frames the next century's approach to mental illness and, in a way, its fear of its own mind. If one cannot control the mind's thoughts, if trains of thoughts can arise unbidden, then one senses the possibility of losing control, and for this reason one must all the more certainly assert it. This search for order and control became paramount in the next century, especially in such literary figures as Addison, Steele, Swift, Pope, and Johnson. In fact, this impulse to order—itself capable of being exaggerated into a form of madness—reached an almost obsessive level in Johnson in his efforts to control and improve his period's conversation, its criticism, its drama and poetry, indeed its very language.

SUMMARY

The Renaissance and early seventeenth century sought the source of error or sin by dissecting the interior life. For want of an adequate faculty psychology or "philosophy," many doctors were content to abuse the bodies of the mentally ill by means of one mechanistic theory or another. Just as the priest identified erratic conduct with demonic possession, so too did the doctor ascribe it to problems with nerves, spleen, the brain, or even the passions, all the while ministering to a tormented mind with emetics, cantharides, and bloodletting and following such practices even when they militated against reason or results. But in the seventeenth century, as seen in the quotation from Milton, writers made a clear attempt to separate the faculties in order to find the source of error. Imagination increasingly became identified as the source of disorder or error. Causabon speculated in 1655 that imagination was the source of madness. The great Cambridge Platonist, Henry More, suggested that mental illness arose from an unbounded imagination when the soul "can neither keep out nor distinguish betwixt her own fancies and reall truths." He spoke of Hobbes's unguided "trayn of thoughts" and how men "become mad and fanatical whether they will or no" (Hunter 1966, 151). As noted in the previous chapter, the identification of imagination/madness/enthusiasm with Quakers and religious dissent embroiled Friends, doctors, and clergymen in a series of religious, medical, and social interrelationships. This same interconnectedness of ideas and issues dominates the history of mental illness into the eighteenth century and beyond.

Philosophical Factors: Locke and the Enlightenment

In the seventeenth and eighteenth centuries a group of secular philosophers began to wrest control of society's intellectual leadership from the clergy. A diverse group embracing Newton, Locke, Adam Smith, Kant, Voltaire, Hume, Lessing, and Diderot led the Enlightenment reexamination of fundamental issues of man and society, body and soul, which for political or religious reasons had been frequently neglected, save for orthodox discussions, or discussed at great peril, as in the case of Giordano Bruno or Galileo. Relying on Bacon and Descartes as models of rigorous inductive pursuit and methodical doubt, these thinkers not only made their ideas accessible to an increasingly wider audience but thereby provided the philosophical underpinnings of later social and political revolutions. At the same time they redefined humanity, seeing people not as eternal captives of original sin but as rational animals capable of change and even perhaps figures of original goodness. If people do exhibit evil, perhaps it is the result not of innate corruption but of societal and environmental influences. The problem of humanity became not a religious problem but a social one; thus at the end of the eighteenth century a rudimentary social science began to appear. The new conception of humanity and an emerging science combined to stimulate a variety of reform movements in all segments of society. Quakers were to take the lead in a number of such movements.

In France, this group of intellectuals and reformers were known as the philosophes, but they drew ideas and reinforcement from a number of British thinkers such as Newton and Locke. The philosophes were essentially scientists and thus often dealt with subjects that kept them from the strong religious entanglements dominating their ages. As Voltaire remarked, there are so sects in geometry. However, the breadth of their writings led them into other intellectual territory, often sparking confrontations that were not of their making and stimulating examinations of diverse fields from a new and exciting perspective. One clear instance of such influence was John Locke's *Essay Concerning Human Understanding* (1690).

JOHN LOCKE

Locke, especially in his *Essay*, dominated the age. As Basil Willey notes in *The Seventeenth Century Background* (1934), if Newton was the physicist for the eighteenth century and Milton its poet, then surely Locke was its philosopher (263). No matter where one turns in the period's writings, be it in the coffeehouse periodicals disseminated by Addison and Steele, the many medical writings considered later in these pages, the poems and essays of England's leading writers, the politically incendiary essays and documents, the thousands of religious tracts that erupted from multitudinous sects—these and numerous other writers, thinkers, and reformers were touched directly or indirectly by John Locke. His sober, straightforward analysis of philosophical problems, open to common sense and conveyed in a clear, nonacademic prose style, made him accessible to the common reader and, as popularized by the periodical press, widely read. As one who ever sought to keep the "pure glass of the understanding" as free as possible from the "gross dew" of the imagination, Locke always sought safety and common sense in his political, religious, and philosophical writings. He perfectly encapsulated a world he helped create: he affirmed a deity to be demonstrated, not enthusiastically embraced; he felt no need in poetry to assert an imaginative apprehension of truth; he was more concerned with truth than beauty. While Milton wanted an educational system to graduate heroes or saints, Locke was content with gentlemen (such as the third earl of Shaftesbury, whose education he supervised). Locke asserted that "Reason must be our last judge and guide in everything" (Willey 1953, 279). Small wonder then that Willey calls Locke a "massive figure" and quotes with approval Cobben, who described Locke as "the writer whose influence pervades the eighteenth century with an almost scriptural authority. . . . For a hundred years Europe continued to live on his ideas" (1953, 186).

Locke and those he influenced were thus particularly resentful of the enthusiastic excesses of the Quakers and other dissenting sects that had caused so much civil and religious chaos during the English Revolution. In his writings, Locke was not prone to trespass beyond the natural bounds of reason. He wished "to prevail with the busy Mind of Man to be more cautious in meddling with things exceeding its Comprehension; to stop, when it is at the utmost Extent of its Tether; and to sit down in a quiet Ignorance of those Things, which, upon Examination, are found to be beyond the reach of our Capacities" (1975, 44–45). How distant from the intellectual bravura of William Blake, who a hundred years later would shout "that which can be made explicit to the Idiot is not worth my care" and who sought "to see a World in a grain of sand" (1966, 793, 431).

Influenced by Locke, more people began to consider not God or external order but the workings of their own minds. For the *Essay* set out "to enquire into the Original, Certainty, and Extent of humane Knowledge; together with the Grounds and Degrees of Belief, Opinion, and Assent" and to consider how "our Understandings come to attain those Notions of things we have . . ." (1975, 44). He attacked the notion of innate ideas and religious enthusiasm, which rises from the "conceits of a warmed or overweening brain." He apparently had the Quakers in mind when he disputed the idea of the "internal Light," concluding *"it is a Revelation, because they firmly believe it; and they believe it, because it is a Revelation"* (702). The notion of the Inner Light cannot be innate; all knowledge, said Locke, must build up in each person from his/her experience. It is based in the senses. Though Locke only casually mentioned the association of ideas in a later edition of the *Essay,* many writers developed this notion, using Hobbes and More for additional support. Locke followed Hobbes and More in other respects. He agreed with More that a violent imagination can take "Fansies for Realities." The mad are not idiots. That is, they do not lack intellectual faculties and are not deprived of reason. Rather, "having joined together some *Ideas* very wrongly, they mistake them for Truths; and they err as Men do, that argue right from wrong Principles" (161). However, in his first edition of the *Essay,* Locke departed significantly from Hobbes and More in seeming to deny the possibility of unconscious thought. Unlike Hobbes and More, Locke refused to concede that one's knowledge can transcend experience, even in inner life. He posed the question: "Consciousness is the perception of what passes in a man's own mind. Can another Man perceive, that I am conscious of any thing, when I perceive it not my self?" (1975, 115). In the fourth edition (1700) of his *Essay* though, Locke did discuss the association of ideas and indicated that feelings as well as ideas could be associated.

DAVID HARTLEY

Influenced by Locke and strongly influential on the writers to be considered in later chapters, David Hartley wrote his *Observation on Man, His Frame, His Duty, and His Expectations* in 1749 and combined a potent and popular mix of ethereal physiology with associationist psychology. Hartley said that the ether in the filaments of the nerves receives vibrations ("vibrunticles") from external objects, and these vibrations in turn are transmitted to the small particles of the medullary substance. By degrees they produce different ideas in the brain, which associate with other vibrations to occasion new ideas and more complex concepts. Matter and spirit both exist in this process, for "the brain is . . . the seat of the rational soul." Hartley was not bothered by his failure to demonstrate such imaginative conjectures. He simply stated: "Let us suppose the existence of the aether, with these its properties, to be destitute of all direct evidence, still, if it serves to explain and account for a great variety of phenomena, it will have an indirect evidence in its favour by this means" (15–16).

THE SCOTTISH PHILOSOPHERS

Medical writers also looked to Scottish philosophers for discussions of the mind. In his *An Inquiry* (1798), Alexander Crichton acknowledged the intellectual debts he owed to Locke, Hartley, Reid, and Stewart for the theoretical underpinning of his ideas. In his preface, he said that he intended to use a method of "analysis" that involves "abstracting his own mind from himself" and examining it (ix). In doing so, he echoed the approach of Thomas Reid (1710–96) in *An Inquiry Into the Human Mind, on the Principles of Common Sense* (1764), *Essays on the Intellectual Powers of Man* (1785), and *Essays on the Active Powers of the Human Mind* (1788). In 1722, John Quincy, in his *Lexicon Physico-Medicum* said that "Experience without Theory will never make a physician." Problems abounded, however, when physicians tried to fit their experience to a theory of mind governed by the Lockean, associationist tradition. At the philosophical extreme was Reid, who opposed the use of hypotheses when not drawn from data and felt that true theories could arise only from careful reflection upon the operations of one's own mind. For instance, in asserting that in any act of perception there is a clear distinction between the mental act and its object, Reid was leaving behind philosophers such as Locke who had blurred this distinction. Unlike Locke, Reid also affirmed the existence of intuitive judgments, or what he called the judgments of common sense.

One chapter from *Intellectual Powers* gives the flavor of Reid's thought and suggests why he appealed so strongly to his contemporaries. In chapter 4, entitled "Of the Train of Thought in the Mind," he mentioned that trains of thought are of two kinds: "they are either such as flow spontaneously, like water from a fountain, without any exertion of a governing principle to arrange them; or they are regulated and directed by an active effort of the mind, with some view and intention." He said that even in a train of thought reason operates under control of the will. A train of thought can be guided and directed "much in the same manner as the horse we ride." He remained the eighteenth-century man in his assertion that even works of poetic genius and inspiration were originally the "offspring of judgment or taste": "What a man himself at first composed with pain, becomes by habit so familiar, as to offer itself spontaneously to his fancy afterward: but nothing that is regular, was ever at first conceived, without design, attention and care" (1785, 455). Thus he disputed the concept of Hobbes and Hume of an aimless association of ideas leading from the simple to the complex.

While allowing for the effect of the body on imagination, as in the taking of opium, Reid confidently asserted the power of the mind to cast out superstition and demons in order to make for itself a happy, ordered life. Reid would agree with Iago that "our bodies are gardens to which our wills are gardeners." Boswell reported that Samuel Johnson, who endorsed the ideas of the Scottish common sense school, put it even more simply: "Sir, we *know* our will is free, and *there's* an end on't." As influential as his fellow Scot was Dugald Stewart, professor of moral philosophy at Edinburgh University from 1785 to 1820, whose lectures, eventually brought together in 1827 as *Elements of the Philosophy of the Human Mind,* were widely quoted throughout this period. Haslam, in fact, called Stewart "the most thoughtful and intelligent of modern metaphysicians" (1809, 11). In doing so, Haslam echoed other commentators on mental illness.

Stewart and Reid represent the culmination of an epistemological tradition having roots in Descartes and Locke. In asserting that education and environment rather than the passions destroy the imagination and reason, Locke removed mental disease from the province of the moralist (DePorte 1974, 20) and became a necessitarian. Suggesting that madness is a disorder over which one has no control, he argued against free will. Hobbes, Locke, and Descartes established a philosophical milieu that emphasized that secondary qualities are not inherent so much as they are constructs of the mind. Descartes radically asserted that one at least knows that one exists and then must reason outward. One begins to test the limits and possibilities of this reasoning process to escape the prison of self. Locke and Hobbes rejected innate ideas and insisted on external standards; imagination must be restrained, and subjective impulses are not to be trusted.[2]

Many doctors confused symptoms with causes and assumed insanity was the result of flawed imagination, since the insane were unpredictable and often fanciful in their thought patterns. They saw the mind divided into reason, feeling, and will. Sanity comes when reason masters the other two. At the same time, many physicians were Lockeans who accepted sensationalism and associationism. Sense impressions rather than innate ideas were the constructs of the mind. Benjamin Rush saw insanity as a somatic disease and was most comfortable treating the mind through the body. He became caught up, like most theorists, in the mind-body debate. Was mind a function of brain, or could mental illness be explained psychologically? This was the overriding question and a constant dilemma. Having conquered the priests in the treatment of the insane, were the physicians now to yield the field to the philosophers/psychologists?

Stewart and Reid provided another, useful perspective for those physicians who wanted to believe that the body was to blame in all cases of mental illness because the soul could not become diseased but who remained uneasy over their failure to demonstrate such a totally somatic view. Reid and Stewart attacked Locke as being too atomistic and denying the unity of soul and innate faculties (Dain 1964, 59). They said there was an objective reality and people had innate faculties of duty, self-interest, and moral taste. Such comforting thoughts appealed to physicians interested in maintaining conventional moral and religious principles. What Stewart and Reid had to say did indeed appeal to the commonsense instincts of their readers. The appeal of their ideas is illustrated as well by the success of their colleague, James Beattie, the author of *Essay on the Nature and Immutability of Truth* (1770). The popularity and influence of Beattie's essay is best illustrated by Joshua Reynolds's painting showing Sophistry, Skepticism, and Infidelity fleeing before Truth. Beattie is at Truth's side holding a copy of his *Essay*.

As an important aside, it should be recalled that in the eighteenth century psychology was a branch not of science or natural philosophy but moral philosophy. One should also remember that epistemology was an area of thought where theology and psychology met; indeed, metaphysics came almost to be identified with epistemology. As William Blake said, "As a man is, So he Sees" (1966, 793). For want of an adequate psychology or "philosophy" of the faculties, many medical practitioners abused the bodies of the mentally ill using one mechanistic theory or another. The lack of agreement about the essential bases of mental illness led as well to constant speculation in medical texts about the nature of mind-body relationships, how faculties work, and how they fail. The philosophers examined here served medicine well by at least preparing a body of material for doctors to use as they took a more active interest in their patients' minds. Many of these physicians were mechanists who wanted to update Newtonian physics in terms of the mind or scientifically explain mind-body relationships but who, barring these possibilities, would settle for feasible if inchoate psychophysical theories of mental illness. It is now time to examine some of these theories and their advocates.

EIGHTEENTH-CENTURY THEORIES

Though designated for crude convenience the neoclassical age or Age of Reason, the eighteenth century was more complex. It was Augustan in its concern for reason and order, enlightened in its progressive optimism and skepticism about tradition, and Romantic in its fascination with the irrational and disordered. It was the century of Pope and Johnson, but also of Cowper, Chatterton, Blake, and Wordsworth. It was the period of a deistic god setting the clock in motion and stepping back from his creation, but it was also a time for discovering the banished god in nature. It was a period of religious sects that enthusiastically embraced the indwelling power of the "spirit," but it was also the time of the jaundiced Whig Lord Melbourne who, after being subjected to an evangelical sermon on the consequences of sin, remarked that "things are coming to a pretty pass when religion is allowed to invade private life" (Cecil 1969, 168).

A similar degree of complexity is apparent concerning medical theories of the day, for while the influence of Locke, Hartley, Reid, and Stewart was keenly felt, a number of other forces—religious beliefs, holdovers from classical medicine, fixations on particular drugs, warring views of body functions—helped shape the theories advanced in the many publications on insanity that appeared partially as a result of the notoriety surrounding the mental breakdowns of George III. As was already suggested, the philosophical and medical speculations of the seventeenth and eighteenth centuries were inseparable. For instance, the following elementary statements about mind-body relationships are revealing:

1. Mind is spiritual.
2. Body is material.
3. Mind and Body interact.
4. Spiritual things do not interact with material things.

The philosopher/practitioner had to make compromises in order to explain what became paradoxes. The dilemma for many doctors, especially if they were traditional Christians, was that they did not want to take the body out of medicine and leave the field to the priests, yet at the same time they did not want to admit that the soul was corruptible. Thus insanity as a physical or spiritual phenomenom was both intriguing and perplexing to philosopher and physician alike. This was why faculty psychology became more art than science. To protect the spiritual aspect Descartes' distinctions were desired; for medical/practical reasons one had to invade and overthrow comfortable compromises. Looking at the list above, for instance, Hobbes gave up number 1, Berkeley, number 2, and Leibniz and Reid, number 3. The latter believed that mind and body move on parallel tracks (i.e., that stubbing the toe does not necessarily cause the pain but is the occasion of one's feeling pain). Descartes gave up number 4 and said that the two interact at the pineal gland (not that the pineal gland was the same as the soul). Hume too gave up number 4; he said things were just conjoined and did not interact (e.g., billiard balls just happen to hit each other).

Assimilating the diversity of philosophical speculation, theorists reduced the cause of mental illness to four possibilities:

1. Physical causes with physical symptoms (this was medicine and did not challenge anyone).
2. Physical causes with mental symptoms (lesions on the brain, for example, might produce strong imagination or an enfeebled state of judgement).
3. Mental causes with physical symptoms (this could be as primitive as seizure by evil spirits or as complex as the notion of tension causing heart disease).
4. Mental causes with mental symptoms (mental causes could include rejection, grief, anger, an overpowering imagination, strong passions, religious enthusiasm).

These were not rigid distinctions but rather convenient categories that often glossed over problems and suited the particular mental construct of the person doing the theorizing. Cartesian theories were quantitative, while humoral theories were qualitative. Burton said that madness was based in imagination so that he could preserve the sense of reason as an immaterial faculty. Locke essentially agreed, and said that one could reason soundly on incorrect fancies. Imagination can control the other faculties, Locke said, and thus the mind is subject to associations of thought. Locke seemed to suggest that madness was the result of unfortunate experiences over which one has no control.

In all of this philosophizing, however, one comes back to particulars and to figures like Samuel Johnson. Johnson feared solitude because it might breed reptiles of the imagination, similar to those occurring in the Goyaesque sleep of reason or the replacement of reason's monitor with the usurper fancy during sleep. Any tendency toward the subjective, the major writers of the time felt, inclined one toward madness. The epistemologists' sense that secondary qualities were constructs of the mind again suggested the power and the danger of the independent self. The affirmation of self through self-reflection opened up an epistemological frontier but one fraught with the risks inherent in any testing of limits. Here as well lies the potential for turning the Enlightenment on its head. One might reason and use reason not merely to reflect sanity but also to escape madness. One might move *toward* order rather than *from* it. Johnson's letter of 19 June 1783 to Hester Thrale is illustrative. He mentioned that he went to bed but then awoke with

> a confusion and indistinctness in my head which lasted, I suppose about
> half a minute; I was alarmed and prayed God, that however he might afflict

my body He would spare my understanding. This prayer, that I might try the integrity of my faculties I made in Latin verse. The lines were not very good, but I knew them not to be very good, I made them easily, and concluded myself to be unimpaired in my faculties (Wain 1974, 359).

The Age of Reason feared nothing more than the loss of this faculty. Johnson's letter makes even more meaningful and trenchant Imlac's remark in *Rasselas* that "of the uncertainties of our present state, the most dreadful and alarming is the uncertain continuance of reason" (Johnson 1958, 595).

As the previous chapter indicated, religious enthusiasm was closely identified with madness. It was no accident that seventeenth- and eighteenth-century religious writings were full of distinctions between enthusiasm and inspiration, mystical and enthusiastic sensibility. Reason provided a standard, an ordered stillpoint to which one might cling, fearful of losing one's grasp and tumbling into a hellish subjectivism. The empiricists were so popular because they upheld the need for standards and discounted the notions of conscience and innate ideas. At the same time they had a problem. They wanted to affirm freedom and deny innate ideas but were left with the question of what standards to follow and how to avoid the dangers of poor environment or faulty education.

The issue was particularly thorny for Hume and Reid and the rest of the empiricists because they relied on nature; what was "natural" for them was good, true, and reliable. Where possible, they tried to ascribe madness to "unnatural causes" such as the fanaticism induced by religious indoctrination. But they left room for a perverted, unhealthy form of natural association as well. In the following passage Hume tried to distinguish between two operations of the imagination, both natural, but one more healthy and useful than the other:

One who concludes somebody to be near him, when he hears an articulate voice in the dark, reasons justly and naturally; tho' that conclusion be deriv'd from nothing but custom [imagination] which infixes and inlivens the idea of a human creature, on account of his usual conjunction with the present impression. But one, who is tormented he knows not why, with the apprehension of spectres in the dark, may, perhaps be said to reason, and to reason naturally too; But then it must be in the same sense, that a malady is said to be natural; as arising from natural causes, tho it be contrary to health, the most agreeable and most natural situation of man. (1888, 225–26)

As we will see, similar mental dexterity was to be found in medical accounts of insanity.

Medical Factors

Having noted the related social and intellectual factors contributing to the establishment of York Retreat, one must examine as well the specific writings on insanity available to Tuke and Jepson, to Fowler and Cappe as they began treating patients. These are some of the same writers to whom Samuel Tuke naturally turned for background when he prepared to write his *Description of the Retreat* (1813). He says in his *Memoirs* for October 1810 that he wished to "collect all the knowledge I can on the theory of insanity, the treatment of the insane, and the construction of lunatic asylums" (151). To this end he vowed to read or reread Stewart, Reid, Locke, Hartley, Haslam, Monro, Battie, Crichton, Ferriar, Beddoes, Pinel, Arnold, and others. The following summaries of the ideas of particularly important writers serve to frame the next chapter's discussion of therapies at York Retreat.

WRITINGS ON INSANITY: WILLIAM CULLEN

On 9 July 1790, Benjamin Rush delivered a lengthy eulogy before the College of Physicians of Philadelphia on Dr. William Cullen, professor of physic at the University of Edinburgh, who had died in January of that year at the age of 78. In doing so, Rush affirmed his respect for his former teacher and confirmed the ties between American psychiatry and the most successful medical school in Europe. Cullen's direct influence on Rush and American medicine, as well as on British and Continential medicine, was pronounced. Of the five original lecturers at the medical school of the College of Philadelphia—John Morgan, William Shippen, Jr., Thomas Bond, Adam Kuhn, Benjamin Rush—all except Bond (who studied in Paris) were educated at Edinburgh and thus came under Cullen's sway (Baltzell 1979, 165). Others among his students were Thomas Arnold, Alexander Crichton, and John Ferriar. On the Continent, Philippe Pinel translated in 1785 Cullen's *First Lines in the Practice of Physic* (1784). These and other influences were alluded to by Rush in his eulogy but were more particularly to be found in Cullen's own writings, specifically *First Lines* (1789).

Cullen himself in *First Lines* provided an historical overview of the history of science leading up to his work at Edinburgh. He noted the historical acceptance of the Aristotelian-Galenic system of humoral pathology that was slightly modified by the Paracelsian chemical system in the early sixteenth century but was also based on the state of fluids in the body. The theory of humors, however, was "exploded" (1789, 1:xvi) in the middle of the seventeenth century by the discovery of the circulation of the blood and the chyle and thoracic ducts. Also influential was the revolution in the system of natural philosophy, especially Galileo's introduction of mathematical reasoning and Lord Bacon's use of induction and experimental method.

Scientists began to move away from Galenic systems. Stahl, Hoffman, and Boerhaave introduced new systems. Stahl, from the University of Halle, believed that the rational soul governed the economy of the body. He believed that the soul excited the body to remove the "noxious powers" threatening it and affirmed the "art of curing by expectation" rather than using medical interventions. Frederick Hoffman, also at Halle, advanced the idea of primary moving powers while remaining a Cartesian humoralist. Boerhaave at Leyden was one of the systematics who produced a new synthesis of simple solid diseases and diseases of fluids.

Although Cullen saw himself as improving on the systems of these three men, in fact it was Boerhaave who earlier had sowed the seeds of change both by his own theories and by the large number of students he influenced. Boerhaave was a transitional figure in the movement from mechanism to vitalism in eighteenth-century English physiology. As professor at Leyden, he developed, in such works as *Aphorisms* (1715) and *Methods of Studying Physick* (1719), a great concern for rational empiricism and an emphasis on fibers rather than fluids. His direct influence on Cheyne and Strother and the presence in England of many of his former students accelerated his influence. During the nearly thirty years of his tenure at Leyden, in fact, Boerhaave touched the lives of 659 British medical students and infused in them his particular blend of mechanism combined with the diversity of experience (Schofield 1969, 48). His work paved the way for the reemergence of Thomas Sydenham, the "English Hippocrates," whose clinical, empirical approaches had never really enjoyed popularity in his own lifetime. A figure such as Richard Mead also offered an interesting blend of Newtonian mechanism and Boerhaavianism. In his *Medical Precepts and Cautions,* found in *The Medical Works of Richard Mead* (1763), he defined health and disease as follows: "Upon the whole, health consists in regular motions of the fluids, together with a proper state of the solids; and diseases are their aberrations." He saw as his purpose to "lay down precepts of the art, and methods of cure, rather than definitions and descriptions of disease; and to propose medicines confirmed by practice, not mere conjectures" (Brown 1974, 211).

It would be difficult to exaggerate William Cullen's influence on this important change; the mechanistic viewpoint gradually yielded to Hippocratic vitalism and to Cullen's scientific medical system. No doubt Cullen was also influenced by Thomas Willis's *An Essay on the Pathology of the Brain and Nervous Stock* (1681). Willis dealt with "psychology" or the study of "nature and essence . . . parts, powers, and affections of the Corporeal Soul." The word "psychology" was also used in theological works on the soul, so the word itself conveyed the shift from mechanism to vitalism. Also influential on Cullen were Robert Whytt's *Observations on the Nature, Causes and Cure of Those Disorders Which Have Been Called Nervous, Hypocondriac, or Hysteric, to Which Are Prefixed Some Remarks on the Sympathy of the Nerves* (1765), and Nicolas Robinson's *A New System of the Spleen, Vapours, and Hypochondriack Melancholy, Wherein all the Decays of the Nerves, and Lownesses of the Spirits, are Mechanically Accounted For* (1729).

An ardent mechanist like Robinson developed a rigorous extension of Locke's ideas of theories of mental illness that moved beyond a simple notion of flawed reason to a suggestion that the brain, diseased, produces such flaws. While both Willis and Robinson threw up their hands as to the precise, ultimate cause of mental illness, the influential Robinson was most emphatic that mental problems "are not imaginary Whims or Fancies, but real Affections of the Mind, arising from the real, mechanical Affections of Matter and Motion, whenever the constitution of the Brain warps from its natural standard" (1729, 408). A theory that would yield such modern terms as "high strung" or "nervous tension" was a clear precursor of somaticists who argued that mental illness arose from problems in the material objects, such as nerves and fibres, that constituted the brain.

Cullen combined mechanism and vitalism in his works. In volume 4 of *First Lines,* he dealt explicitly with "Vesaniae or of the Disorders of the Intellectual Functions." He first distinguished between purely topical hallucinations and diseases that affect judgment. Delirium affects people while awake and produces wrong judgment, while fatuity is a weakness or imperfection of judgment and also an "unusual association of ideas" (117). Cullen affirmed that the mind was affected by the body, especially the nerves (or brain), yet he admitted that it had not been discovered which parts of the brain relate to particular intellectual functions. He believed that the operations of the brain relate, however, to a "Nervous power" or a "subtle very moveable fluid, included or inherent, in a manner we do not clearly understand, in every part of the medulla substance of the brain and nerves, and which in a living and healthy man is capable of being moved from every one part to every other of the nervous system" (1793, 2:261). This power moves from the extremities of the nerves toward the brain and as a result produces sensations; equally, through the will, this nervous power instigates a motion from the brain to the muscles and produces motion. Cullen concluded: ". . . as sensation excites our intellectual operations, and volition is the effect of these, and as the connection between sensation and volition is always by the intervention of the brain and of intellectual operations; so we can hardly doubt, that these latter depend upon certain motions, and the various modification of these motions, in the brain" (1793, 2:261-62). Cullen used the terms "excitement" and "collapse" to indicate the different states of nervous power in the brain and nervous system.

Cullen then indicated that while dissection revealed the brain of the insane to be drier and harder or softer and more humid than that of normal individuals, he felt it was a mistake to consider insanity the result of organic lesions. Since people have recovered from insanity, he believed it to be a "state of excitement" that could be changeable by various causes that occasion temporary insanity. For instance, such increased excitement might cause mania, a "hurry of the mind" in which misjudgments feed on each other and are compounded by anger and sometimes violence, often toward loved ones. Complete restraint is an effective antidote to avoid reinforcing passions by movement. The patient should be placed in an erect position to avoid increased blood flow and thus increased excitement in the brain. This should be done within a closed place with familiar objects removed from the patient's view. Fear is also useful, with "stripes and blows" (1789, 4:154) if necessary, as is the use of evacuants, especially bloodletting, to reduce the "fullness and tension" of the brain. One may also use emetics, shave the patient's head, and promote perspiration to reduce "excitement of the internal parts" (1789, 4:159).

Throughout his listing of treatments Cullen relied on his experience to praise some and discount others. He liked soluble tartar, but not hellebore as an evacuant; bloodletting was necessary, but not over a prolonged period if improvement did not occur; cold should help, but did not appear always to relieve the metaphorically fevered brain (though he had seen successful use of the clay cap and surprise dunkings of mad people in cold water); camphor and opium relaxed patients but must be used with care.

Finally, Cullen divided mania into sanguine and melancholic personalities. The former was best bled and given cold treatment. Melancholics needed their "disordered imaginations" distracted. It was a partial insanity but affected other intellectual operations through "false imagination of judgment" on one subject (1793, 2:284). It was a disease in many cases not accompanied by any "morbid affections" of mind or body, yet it may affect both, particularly the mind. Dissection of the melancholic brain should show dryness and hardness in the medullary substance of the brain from want of fluid in that substance.

In his *A Treatise of the Materia Medica* (1789), Cullen provided a more definitive explanation of the nervous basis of disorder. The brain controls everything; it is an "energy" that "supports fullness in every part of the nervous system." But the basis of will is sensation. Impulses from other bodies impress the nerves and set up a nervous motion to their origin in the brain or "medulla spinalis," producing a sensation, then a volition, or another motion to muscles or "moving fibres." The body is affected in this way or more directly by sensation upon certain parts ("irritability"). Medicines depend upon "the sensibility and irritability of the human body; or, in other words, . . . upon motions excited and propagated in the nervous system" (1:42). The motions in the nervous system are those of a "subtle elastic fluid somehow connected with their medullary substance." These motions vary in people—the more elastic the fluid, the greater a person's mobility and sensibility. Sensibility as well depends on tension, or the pressure of blood flow in different parts of the body. As an "Energy" that "supports fullness in every part of the nervous system," the brain controls everything. An excess of fullness in the blood vessels of the brain may, however, destroy sense altogether. Cullen thus correlated temperaments with physical makeup. For instance, melancholics are thick-blooded; manics exhibit excessive strength of the medullary fibre.

For Cullen then, and for the many writers on insanity influenced by him, the nervous system became a critical point in the debates swirling about Cartesian mind-body dualism. As a fervent mechanist, Robinson said that mental illness resulted from perverted motions of the nerve fibres of the brain and not from any fault of the passions, imagination or reason. Cullen, however, while stressing the importance of the nerves in unequal state of "excitement" and "collapse" (though without an identifiable pathology), ultimately said that the reason for madness was faulty intellect and argued for a treatment combining fear and traditional emetics, bloodletting, and (his favorite) Peruvian Bark, Cullen moved toward a more monistic view of nature, in which he posited a sense of active matter unable to be labeled either mechanistic or spiritualistic.

WILLIAM BATTIE

A number of other important theorists and practitioners set down views that would ultimately shape directly or indirectly the mode of treatment developed at York Retreat. One of the earliest was William Battie. Battie, a physician at St. Luke's Hospital for Lunatics and a Fellow of the Royal College of Physicians, wrote *A Treatise of Madness* (1758) to promote as a distinct discipline the study of madness. As an established physician with a solid reputation, he dignified the treatment of the insane by establishing St. Luke's Hospital and devoting himself to the care of the insane both at St. Luke's and at a private madhouse in Wood's Close. His treatise was the first by a practicing psychiatrist with wide practical experience and stimulated others to write on the same subject. He made his mark as well by not confining himself to set theories and displaying a willingness to observe and treat individuals in terms of what they needed, not what the doctor desired.

Using the notion of sensibility being tied to nerves, Battie defined madness as "deluded imagination" or "false perception," tracing the problem to "some disorder of that substance which is medullary and strictly nervous" (1758, 41). The disorder can arise internally ("original madness") or externally ("consequential madness"); the latter could arise, for example, in a *coup de soleil* where the sunbeams dart perpendicularly upon the head of a sailor. In such a case it is important that membranes recover their elastic tone and not become too lax. Battie also anticipated Friends' moral treatment by agreeing that "management did much more than medicine" to effect cures. Confinement is necessary to remove the patient from objects that might act forcibly upon the nerves and cause misperceptions of things, but one should not then follow a rigorous medical regimen; there is no medical cure for original madness, though medicine can help make consequential madness manageable. He concluded that madness was a complex illness that resisted all general methods such as bleeding, blisters, opium, and emetics.

JOHN MONRO

John Monro perceived Battie's work as a personal attack and immediately responded in the same year in his *Remarks on Dr. Battie's Treatise on Madness* (1758). As physician to Bethlem Hospital from 1751 to 1791 and son of James Monro, who held the same position from 1728 until his death in 1752, John Monro became along with Battie the leading "mad-doctor" of his time. If Battie saw madness as a disease of the imagination and thus open to a psychological approach, Monro saw it resulting from "vitiated judgments" (1758, 4) that can be cured by a regimen of fear, restraint, and physic. Monro allied himself with ancients such as Aretaeus of Cappadoci whom, he indicated, Battie had censured undeservedly. Like Aretaeus, who was famous for anticipating the Galenic approach to the whole person rather than merely treating one part of that person and expecting results, Monro said that the Bethlem physicians never regarded certain nostrums, such as antinomial emetics or hellebore, as being specifically antimaniacal. Nonetheless, the use of bleedings and emetics was certainly widespread at Bethlem Hospital, as noted in the oft-quoted and damning account provided by Thomas Monro (John's son and successor) in his 1815 testimony before the parliamentary committee examining conditions and treatment in madhouses:

> They [the patients] are ordered to be bled about the latter end of May, or the beginning of May, according to the weather; and after they have been bled they take vomits once a week for a certain number of weeks, after that we purge the patients; that has been the practice invariably for years, long before my time; it was handed down to me by my father, and I do not know any better practice. (Hunter and Macalpine 1963, 702)

In the same testimony, Thomas Monro noted that the rich were more likely to be irritated at being in chains than pauper lunatics.

ALEXANDER CRICHTON

In his *An Inquiry into the Nature and Origin of Mental Derangement* (1798), Crichton frequently distinguished between imagination and true inspiration. Imagination consists of voluntary images summoned by a writer or painter from the representative faculty. This is larger than the faculty of judgment and potentially a source of error if the images are involuntary and force themselves on the brain, thus obstructing the possible balancing forces of external impressions. The genius, in addition to having a fertile representative faculty, also has judgment. Fiction writers are particularly prone to passing from the real world into their ideal realms, where they take fancy for reality, or peevishly returning to reality. This happens, said Crichton, because the image moves from the brain to the circumference or external sense. Religious enthusiasm is a particular train of thought gone awry and may result in a deep melancholy, a strong desire for eternal happiness, or absolute frenzy.

Crichton admitted that he had been influenced by numerous associationists. He envisioned the brain at the center of a great circle with the nerves at the circumference. Thus external impressions move from the circumference to the center, while internal ones operate in just the reverse. In this way, he said, "one and the same impression may be both external and internal as to its ultimate effects . . ." (59). Crichton also distinguished between creative aspects of understanding, such as the genius of poets and painters, which were erroneously termed imagination. Images may be voluntary or involuntary. Involuntary images arise through association; in delirium the images of imagination force themselves on the brain and obstruct the possible balancing forces of external impressions (9). The representative faculty goes awry from (1) arterial action being influenced by fevers,

brain inflammation, poison, or drunkenness; (2) causes that coun-
teract external impressions (such as sleep or "diseased viscera"); (3)
causes, such as fiction or strong passions, that distort judgment by
exalting imagination. Judgment is necessary to restrain the "stream of
ideas . . . lest they break down the natural banks of reason" (22).
Artists are particularly susceptible to insanity because they frequently
exercise their imaginative powers. Crichton even provided a perfect
neoclassical definition of genius: "new combinations of thoughts,
which . . . do not shock our judgment by their extravagance, but
appear as the glowing emblems of probable existences, or probable
truths . . ." (23).

THOMAS ARNOLD

   Without a clearly delineated mind-body schema and rigorous sense
of the effect of one on the other, it was only natural that as educated,
humanistically trained scientists, some of these writers would rely on
contemporary literary and social critics to guide them through this
philosophical maze. Thus works on mental illness abounded with
references to literature and philosophy. As Richard Hunter notes,
what makes psychiatry so difficult and complex is that it belongs both
to the natural sciences and the humanities (1966, vii). Like Crichton,
Thomas Arnold in his *Observations* (1782–86) discussed madness by
making consistent reference to the contemporary world of literature
and philosophy.
   In his first volume, Arnold stressed imagination run amok, a world
in which "imagination bodies forth the forms of things unknown" and
where (said Pope) "men prove with child, as powrf'l fancy works /
And maids turn'd bottles, cry aloud for corks." Arnold wrote that just
as wine and opium may disorder the mind through the body, so too
can passions affect the body; but all effects are ultimately reducible to
Hartleyan motions and vibrations. He found Hartley more useful than
Locke because of the former's greater emphasis on ultimate origins of
knowledge in the senses (62); for Arnold an "idea" was the "immediate representation in the mind of objects of sensation only" (62). But
the primary enemy remained a too active imagination, which excited
the brain and gave strength "to every other agent which may concur in
the production of that disorder," such as aggravating the passion and
confirming prejudice of error. Like many writers during this period,
Arnold distinguished between genius (which is rare), and imagination
(often the "parent of folly"). Unless judgment regulates the energies
of imagination, the imagination remains a blind, demonic faculty
producing disorder, lacking in discrimination, and leading to madness. Imagination produces "very active vibrations . . . in the fibres

and vessels of the brain." One antidote is "rational views of God and Religion; free from superstition, enthusiasm, or despondency" (509). One should also avoid writers on subjects of imagination or who misuse their imaginations on the subject of reasoning. "In short," says Arnold, "the imagination should be subdued . . . that the mind may be able to attend to reality and the nature of things, and not suffer itself to be seduced by fancy" (523). A firm mind arises from governing passions and restraining imagination.

This theme of the fear of imagination came at a point in literary history when writers were beginning to deify the imaginative faculty and see it as capable of disrupting a Lockean-Newtonian universe that was precise, limited, and restrictive.[3] Imagination became the particular bogeyman for the eighteenth-century thinker because of the shadow of the chaos and destructiveness of a seventeenth-century civil war that itself seemed to stem from religious enthusiasm and in particular the imaginative, innate ideas or inner-light convictions of so many self-styled prophets and dissenters.

Accompanying this fear of imagination was a desire on the part of the philosophers/psychologists to separate the faculties in order to find the source of error. A touchstone work, Plato's *Phaedrus* exemplifies the classic ambivalence toward the imaginative faculty—an ambivalence that is present in such writers as Addison. Addison saw that imagination was a two-edged faculty "as liable to Pain as Pleasure. When the Brain is hurt by any Accident, or the Mind disordered by Dreams or Sickness, the Fancy is over-run with wild dismal Ideas, and terrified with a thousand hideous Monsters of its own framing" (3:579). All pleasures of imagination arise from visible objects, either on immediate apprehension (primary imagination) or recollecting and recombining them at our leisure (secondary imagination). The source of both is the senses:

> We cannot indeed have a single Image in the Fancy that did not make its first Entrance through the Sight; but we have the Power of retaining, altering and compounding those Images, which we have once received, into all the varieties of Picture and Vision that are most agreeable to the Imagination . . ." (3:537)

Though aware of fancy's potential for being overrun with wild dismal ideas because of the mind's disorder as a result of dreams or sickness, Addison dwelt on the pleasures. It remained for that more troubled neoclassical spirit—Samuel Johnson—to voice the period's fear of imagination.

ANDREW HARPER

Andrew Harper's *A Treatise on the Real Cause and Cure of Insanity* (1789) blended several of these influences. On the one hand, he seems overwhelmingly mechanistic in asserting:

> Every impression, image, or idea, that exists in the mind has a peculiar note, pitch, or modulation. . . . Every idea may be measured by its elevation, or its depression, and in this point of view, every idea has its regulating or attempering idea that can restore it to mediocrity, or unison. The elevation and depression of ideas is adequate and parallel to the degree of pleasure and pain which ideas yield. (1789, 29–31)

One needs a balance of ideas yielding pleasure and pain to have "equilibrium of mental or rational mediocrity. Either of these extremes constitutes a degree of mental irritation; and the medium is the point of apathy, or composure" (31). Yet what impresses the reader as a literal rendering of Hartleyan psychology becomes basically a plea for balance and order in one's life. Insanity arises from the "sudden invasion of some deep, intense idea, or the rapid succession of several exorbitant ideas or affections, whether relevant or depressive" (41). Physically, one corrects imbalances by diet, bleedings, and purgings. A moral cure would be to practice moderation and the management of passions in one's daily pursuits. One should never allow one idea to dominate (such as love, pride, grief, enthusiasm) and destroy the balance.

JOHN HASLAM

A work mentioned by Samuel Tuke as particularly important to early development of the Retreat was John Haslam's *Observations on Insanity* (1798), probably because of Haslam's reputation and years of experience as medical officer at Bethlem Hospital before his dismissal in 1816 following investigation by the Select Committee of the House of Commons on the Regulation of Madhouses. Haslam served twenty-one years at Bethlem, the largest and oldest asylum in England, and as a result had more practical experience with the insane than most British doctors.

He defined insanity as "an incorrect association of familiar ideas" (1789, 10); Haslam could not imagine a disease of the mind and always traced the problem to physical causes, i.e., diseases of the brain and its membranes. He believed that dissections proved such deterioration and thus provided an orthodox conclusion: "When we find Insanity uniformly accompanied with disease of the brain, is it not more just to conclude, that such organic affection has produced the incorrect association of ideas, than that a being, which is immaterial,

incorruptible, and immortal, should be subject to the gross and subor-
dinate changes which matter necessarily undergoes?" (106). These
continuous incorrect associations need to be broken by change of
venue and a more regular regimen. Haslam was traditional with
respect to medical care, arguing for bleeding and purging although
denigrating the value of vomiting and opium. He found it "manifestly
asburd" to whip patients, but believed that the caretakers should gain
a firm ascendancy over their charges and sometimes keep them in dark,
quiet rooms, to avoid "a strong propensity to associate ideas." He also
urged kindness of treatment, gentle manners, and restraint that was
"not incompatible with kindness and humanity." In another major
work, *Observations on Madness and Melancholy* (1809), Haslam noted
that madness was not a complex idea but a "complex term for all the
forms and varieties of this disease" (1809, 4). He used, albeit incon-
sistently, division between mania and melancholia whose source ultimately was probably Cullen (and Linnaeus)—a nosology that
dominated the period. By mania Haslam meant false perception and
by melancholia he referred to an intensity of ideas.

As already noted, such writers as Crichton and Harper, as well as
Haslam, tended toward mechanism, following the empirical influences of the philosophers; however, these writers were obviously
uncomfortable with a purely mechanistic approach because they could
not demonstrate it. They also strained to avoid tracing the conditions
to the mind. They resorted to saying that insanity is based in the body,
not the mind but then proceeded to advance the conjecture of a
disease of ideas and how to treat it. Such a hypothesis reflected their
own confusion as to causes and cures. Bryan Crowther, in his *Practical
Remarks on Insanity* (1811), was more frank: "As to the general cause
of insanity, I know nothing," adding that to those who are insane, "it
matters not, whether they possess one condition of the brain or the
other; and whether it be the cerebrum aridum of Morgagni, or the
mania corporea of Dr. Cullen" (21). The construction of nosologies,
while providing pathways for future researchers, did not result in
cures. Crowther did believe, however, that enthusiasm and madness
were closely related and that the insane were "more frequently disordered in their health, than is generally imagined . . ." (1811, 88).

Several other works are also worth mentioning, since Tuke refers to
them. James Makittrick Adair, in his full, orotund style, described
how blood forms humors and supplies matter for solid body parts
composed of fibres and threads of different degrees of strength and
firmness. Medicine and psychology converged in his *A Philosophical
and Medical Sketch of the Natural History of the Human Body and Mind*
(1787). In a posthumous edition of his *An Essay on Diet and Regimen*

(1804) and in his earlier *Medical Cautions for the Consideration of Invalids* (1786) he ridiculed the hypochondriac tendencies of those who complained of "nerves" and frequented the spas at Bath. He attributed this phenomenon in part to Whytt's works (1751, 1765), since before they were published, Adair maintained, people of fashion did not even realize that they had nerves. Another work, William Pargeter's *Observations on Maniacal Disorder* (1792), shows the influence of Cullen and contains an extensive listing of the various medicines used in the treatment of madness—from cathartics such as black hellebore of Anticyra (Horace told the mad to *naviga ad Anticyran*), emetics like white hellebore or tartar emetic, antispasmodics like henbane, and medicated snuffs (errhines and sternutatories) used for ridding the nostrils and sinuses of the brain of mucid lymph secreted in the pituitary membrane.

JOSEPH MASON COX

The impact of the school of nervous sensibility extended into the next century, so that by 1806 Joseph Mason Cox, in his *Practical Observations on Insanity* blithely took it for granted that "the brain and its emanation, the nervous system, are the parts most intimately connected with the intellect, and that some morbid changes of these exist in every case of Insanity" (xi). Cox avowed that insanity was caused by "early dissipation, unrestrained licentiousness, habitual luxury, inordinate taste for speculation, defective system of education, laxity of morals; but more especially, promiscuous intermarriage, where one or both of the parties have hereditary claims to alienation of mind" (v). He thus affirmed a sympathetic correspondence of action between body and mind, where these causes or other predisposing ones (such as "excessive venery") included the proximate cause of morbid changes in the brain and blood circulation.

It is worth noting, as does Vieda Skultans, that toward the end of the eighteenth century and in the early years of the nineteenth, there arose a period of "psychiatric romanticism" in which the individual was perceived as being able by strength of will to combat the forces of unreason afflicting her; this view culminated in the idea of moral management developed by Friends at York Retreat (1975, 1). Gradually, however, as the number of patients increased and the possibility of individual attention waned, and as an increasing pessimism over the low rate of actual cures began to overtake many practitioners, the nature of insanity itself was reappraised. Words such as "force" and "will" in writers and theorists began to yield to terms such as "heredity" and "character." Gradually, too, the larger asylums moved away from individual treatment to simple custodial care. David Rothman's

Discovery of the Asylum (1971) and Hunter and Macalpine's *Psychiatry for the Poor* (1974) discuss this phenomenon at institutions in America and England.

It is worth noting that much of the British experience was replicated in America: for instance, the impact of Cullen's views was promoted by Benjamin Rush in his *Medical Inquiries and Observations Upon the Diseases of the Mind* (1812). Many of the ideas of the various medical writers of the eighteenth century examined here came together in Rush's influential work; he cited among others Cullen, Haslam, Pinel, Locke, Berkeley, Hartley, and Pope. At every point Rush affirmed himself as the quintessential eighteenth-century man.

Rush began his work by asserting that the faculties of the mind are "internal senses" and depend wholly upon bodily sensations for their operations. He defined derangements in the understanding as "every departure of the mind in its perceptions, judgments, and reasonings, from its natural and habitual order; accompanied with corresponding actions" (1812, 9). Rush refuted the idea of madness as caused by liver, spleen, intestines, nerves, or the mind. Regarding the latter, Rush said that were this so, the brain would appear in a sound state after death. He said that mind problems can provoke bodily changes. The primary seat of madness is in the blood vessels of the brain and is associated with the same kind of morbid actions related to other arterial diseases.

He then classified the causes of mental illness. Causes exciting madness are those (1) acting directly on the body (such as lesions; diseases such as palsy, vertigo, epilepsy; and certain odors); (2) acting on the brain in common with the whole body (onanism, ardent spirits, inordinate sexual desires and gratifications, extreme temperature, unusual labor or exercise); (3) bodily causes acting sympathetically upon the brain (narcotics, worms in alimentary canal, decayed teeth); 4) metastasis of some other disease to the brain (dropsy, consumption, St. Vitus's dance).

Causes may also act on the body through the medium of the mind, either directly (such as intense study, rapid transition of mind from one subject to another) or indirectly (imagination, joy, terror, love, grief, ridicule). He noted that intellectual derangement from mental causes was more common than that arising from corporeal causes and cited the figures given by Pinel of the 113 patients at Bicêtre; thirty-four suffered from domestic misfortune, twenty-four from disappointments in love, thirty from the French Revolution, and twenty-five from fanaticism.

Predisposing (i.e., long-standing) causes included (1) hereditary organization of nerves, brain, and blood vessels; (2) dark-colored hair and light-colored eyes; (3) an age of 20 to 50 years; (4) sex—women because of menstruation, pregnancy, and parturition; (5) marital status—single persons being more susceptible; (6) wealth (7) walk of life—poets, painters and other artists who exercise imagination more than understanding; (8) climate; (9) different religions and different tenets of same religion. The treatment for these various forms of mental illness was suitably physical and predominately antimaniacal— ranging from extreme bloodletting (twenty to forty ounces), darkness, solitude, Cox's gyrating chair, and (inspired by Cullen) the tran-quilizer chair.

SUMMARY

Prevalent in this period is a series of commonplaces that have evolved from a shared tradition of humoral psychology, common-sense epistemology, etc. These include: (1) associationist ideas; (2) the imagination problem; (3) mania-melancholy nosology; (4) therapeutics of bleeding and purging; (5) the dominant influence of Locke; (6) the relationship between enthusiasm and madness; (7) an emphasis on social order and moderation. It is odd, then, to juxtapose these emphases on moderation, control, and order with the simul-taneous Romantic revolt in literature and its accompanying idealiza-tion of the imagination, eccentricity, and creative disorder. It is, in fact, doubly odd because the Romantics, led by Wordsworth and Coleridge, were formulating a theory of the mind and the creative act that was distinctly anti-Lockean. No writer was more strongly critical of Locke and the world view he helped create than William Blake. Blake saw Locke and Newton as philosophers of limitation and con-finement. In "There is No Natural Religion" (1788), Blake overstated Locke's position to assert that if man is confined only to sense percep-tion he can only have organic or natural thoughts and will be unable to desire what he has not perceived. Blake concluded that "if it were not for the Poetic or Prophetic character [imagination], the Phi-losophic & Experimental would soon be at the ratio of all things, & stand still, unable to do other than repeat the same dull round over again" (1966, 97). And in *The Marriage of Heaven and Hell* (1970, 93), Blake boldly announced that "Man has no Body distinct from his Soul; for that call'd Body is a portion of Soul discern'd by the five Senses, the chief inlets of Soul in this age," concluding that "Energy is the only life, and is from the Body; and Reason is the bound or outward circumference of Energy. Energy is Eternal Delight" (1966, 149).

These ideas have been summarized because of their varying influ-ence throughout the period. Modern discussions that are revealing in this regard are R. E. Schofield's *Mechanism and Materialism* (1969) and the essays by Christopher Lawrence, "The Nervous System and Society in the Scottish Enlightenment" (1979) and Karl Figlio, "Theories of Perception and the Physiology of Mind in the Late Eighteenth Century" (1975). These scholars chart the movement from a world view captive to the simple Lockean impress of objects on the nerves to a more complicated sense of the active mind—a sort of reconciliation of opposites explored by Coleridge in his essays and poems dealing with the imaginative faculty and suggested too in his naming his children Hartley and Berkeley. In this interplay of the philosophical and physiological, the nervous system became the mediator. The idea of the "sensorium commune" became important at the end of the eighteenth century as a way of locating the mind in the nervous system tied to the body. This faculty presented sensations to the mind and made possible the imposition of the will on the body. Descartes located it in the pineal gland, while others (like Cullen) had more tolerance for ambiguity. As Figlio notes, the "sensorium commune" was a convenient idea that was both mental and physical—partly philosophical, partly anatomical. Such ambiguity was both satisfying and useful, since as a metaphor it permitted further researches without the need to resolve the mind-body dilemma.

Boerhaave strictly separated mental and physiological activities, while the idea of sensorium commune permitted a blending of the two. Figlio provides a useful summary of this faculty: it was "a precisely, though variously defined part of nature, with an indefinitely specified relationship to the soul. . . . A way of visualizing the nervous system rather than a way of observing it" (1975, 185). This sensibility theory of sensation became widespread and even led to a rationalization of class distinctions. Lawrence notes that sensibility was the foundation of Edinburgh physiology and could be affected by such factors as heredity, temperature, previous impressions, the state of the nerves and brain, the anatomy of the sense organ—in brief, ultimately by the quality and mode of one's life. Thus the upper classes were perceived as having more refined sensibilities, qualifying them as the proper custodians of civilization. Wordsworth modified such views to suggest that the finest sensibilities and moral natures result from a deep association with nature, but only with the better classes; do not build railroad lines to the Lake Country, he would argue later in his life, since the poor do not have the sensibility to appreciate and benefit from the landscape.

Figlio concludes his essay by asserting that in the eighteenth century sensualist ideas became intermediate between mind and the external world, not agents of the former. "It was in this intermediate domain that the eighteenth century physiological theories emerged" (1975, 199). The physiological correlate of this environmentalism was, as Lawrence notes, the "development of the concept of the reactive organism. Given a sensualist epistemology, the nervous system was clearly going to be of importance as the mediator between man and his environment" (1979, 19).

Robert Whytt (1765) was one of the first to move away from a Cartesian sense of automation and reintroduce the soul into the body. He said that the source of the body's purposeful behavior was the "sentient principle"—an "immaterial, undivided substance that could 'feel' stimuli and necessarily direct the appropriate response." This sentient principle was seated in the nervous system, with which it was coextensive. The death sentence for Boerhaavean physiology had been given.

Cullen, however, hesitated to administer the coup de grace. He flirted with Whytt's ideas by talking about a "vital principle" or nervous energy that is the source of sensibility, but he hesitated to go beyond natural law in analyzing this immaterial sentient principle. He perhaps would agree with Dugald Stewart that one should not extend "physiological modes of the nervous system to include the activity of the mind" (Figlio 1975, 184). In any case, Cullen would agree with Whytt about the importance of the nerves and sensibility. As Cullen said, "the nerves are more or less concerned in every disease" (Lawrence 1979, 28). Lawrence provides two important conclusions in the Scottish move to a more vitalist theory. One, that it became in principle the conceptual basis of nearly all midcentury Edinburgh pathological theory. Two, that clinical practice remained almost identical under the influence of this theory.

As will be seen in the next chapter, the managers of York Retreat began not merely with theories but with commonsense observation and a humanitarian spirit; this led them to changes in clinical practice. But while they did not remain captives to any abstraction, they had clearly synthesized much of the theory that had been developed during this period. That they chose to absorb it yet move in different directions was the result of many factors.

4

YORK RETREAT AND MORAL TREATMENT

This chapter is concerned with York Retreat and its adoption of moral, family-oriented treatment of the mentally ill. It will show how this modality of treatment grew out of philosophical and medical influences discussed in chapter 3 and, more importantly, out of Quaker religious history and the psychosocial organization of Quaker society. Particular attention will be paid to the Tuke family in its role as founder and promoter of the Retreat.

Pinel and Tuke

On Thursday, 21 July 1892, the members of the Medico-Psychological Association of Great Britain and Ireland held their fifty-first annual meeting at the York Retreat in honor of the centenary of the founding of that institution. A fact irresistible to the historian of psychiatry was that sharing the platform that evening were Dr. Rene Semelaigne, the great-grandnephew of Philippe Pinel, and Dr. Hack Tuke, the great-grandson of William Tuke. One hundred years earlier, Tuke and Pinel, without knowing what the other was doing, resolved to establish a humane system for the treatment of the insane. That each acted during a period of social instability and often without the support of government and professional leaders makes all the more remarkable both their accomplishments and the parallel nature of their efforts, but it is important as well to keep in mind the different backgrounds and motivations for their work.

Philippe Pinel (1745–1826) became director of the Bicêtre, the Paris hospital for insane men, in 1793, and in 1795 professor of internal pathology and director of Salpêtrière, the corresponding Paris hospital for insane women. As recounted in his *Traité médico-philosophique sur l'aliénation mentale*, published in Paris in 1801 and translated into English by D. D. Davis in 1806, he struck off the

chains of his patients, inspired more by compassion than any theoretical impulse, and with the cautious approval of the Comité de
Salut Public, since the chaining of such patients was required by law.
Like the Tukes, Pinel sought "to divest myself of the influence, both of
my own prepossessions and the authority of others"[1] while relating
his experiences, successes, and failures in his use of common sense and
humane judgment in treating the insane. Like the Tukes, he came to
attach little importance to the variety of pharmaceutical preparations
used in treatment and to place greater stress on the "physical and
moral regimen" of the patients.

It is significant too that Pinel paid particular attention to the difficulties of treating religious enthusiasm. Were he able, he mentions, he
would have isolated this class of patient and had them attend to their
own patch of ground while removing from their sight every object
pertaining to religion, to have them devote themselves to philosophical reading while drawing their attention at every opportunity to
comparisons between "distinguished acts of humanity and patriotism
of the ancients, and the pious nullity and delirious extravagances of
the saints and anchorites; to divert their minds from the peculiar
object of their hallucination, and to fix their interest upon pursuits of
contrary influence and tendency" (1806, 78–79). This group, he says,
is particularly susceptible to *"folie raisonnante,"* i.e., being fixated on
one idea while reasoning well on others.

Unlike William Tuke, Pinel was a rational humanitarian interested
in religion only as an aberrant expression of the internal stresses of his
patients. He was an arch empiricist who emphasized not hypotheses
but detailed analyses of a patient's behavior and elucidation of symptoms. He saw that insanity was a term applied to a broad range of
abnormal conduct and sought through the detailed descriptions and
analyses of his patients to be more discriminating. He admired the
writings of Willis and Cullen, but he felt that individualized moral
treatment had ultimately more effect on curing patients than any
preconceived regimen of bleedings and physic. In the second chapter
of his book, entitled "The Moral Treatment of Insanity," he appraised
the work of the English in moral treatment and singled out for
comment an account of York Retreat as given in the *Bibliothèque
Britannique* of 1798, though wrongfully attributing the article to Dr.
Thomas Fowler and placing the location of the Retreat in Scotland
(Hunter and Macalpine 1963, 605).

Other analogies with Tuke's work beyond the emphasis on moral
treatment can be seen. Neither man disavowed the use of restraint but
sought to minimize it, and both saw that oppression of patients might
lead to increased violence. Both acknowledged the need for compe-

tent, experienced managers of the insane with a trained nursing staff reporting to them. In both cases, they found such figures—George and Katharine Jepson in the case of the Tukes, Jean-Baptiste Pussin and his wife for Pinel. Pussin was a former patient of Pinel's, and the bonds were so strong between them that when Pinel left Bicêtre to move to Salpêtrière, the Pussins moved with him.

The obvious point of difference between Pinel and Tuke is that one was a doctor working in his chosen profession, while the other was a tea merchant acting to meet a need that he saw as important. Also, while the one man was a rationalist, the other was a committed Christian motivated in part by a sense of religious exclusivity. To trace Tuke's involvement in the movement for asylum reform is to see a variety of influences at work, not least of which was the social and religious heritage of Quakerism. What follows in this chapter is an effort to articulate those influences as they related to the establishment of York Retreat and, by implication, the involvement by Friends in the entire American and British reform movement.

William Tuke and the Establishment of York Retreat

Why, it may be asked, did Quakers, particularly William Tuke, involve themselves so energetically not only in the establishment of York Retreat but in the founding and promotion of similar institutions at home and abroad? As I suggested in an earlier chapter, because of their own enthusiastic roots, Quakers remained sensitive to charges of extremism or eccentric conduct in the practice and expression of their faith. As a close corporate body, they feared any dimension of public scandal that would bring the force of opprobrium of the community down on Friends as a whole. While a belief in the Inner Light had earlier presupposed following "leadings" that were not always socially acceptable—such as running naked as a sign or decrying the sinners of Lichfield—Quakers gradually lost confidence in such expressions and began to identify them as embarrassing excesses and dangerous vulnerabilities that left the entire Society open to charges of deviant behavior.

Certainly by the time of William Tuke a more conservative period has been reached, marked by a sense that the Inner Light must be balanced by the Bible and by experience and common sense. The turning point for Quakers was undoubtedly the writings of Robert Barclay. Barclay had a formidable sense of the primacy of inward revelation that contradicted neither Scripture nor reason. While Barclay clearly had mystical leanings, especially in his forceful arguments for the need of personal religious experience, he stressed the Cartesian need for both intuition and deduction and believed that there was no salvation outside the Church. An individual who accepts Christ in his heart is driven to find the fullest expression of that faith through a committed community of fellow worshippers. The group experience, to which Quakers were committed, thus acted both to reinforce and discipline their convictions.

William Tuke's life (1732–1822) gives ample evidence of the twin impulses of commerce and religious community that motivated many Friends during the eighteenth century. As such, his life may be seen as the culmination of the changes started by Barclay. No lengthy biography of William Tuke exists, and not much is known about his life, especially his early years. What is known has been developed in "A Sketch of the Life of William Tuke" by Harold C. Hunt (found at the University of York's Borthwick Institute of Historical Research), in Mary R. Glover's *The Retreat York; An Early Experiment in the Treatment of Mental Illness* (1984), and in the useful *The Tukes of York in the Seventeenth, Eighteenth and Nineteenth Centuries* (1971) by William K. and E. Margaret Sessions. These sources draw their primary materials from *The Memoirs of Samuel Tuke* (2 vols., 1860) and a work by William's great-grandson, Daniel Hack Tuke, *History of the Insane in the British Isles*.[2]

A sketch of William's life, as drawn from the records at the Borthwick Institute and the sources cited, is illustrative of the life of a typical eighteenth-century Friend and of the particular reasons and background for William's involvement in asylum reform. The twin poles of his life were his commercial activities as a tea merchant, a business inherited from his aunt, and his activity with the First Day, Preparative, Monthly and Yearly meetings of the Society of Friends in York, Yorkshire, and London. At the age of fourteen, William left school and became apprenticed to his aunt, Mary Tuke, who in 1725 had set up in York as a tea dealer. His natural inclination for hard work and his kind attentions to his aunt endeared him to her so that when she died in 1751, William inherited the business. It seems, however, that William had reservations about going into the tea trade, perhaps thinking that another profession would insure greater material success. He later castigated himself on this point: "I not only most anxiously grasped after the greatness of the world, and to obtain a name amongst men, but my corrupt inclinations so far prevailed as again to push me on to seek delight in forbidden gratifications." He confessed this following an experience at Sheffield Meeting where he was "much broken" and sensed that if he "first sought the Kingdom of heaven and its righteousness, all other things would be added."

These comments from a letter to Esther Maud of 28 November 1764 are worthy of reproduction because they illustrate the almost morbid sense of analysis and self-flagellation into which Quakers had descended during this period. Quakers had become conscious of the letter rather than the spirit of the law, and there is much evidence of their self-criticism over minor matters: falling asleep in meeting, for instance, was tantamount to a denial of the Inner Light; slight thoughts of personal adornment was clear evidence of Satan at work. Critical energies were directed toward themselves and their neighbors, as if moral perfection were to be attained by attention to religious minutiae. Quakers had become so inbred and self-critical that they needed an ennobling cause and spiritual uplift to give them new vitality. William Tuke was conscious of this. This surely was one of the motivations for his involvement in asylum reform.

During this period William also experienced some of the harassment and minor persecution of Friends that were carryovers from more severe, serious repression of the earlier days. In 1750 wardens of the town of York had visited William's aunt with a warrant from the mayor demanding 12/7 for Church repairs. They took 12/10 out of her change box and an additional 6-1/2 lbs. of loaf sugar for charges. Similar demands were made on William in 1753 when a warrant was issued to him in the amount of 4/9 for "Steephouse" rates and 5/- for charges (Hunt 1932, 5). No doubt, being forced to pay such church taxes made William sensitive to the isolation of Friends and the increased need for community solidarity. He also found a link to his own past, for his great-grandfather, William Tuke (c. 1600–1669), a blacksmith, was twice imprisoned for his Quaker beliefs in the York Kidcote or jail; he also suffered loss of property. Joseph Besse's *Sufferings of the People Called Quakers* (1753), with its detailed accounting of the Friends who suffered persecution from 1650 to 1689, mainly for their religious testimonies and refusal to pay church tithes, mentions that in 1660 alone 535 Quakers were imprisoned in various parts of Yorkshire, five of them dying in York Castle (Sessions 1971, 1).

William too would have faced many of the legal and social restrictions against Friends advancing themselves in the world. The 1673 Test Act barred them and other Nonconformists from public office and university education. The Quaker peace testimony prevented their following a military career. They tended not to own large estates, nor did they dance, drink, or gamble. While many early Friends were farmers, their persecution for not paying tithes often cost them their land and forced them to flee to urban areas, where career opportunities were greater and they could associate with a larger, more concentrated group of Friends. Quakers thus tended to become merchants and shopkeepers. Their reputation for honest dealing and for setting a single price instead of haggling eventually insured their commercial success. Their outlets beyond commerce were natural science (the liberal arts were frowned upon as an extravagant indulgence and a possible temptation of the spirit) and humanitarian causes. Thus their involvement in asylum reform, like their efforts in the antislavery movement and prison reform, were natural outgrowths of their interests and inclinations.

In 1754 Tuke married Elizabeth Hoyland of Sheffield, a woman of "very respectable connexions" who "united much that was pleasing in aspect and manners with good sense and sound principles" (Tuke 1860, 1:26). Then after six years of marriage and but a few days after the birth of her fifth child, Elizabeth Tuke died. Her death cast William into a guilty depression, feeling that the loss was a judgment on him for past sins. But after a period of mourning he recovered his emotional health and resolved to continue his attention not only to business but also to Quaker affairs. York Meeting at this time, like many meetings throughout England, had lost much of the fervor typical of the early Friends and too often had a leadership resistant to change. Samuel Tuke remarked that the leaders of York Meeting were dry formalists unsympathetic to any proposals for change and greatly wanting in tact. William Tuke also apparently lacked tact in reproaching them for what he perceived to be the failures of the meeting, but eventually his recommendations for change were supported by a commission from London Yearly Meeting.

During this period he was courting Esther Maud, whom he eventually married. She proved to be an ideal choice, not only as a mother to his children (winning them over through her strong sense of humor), but as a spiritual helpmate and independent force. She was an acknowledged minister in the Society and went on numerous preaching journeys to visit monthly and quarterly meetings. In 1784 she headed a deputation seeking to have the women Friends meeting officially recognized by the men's meeting. The clerk of yearly meeting was so moved by her dignified mien that he supposedly addressed her: "What wilt thou, Queen Esther, and what is thy request? It shall be given thee to the half of the kingdom." She also helped establish what became the Mount School to provide female Friends a fuller education than that available at Ackworth (Hunt 1937, 11).

Another fact worth mentioning is her authorship in December 1792 of an untitled broadside of three pages, twelve hundred copies of which were printed by York Quarterly Meeting for distribution throughout the county. In this pamphlet she obviously has in mind the domestic turmoil brought about by the impending conflict with France. She says in it that the meeting advises its members to "gather to that true quietude of mind, which will enable them to act consistently with our peaceable principles, in the state of unsettlement which at present exists in the nation." She talks of impending "times of trial." Too many Friends have been caught up in worldly pursuits; the land is in a "fermented state," but Friends must follow the "Shepherd" of peace. Shortly before her death she also published "An Address to the Inhabitants of the City of York With Some Remarks on the late Illumination and the Excesses Attending it. By a Lover of Peace and Order" (1794).[3]

Related to the expressions of unease found in Esther's broadside is the general turmoil in the period, from the outbreak of the French Revolution to the Battle of Waterloo (1815), i.e., the period of the Retreat's establishment and the publication of the Samuel Tuke's *Description* (1813). An atmosphere of disorder and chaos reigned throughout the nation because of the French Revolution, with its resultant civil and political chaos; the Corn Law and Luddite Riots that occurred in sections of England and led to hangings in the Tukes's East Riding district; the Nore and Spithead Mutinies at the end of the eighteenth century that bespoke the breakdown of order in the armed forces of England; Tuke's feeling that the prince, filling in for his supposedly mad father, could not cope because of his "indolence"; and the assassination on 12 May 1812 of the prime minister, Spencer Perceval, by a businessman named John Bellingham.

These turbulent times provoked the following outburst from Tuke: "*Reason,* as well as *life,* hangs upon a thread, exposed to ten thousand jars and violences which we can neither see nor prevent" (1860 1:283). Considering their history, it was only natural that Quakers would be particularly sensitive to such signs of disorder, especially among their members, and to the possibility of acting in such a way as to be the source of scandal. External events that would make the general populace, especially Friends, nervous about deviant conduct, resulted in a tightening of theological standards among Friends.

In the *Memoirs* Samuel Tuke recalls that while the fundamental principle of the Society of Friends is the doctrine of the immediate revelation, it is also important that the Scriptures be seen as the inspired word of God, including belief in the Trinity and original sin (here Samuel, like William, is countering the notion that early Friends agreed with Socinus and his antitrinitarian movement). Even at this late date, Tuke took pains to answer the charge that Friends' doctrine of Christ within was a subversion of scriptural authority, and in doing so he reinforced the notion of reliance by Quakers on standards other than personal revelation.[4] He said that "Friends are one with the Christian church at large" (Tuke 1836, 5). He restated his sense of the early Friends, saying that while they did stress the inward knowledge of Christ, "it was not in opposition of the outward knowledge but certainly, in opposition to the *resting* in the outward knowledge, which the Early Friends pressed so earnestly" (1836, 9). He then emphasized the need for order and standards: "They [Friends] do not set up any private revelation in opposition to the Holy Scriptures, but admit it as a positive certain maxim, that whatever any do contrary to the Scriptures, pretending to the Spirit, be accounted and reckoned a delusion of the devil" (18). As if to prove his point, Tuke later cited the hard work done by Quakers in the British and Foreign Bible Society to promote the Scriptures.

Two reasons, then, can be seen in William Tuke's life for the establishment of York Retreat and his own efforts in that regard: (1) a traditional Quaker sensitivity to breaches of public or personal order, and (2) a perception of humanitarian efforts as a creative outlet for an ambitious, intelligent segment stifled in many other avenues of achievement. A third reason for his and Quakers' work in asylum reform followed directly from their religious convictions. Quakers value all souls and esteem it a religious duty to seek and cherish all that is good, useful and rational in their fellows—to, as Fox urged them, "walk cheerfully over the world, answering that of God in every one." Quakers believe that there is that of God in every person, an indwelling force expressed as the "Inner Light," and that it is a matter of strict religious duty to see that expressions of that Light are not hindered, either by slavery or other forms of physical and mental oppression. Even the most severely afflicted of the mentally ill, Quakers believe, retain that spark of the Light which makes them God's children and part of a religious community. Quakers pay special heed to Paul's injunction in the epistle to the Romans: "Be ye transformed by the renewing of your mind, that ye may know what is the good and acceptable and perfect will of God." (Romans 12:2)

In this regard, it is interesting to track the conversion of Mary Maria Scott, later to become the wife of William's son Henry. She first became interested in Quakers by reading at the age of twenty-nine William Penn's "No Cross, No Crown." During this time she sent a letter to her mother from Bawtree, at the edge of Nottinghamshire, where she had attended meeting while visiting her grandmother. The letter states:

And I hope to stand ever in that light, which shows me all my enemies, and the way to escape and leads with unerring steps to that blessing which

Christ died to purchase for true believers. The Quakers profess a knowledge of the power of the spirit, and I profess that I would be guided in all
things by it; to eat, to drink, to fast, to watch, to pray, to sleep; if the Lord
will be so merciful to me as to grant that no early or devilish power shall
delude me from it; but give me light to make me resist all my enemies with
all my strength. . . . I hope to strive with all my natural gifts to obtain the
cross; the light of the Holy Spirit shows me—[that] without it I have no
right to obtain heaven. (1860, 1 : 43)

This quotation forms part of a two-page letter in which Mary Maria
uses the term "light" twenty-two times. It reveals how quickly even a
convert became steeped in Quaker rhetoric, how influenced by the
mystical dimension of John's Gospel the average Quaker was, and
how important the concept of Inner Light was to the average Friend.
Mary Maria's prose is that of a logical, rational eighteenth-century
woman, not the sociolinguistically revealing, introspective process
writing that is found in so many Quaker tracts and diaries earlier in
the period. Yet even for her the concept of Inner Light is more than a
spiritual metaphor. It is a living, redemptive force that guides the
individual, and it is the indwelling God. Quakers had a special moral
impulse to remove any blocks to that Light, especially mental illness.
    A fourth, perhaps less noble reason for Quaker involvement in the
care of the insane was their sense of religious exclusivity. Because of
the large amount of oppression and ostracism they had received,
Quakers in the eighteenth century tended to turn inward. They exhibited a growing quietism in religious thought and practice. No
longer directly persecuted and less evangelical in spreading their message, they withdrew to refine their discipline in matters of conduct and
dress and to direct energies toward personal and group development.
Too often this became a form of religious isolation. They reaffirmed
the ideas of George Fox by stressing simplicity in plain dress and
furniture, emphasizing the education of youth, and dutiful attendance
at meetings. They had fewer dealings with non-Friends and began to
disenfranchise those who consorted with or married non-Friends.
    It is important to place William Tuke's commitment in the context
of late eighteenth-century Quakerism and to see in his life a model
duplicated so often in the period. It was, of course, a much more
subdued Quakerism into which William was born in 1732 and a
significantly different one that he left behind when he died at age
ninety in 1822. It was a period in which Samuel Tuke would tepidly
note the merits of the founders of Quakerism while taking pains to
excuse their "extravagant" conduct. Tuke admitted that their "zeal was
a rough hairy garment, which suits but ill these days of silken ease and
nicely regulated habiliments," that they were "not gentle or prudent,"

but he commended their zeal and felt that they grew in the "graces of the spirit" until "the richer and softer tints of Christian character were seen spread over their later years" (1837, 39).

As noted earlier, William exhibited the almost morbid consciousness of his fellow Friends that was prevalent in this period; i.e., a tendency to examine in minute detail inward and outward failings. For instance, he perceived his first wife's death in 1760 as somehow a punishment for his wrongdoings, just as he had chastised himself earlier for his sin of ambition. In a letter of 14 September 1764 to his future wife, Esther Maud, he says: "I have compared myself to ground wherein wheat had been sown, which came up into green and promised for a crop, but winter passing over and spring approaching, when the husbandman began again to look for a fresh growth of the blade, behold all was become dead." He saw himself as barren ground in need of ploughing and harrowing, with wild roots needing to be gathered up and burnt.

This sort of critical self-appraisal was prevalent among Quakers during the period. One need but examine the journal of Elizabeth Fry to see a self-skewering on what are perceived to be violations of fine points of conduct and form: whether one, for example, was fully attentive to the leadings of the spirit during meeting; whether one was tempted to desire superficial things of the world; whether one took too much delight in the material; whether one's conduct toward another was all that it should be. A moral and formalist rigidity attended these self-doubts and led both to a regular attendance at meetings and rigorous oversight of the conduct of others. Many Friends were disowned for marrying out of meeting, or bringing scandal upon the Society, or for conduct the meeting found to be un-Quakerly.

The word "quietist" accurately describes this period in Quaker history. It was a vigilantly reflective period in which Quakers moved away from their proselytizing spirit, separated themselves from the world and found security in contacts among themselves, were still subject to mild forms of persecution and harassment, and sought to impose a scrupulous kind of religious and doctrinal order on those around them. Quakers needed to break out of this inner-directed, unhealthy self-consciousness. In their preaching journeys to various meetings, William and Esther Tuke discovered a distressing amount of vacant formalism. Samuel Tuke noted in his *Memoirs* that throughout England the Society of Friends "had come in many places (and York truly was not an exception) to be managed, not only by a few, but also by dry, formal members, wholly unable rightly to sympathize with the awakened, or with those who err and are out of the way. . . .

[William] saw that laxity, partiality, formality and perhaps spiritual pride, had crept into its proceedings. . . . The old men sometimes treated his expostulations with contempt, telling the Clerk not to mind what he said" (1860, 1:6). William's attacks on moral laxity (for example, the wearing of smuggled shawls by Quaker women) eventually found confirmation when a visiting commission from yearly meeting endorsed his call for a stricter adherence to Quaker principles (Hunt 1937, 7). Armed with more assurance, William then sought for ways to instill a more rigorous, energetic spirit into Quakerism.

One direction was the education of the young. It was perceived that too many Quaker children lacked sufficient instruction to prepare them for their lay and religious lives, especially those children whose parents were (as yearly meeting stated) "not in affluent circumstances." Under the leadership of Dr. John Fothergill, the noted Quaker physician, Quakers purchased an empty house at Ackworth about twenty-five miles from York, which had been built for the London Foundling Hospital. The school opened on 18 October 1779, with government of the school entrusted to two committees, a London one and a county one. William Tuke was on the latter and devoted a considerable amount of time and effort to insure the school's success. Ackworth was established on the principle that the teachers and children were a "family," thus joining together as a model a well-regulated combination of home and school.

Stirred by this success, William and especially Esther then set out to establish another school in York for the "guarded" education of young women. They became the school's first superintendents and were assisted by William's daughter Elizabeth and later their children Ann and Mabel. Lindley Murray, an American friend of the Tukes, also participated by instructing the teachers in formal grammar. His lessons evolved into Lindley Murray's *English Grammar* (1795) a successful text whose royalties were dedicated to Quaker education. The Tukes continued to be involved in this venture until its close in 1812. York Quarterly Meeting then reestablished the school in 1831, and it became known as The Mount when it moved in 1857 to a house of that name in Dalton Terrace in York.

York Retreat

Another even more significant direction for William's formidable energies was to arise from the death on 30 April 1790 of Hannah Mills, a forty-two-year-old Quaker widow at York Asylum. She had been placed there by her family who, because they were some distance away, asked York Friends to visit her. When they attempted to do so, they were refused admission, being told that the patient was not in a suitable state to be seen by visitors. She died shortly after this incident. When William's daughter Ann suggested that Friends should have their own asylum—so, as Samuel says in the *Description,* they "might enjoy the society of those who were of similar habits and opinions" (23)—William knew he had found a new mission.

Samuel saw this religious separateness as a primary motive for the establishment of York Retreat: "It was thought, very justly, that the indiscriminate mixture, which must occur in large public establishments, of persons of opposite religious sentiments and practices; of the profligate and the virtuous; the profane and the serious; was calculated to check the progress of returning reason, and to fix, still deeper, the melancholy and misanthropic train of ideas, which in some descriptions of insanity, impresses the mind" (1964, 27). In drafting a notice to raise money for the Retreat, such sentiments were foremost in William's mind.

On the back of a 1793 letter from Joseph Hadwen, Jr., William Tuke scribbled two rough drafts of a paragraph for the issue of a further appeal for funds for the establishment of York Retreat. The religious impulse was clear. He wrote: "And as it is mental disorder and People of regular conduct & even religiously disposed minds not exempt therefrom it is easy to suppose that the exposure to such a Company as is mostly found in public Institutions of this kind must be peculiarly disgusting & impious, indeed it is well known that the Situation of some of these hath from this cause been undescribably afflicting & must not such additional wretchedness greatly retard the cure?"

His second version reads: "People of regular conduct & even religiously disposed minds are not exempt on whom the exposure to such a mixed company must be peculiarly disgusting & Impious for as the Disorder is a Mental one a Situation so deeply afflicting to the minds of the Patients as is well known in many Instances have been distressingly the case must greatly retard the cure if not increase the Disorder."

The correspondence regarding admission of patients is also filled with concerns about the desirability of Friends living with Friends. Many applicants stressed membership in the Society of Friends by way of indicating the suitability of a relation for membership at the Retreat. Elizabeth Branne, in a letter of April 1802, petitioned William Tuke to enroll her son at the Retreat, saying: "May not my whole family being members of great Sobriety among friends, my Grandfather Isaac Turnell a publick friend My Mother Catherine Triffen by change of fortune a hidden character, but an honour to friends to her latest moment, Her House received the friends & her solid steady conduct kept the few friends together & the Meeting open so long as she lived at Marlbro' in Wiltsh—My Sister a varey useful & much Respected Member of friends—May not these things plead a little towards the extension of accommodation beyond strict Membership?" In an earlier letter she had felt the need to explain why she had married a non-Friend. She indicated that her sister, Catherine West, kept the Boarding School at Wandsworth, that she [Elizabeth] had married young and was never visited or spoken to by any Friend on her marriage to a non-Friend; that when she was finally visited she was not disowned because she had been "preserved in the fear of the Lord & His spiritual in Meetings with the Members of John Wesleys Society."

The final resolution as put forth at a York Quarterly Meeting on 28 June 1792 spoke directly of the need to establish an asylum "for the Members of our society, and others in professions with us." Friends with mental problems should not be subject "to the government or people of other Societies." Being with and under the care of fellow Friends would "alleviate the anxiety of the relatives, render the minds of the Patients more easy in their lucid intervals, and consequently tend to facilitate and promote their recovery." Further discussion led to amendments concerning the benefits being extended to "those who are not strictly Members of our society," but in theory and practice this would be a rare event. Thus was the scheme for building the Retreat launched (Tuke 1964, 26–31).

Such an undertaking was not easy. First, there was the need to galvanize support among Friends both in the immediate vicinity of York and ultimately throughout England. Something of the difficulty and frustration faced by William Tuke and his allies can be seen in a letter sent to Tuke by Samuel Birchall on 1 April 1793 outlining objections to the project as raised by members of the Meeting at Leeds. He provided four basic reasons for their refusal to contribute to its construction: (1) that the scheme was too bold an undertaking for a quarterly meeting and one that might eventually be copied by yearly meeting, thus perhaps rendering York Retreat redundant; (2) that Friends had no need for their own establishment and would be better advised to liberally support local public asylums, such as the Asylum at York; (3) that some had not considered the scheme at all, but merely reacted with a "noli me tangere negative"; (4) that some Friends had not contributed merely because other Friends of their acquaintance had not done so.

This letter echoed the kind of problems faced by Tuke throughout yearly meeting in attempting to engage the interest and support of fellow Friends in establishing York Retreat. Other letters spoke of York as being too distant from every part of quarterly meeting so as to render travel (especially with a patient) both arduous and expensive. William Alexander also sent a list of objections in his 16 March 1793 letter from Needham Market. His main points concerned the distance to York, but there was also a clear feeling that the terms for non-subscribing counties were too high and that Yorkshire perhaps had some exclusive privileges it ought not to have. Indeed, Tuke faced objections even from his home meeting. Some felt that mental illness could not be helped and that it was foolish to try. Others simply did not like the idea of having an asylum in their town.

Tuke also apparently irritated many of his fellow Friends by becoming annoyingly aggressive in advancing his case in support of the Retreat. Eventually, however, after his more diplomatic son Henry convinced them to at least consider his father's ideas, the meeting asked Tuke to prepare some plans. Appeals were then sent out, but many of the objections already cited led to little money being raised; however, a list of subscribers was compiled, and money was borrowed to advance the project. A site of eleven acres outside York was purchased, and a London architect was hired to design the asylum, based on what Mary Glover has called the "architecture of compassion." Namely, the building was designed to have long wide corridors to enable restless patients to move about freely. The floors were wood, not stone, to soften patients' falls, and the windows had small panes framed by iron bars, so they would not have the appearance of prison windows typical of so many asylums.

What made all of this possible, of course, was the determination and single-minded commitment of William Tuke. In fact, reading through the large correspondence to William Tuke, one is impressed with the magnitude of his labors in establishing the Retreat. As treasurer and early superintendent of York Retreat, he was responsible for payment of all bills and, in addition, the handling of correspondence with regard to admission of patients and reports on their progress once admitted. He also handled many of the details of hiring and firing staff members and haggling over the cost of treatment. The demands on his time for correspondence alone were considerable. One wonders how he was able to find time away from asylum matters to keep his prosperous tea business going.

Yet Tuke did manage to raise enough money and eventually did build an innovative structure on a hill just outside the town limits of York. It was an accessible structure, using much of the technology that had been developed nationally in the treatment and housing of the insane, as well as having some innovations such as the special windows mentioned above. The entire structure still stands today on that hill outside York. The Retreat remains a working asylum, though not as celebrated as it once was.

York Retreat, which early espoused moral management of the insane, had its genesis in both humanitarian zeal and religious exclusivity. The 1792 declaration of purpose clearly stated the need for the Society of Friends to shelter and care for its own afflicted souls. Although there was no true equality in treatment (wealthier patients received better quarters and the right to have their own servants), there was a desire for religious homogeneity in the institution. True, the benefits of the institution, according to the 1792 statement, would be extended to those "who are not strictly members of our Society," yet from the discussions of the commission we see that the latter statement was taken to mean members who were Quakers and had been cast out through marriage to non-Quakers or who at least attended Quaker services.

Description

Samuel Tuke gave up his Hebrew lessons in 1811 when his father Henry asked him to write a history of the Retreat, which had opened in 1796. As recorded in his *Memoirs,* Samuel set about the task with characteristic determination and detail. On 7 January, four days after noting the charge from his father, he "made selections from Pinel" using Davis's translation of 1806, and "had George Jepson to dinner, and had much conversation on the subject of insanity." He read as background material many of the works on insanity mentioned in chapter 3 of this book, he interviewed superintendents of other asylums, and he studied the architecture of asylums. A favorable review by Sydney Smith in the *Edinburgh Review* (1814) helped sell out the first edition of the *Description* within three years of its publication in 1813 and extended its impact beyond England to America and the Continent.

Tuke's essential motivation in writing the book was to contrast the successful application of a benevolent theory of care with the then standard "terrific" approach to treating the insane. The first two sections provide a historical account of the founding of the Retreat, its initial reception of patients, and the various staffing problems, while the third chapter describes the grounds and house, or "family establishment." Chapter 4, "Medical Treatment," is a record of those "pharmaceutical means" that have failed, rather than a record of those that have succeeded. Tuke first discussed the work of Dr. Thomas Fowler, the first visiting medical officer to the Retreat from 1796 until his death in 1801 in London as a result of a fall from a horse. Born in York and a graduate of Edinburgh Medical School, Fowler was famous for the introduction of arsenic to the British pharmacopoeia as a remedy for ague.

As described by Tuke, Fowler was a man with an "unprejudiced" mind determined to test on patients those medicines he thought likely to benefit them or that had been recommended by those with superior knowledge and experience in dealing with the mentally ill. He tried bleeding, blisters, emetics, evacuants, and other prescriptions—all highly recommended—but he found all of them wanting in terms of curing the patient and indeed often harmful to the patient. He thus became reluctant to use medicines, being aware that "the probable good would not be equal to the certain injury" (1813, 112). The one remedy that he did find efficacious was the warm bath, especially for melancholics. These discoveries do not mean, however, that medicine did not have a place at the asylum, nor the physician a role to play. Tuke noted that the physician often possesses a great deal of influence over the minds of the patients, more so than the other attendants. The doctor's presence is also helpful when mental disease is attended by bodily disorder, for there is a clear connection between a sound mind and a healthy body. Finally, Tuke noted the use of large meals and porter in promoting sleep among the maniacal patients; he derided as foolish the notion that the insane are inured to hunger and cold.

Nearly three times as much space is devoted in the *Description* to moral treatment as is given the discussion of medical treatment. Tuke takes it as a given that mental illness arises either from the mind, in which case applications made to it are the most natural, or from the body, in which case the source must be determined. But owing to general ignorance concerning the working of the body, the physician when dealing with the mentally ill can only address himself to alleviation and supression of symptoms. Judicious modes of management or moral treatment are therefore deemed most suitable for such an approach. Moral treatment of the insane was treated under three parts: (1) how to assist and strengthen the power of the patient to control the disorder; (2) the kind and degree of necessary coercion; (3) the means of promoting the general comfort of the insane.

With regard to the first point, Tuke discusses the use of fear. He notes its value in the education of children, but affirms that the desire of esteem has more effect than fear in dealing with the mentally ill. Such desire when properly cultivated "leads many to struggle to conceal and overcome their morbid propensities" so they do not become "obnoxious to the family" (1964, 157). Adherence to religious principles also enables the patient to restrain harmful impulses; thus attendance at meeting is encouraged. As for restraint, the less the better, though Tuke notes that on rare occasions it is necessary to use a strait-waistcoat, to confine a patient in a dark room, force-feed her, or to use ankle or arm straps. In all cases it is important to teach attendants that any restraint or coercion is to be employed as a salutary rather than a punitive measure.

The chapter concludes with several suggestions on ways to improve the general comfort of the insane. The first and the most famous has to do with the tea parties arranged by Mrs. Jepson where the patients were invited to a formal party and were expected to conduct themselves with "politeness and propriety." There was also a constant effort to occupy the mind and combat indolence by drawing, chess, playing at ball, and reading (especially mathematics and natural science).

The final chapter in Tuke's work provides statistics and comments on all patients admitted to the Retreat from 1796 through 1811. He takes care to mention that of the 149 patients admitted, only a few seemed to have as their source religious impressions as the cause of their madness. This observation ran counter to the notion expressed by the apothecary of Bethlem Hospital that he owed great obligations to the Methodists for sending him many of his patients. Tuke disavowed such remarks, adding that religion may be the *apparent* cause of insanity, but that more proof was required before one could state this with conviction. Still, he could not resist stating that "the habits and principles of the Society of Friends are at least not more unfriendly to mental sanity, than those of other societies" (1964, 211), as indicated by the large number of cases among Friends that are constitutional or hereditary.

The actual records, however, would seem to contradict several of Tuke's observations, for it is possible to observe a pattern of remarks revealing a connection between religion and insanity. This sensitivity to religious distraction may be seen in the early correspondence affecting patients at York Retreat. There are frequent references to insanity manifesting itself in religious terms or in religious delusions. In a letter to William Tuke dated 15 February 1804, Thomas Crowley complained of Samuel Waring's sister Mary that she was in "a very visionary way, apprehending a Number of divine communications"; William Farrer from Liverpool regarding Ann Lawton who missed meeting and "laid claim to revelation in such a manner as clearly to manifest her disorder. . . ." (22 August 1808); Jasper Capper regarding Jane King and her conduct: ". . .she had been much amongst the Methodists and had disturbed the meeting of Friends" (25 January

1809). The need was felt to minister not merely to the mind diseased but often to those who could be sources of embarrassment to Quaker family and friends because of their religious delusions and public expressions of belief. There was also a sense of decreasing tolerance for eccentric conduct and the need to impose clear codes of normality in order to avoid potential scandal. For instance, in filing certificates for admission (required as of 1818), usually the reason for admission was noted; there was frequent mention of disorder and religion. It was said of Joseph Rushton in August 1818 that he had "strong religious impressions, producing great despondency"; of George Orger in April 1819 that he "has always been an eccentric man . . . fond of running after particular preachers"; of Jane Biggs that she had a "peculiarity of manner"; of James Kingston (17 March 1820) that he was "subject to strong passion"; of Rebecca Bland that she displayed "great singularity of character" (20 April 1820). In a period sensitive to a need for order, there was an increasing intolerance of disorder.

The Retreat case books from 1798 to 1828 also document the pervasive preoccupation with religious enthusiasm and concern over conduct that would have been routinely accepted in the early days of Quakerism. John Grundy, admitted February 1798, imagined he was "commanded by Angels to walk naked to pronounce woes and judgments to the King and nation in general." Hannah Middleton had a tendency to melancholy, but it was never actively developed "in consequence of the well regulated state of her feelings under the influence of religion" (24 January 1810). Interspersed among the case analyses are frequent remarks of a religious nature, such as those designating the cause of madness as "religious melancholy"; of people speaking in meetings, though not ministers, and often speaking incoherently. Elizabeth Bass, admitted in 1811 and released in 1812 "continued singular and enthusiastic, riding about London on an ass, endeavoring to convert the Jews." Edwin Swan Rickman was "rashly enthusiastic and a writer of verses" (11 April 1820).

Another recurring phrase is "very singular" or "something singular," suggesting a dislike for abnormality. Ann Lees entered in July 1821, left 11 September 1822, and was readmitted in 1824: "a great talker about religion, preaching, etc. and pretended to be a saint." The comments continue about Ann Lees by way of explaining the basis of her illness: "Her friends were Methodists and she was addicted to preaching and praying when deranged in the style of the Ranters. Her coming to friends' meeting, etc., was probably indicative of the unsettled state of her mind, and premonitory of insanity." Frederick B. Tolles later notes such remarks by American Friends as indicative of Quakers rejecting their origins. In his *Quakers and the Atlantic Culture*

(1960), particularly chapter 6 entitled "Quietism versus Enthusiasm: The Philadelphia Quakers and the Great Awakening," Tolles argues that social and cultural change within the Society of Friends moved it from an enthusiastic movement of the lower classes or petite bourgeoisie to developing a more quietist character adopted by wealthier American Friends, i.e., into a period "characterized by a less prophetic ministry, a more introspective mysticism, and a fear of "creaturely activity' "(94).

Tolles notes the reception given by Philadelphia Quakers in 1739 to the preaching of George Whitfield, the foremost evangelist of the Great Awakening. Whitfield disparaged the Quakers for identifying the light of conscience with the Holy Spirit and thus representing Christ within instead of Christ without as the foundation of faith. The Quakers, in turn, ridiculed Whitfield for stirring his audiences into a false sense of being led by the Spirit. James Logan, erstwhile secretary to William Penn, felt that by encouraging the "most hot-headed predestinarians . . . he and they have actually driven divers into despair, and some into perfect madness." Logan was most concerned, says Tolles, over the "emotional excesses and the psychological disorder which they [Whitfield and other revivalist preachers] induced" (100).

Studies of religion and culture frequently reveal a tension between enthusiasm and mysticism. Using the terminology of Joe Lee Davis, it can be argued that George Fox was enthusiastic rather than mystical, that he came to God through "inspirational automatism" rather than the mystic's "regenerative gradualism." As Quakers disavowed their enthusiastic roots, they moved in the eighteenth century into a period of quiet withdrawal and diminished "creaturely activity." They continued to assert that the basis of religious authority is inward experience rather than outward belief, but they became more cautious about the promptings or openings of the spirit lest they be carnally inspired rather than inspired by legitimate "movings" from the Holy Spirit. They became skeptical about religious emotionalism and moved toward a more peaceful introspection and refinement of form. Thus while avoiding the Scylla of a frenetic, misguided enthusiasm, they risked the Charybdis of a self-satisfied formalism.

The Methodists came in for particular attack from Friends, who regarded their energetic forms of worship as undignified and unduly enthusiastic. By contrast one often encounters moral comments that cast a favorable, even smugly elitist light on Friends. Typical was the case-book comment (3 September 1826) on Isaac Taylor: "He has been very rigidly educated both as regards principles of friends and generally has been quite shut up from the world. . . . The effects of a different mode of education exemplified in children of a brother of I. T.'s who were brought up laxly and nearly all fell into some gross vice." The emphasis on personal experience in both Quakerism and Methodist evangelicalism suggested the possibility of an extreme individualism—for the danger cited by Barclay of an antirational element and "enthronement of the experiential element in religion." While having a reputation in the seventeenth century for being dangerously individualistic in their beliefs, especially as expressed by a faith in the promptings of the Inner Light, the fact is that the Quakers remained a viable sect because they were so strongly community based and conscious of the need for structure and organization.

As mentioned earlier, Quakers established York Retreat in order to segregate their insane from non-Friends. Certainly this sense of religious exclusivity was reflected in the tabulated return of persons admitted to the Retreat beginning in 1796. In that first year, it was recorded, fifteen individuals were admitted, thirteen of whom were members of the Society of Friends and two of whom were "connected." Regarding the latter, the original charter stated that the benefits of the Retreat would be extended "to those who are not strictly Members of our Society." This probably meant in practice that spouses of members could be admitted. In any event, it was not until 23 June 1820 that an individual was admitted (Owen Weston) about whom the records show an uncertainty as to a connection with the Society, though doubts had been expressed earlier as to the membership of some. Then on 12 November 1820 a patient was admitted without a connection to the Society of Friends. The number of unconnected members then increased, but not dramatically. Of the twenty-one patients admitted in 1830 only three were unconnected; in 1840 of twenty-three, six were unconnected; in 1850 of seventeen, one was unconnected; in 1860 of fifteen, seven; 1870, of nineteen, eight; 1880, of thirty-six, twenty-one; 1890 of twenty-six, nineteen; and by 1900, of forty there were only four members. It is even recorded that in November 1807 a patient was dismissed from the Retreat in order "to make room for members."

Family

Whenever Samuel Tuke talked about the patients and their caretakers at the Retreat, he referred to them as a "family." For instance, in talking about a patient who had a tendency to wander from the grounds, he said that such actions "excited considerable anxiety in the family" (1964, 154). This term had more than metaphoric value and was suggestive of more than just a coterie of Friends with shared values (though this is important). As Anne Digby notes in her insightful *Madness, Morality and Medicine* (1985), the family concept was important to the sense of moral management. It was related to the discipline of the Society of Friends, "which aimed to inculcate in the young a habitual Christian self-denial, moderation and uprightness of character." In some situations where these virtues had not been taught in the home, the Retreat provided a "surrogate home and family in which to resocialize the patient" (34). As such, the managers had certain preconceptions about character, society, and religion—patterns of "normality"—that they hoped the patients would adopt or at least not grossly violate.

Mention has been made of Scull and Foucault's contention that Quakers were in fact coercive in manipulating the minds of the patients to a bourgeois sense of esteem and work. Digby finds that Foucault's conclusion that moral management was only made possible when madness was alienated in guilt has a "kernel of truth," but she feels that Foucault's and Scull's works apply more to larger nineteenth-century pauper asylums than the small elitist institutions of the eighteenth century.

As discussed above in chapter 3, many of Locke's ideas helped influence the philosophy of care at the Retreat. The notion, for instance, of sheltering disturbed patients in small, dark rooms in order to curb any "strong propensity to associate ideas" (164) was clearly influenced by a Lockean, associationist psychology. Even more important perhaps than Locke or Hartley's epistemology, are Locke's views on education. As Digby notes, patients are like children, and the use of Locke's theories and sense that education would "help to re-create correct patterns of thinking and thus establish appropriate standards of behaviour" (1985, 69) is apparent. By having a stable staff and an accessible structure closely approximating a home, the stress was on the normal and domestic. One thus had an appropriate environment in which to emphasize self-disciplined living in a system inculcating both religious truth and correct principles of behavior.

An emphasis on the family had been one of the most abiding characteristics of Quakerism from its roots in the seventeenth century through its period of persecution to the more quietist, reserved period of the eighteenth century. Here the Quakers deviated somewhat from Locke. While he ultimately defined the family as a private contractual social space, one almost with a life apart from its dealings with the rest of society, the Quakers, like the early Puritans, saw the family and by extension the larger religious network as an important buffer to the persecution around them and, more important, as a bulwark of social and psychic order. This certainly was the kind of mindset at work when William Tuke founded the Retreat and one that consistently emerged in his grandson Samuel's *Description.*

The Quakers survived the religious imbroglios of the seventeenth century primarily because of the organizational skills of Fox and Margaret Fell and because of the strong familial bonds among the followers. There are constant references throughout meeting records of funds being collected or personal counseling being offered to members going through difficult personal or financial problems. Such aid was extended beyond individual meetings to those in other counties, states, or countries. For instance, the Minute Book of the Monthly Meeting of the Society of Friends for the Upperside of Buckinghamshire (1669–90) records numerous instances of support provided Friends, either through gifts or counseling—the principle of help leading to self-help—as well as numerous censures of those Friends whose actions brought disrepute on the Society. It is as if a system of rewards and punishments were at work. If one was a loyal, abiding member of the Society or Family, then one reaped the rewards of community, but one was also subject to punishment or censure for violating the rules. Much the same impulse was at work, though in a kindly, more subtle manner, at the Retreat.

The concept of the extended family was alluded to by Elizabeth Allis Pumphrey, the daughter of Thomas Allis, who was superintendent of the Retreat from 1827 to 1841. Her "Recollections," read at the Centenary Celebration in 1892, recalled the Retreat fifty years earlier,[5] that is, when it was a "much smaller place, simply intended as a kind home for members of our own Society (with the exception, later on, of a few high class patients)." She made a distinction between the period before the law compelling the appointment of a medical man as superintendent and the period after when the Retreat essentially became "a medical institution and very much losing its character of domesticity." She recalled in particular the Plough Monday parties with Morris dancers and the quarterly meeting day parties when tours of the asylum were provided.

Moral vs. Medical

It was not until the Madhouse Act of 1828 that physicians were required to head mental institutions of more than one hundred patients and that all patients were required to receive visitati doctors. Up to that point the interested, sometimes experier teur was superintendent. York Retreat had George Jepson, a earnestly sought out assistance and at the same time had a sound, practical, empirical mind; he weighed on his own what was therapeutic and what was not, in much the same way that the more experienced Dr. Fowler proceeded. Tuke had some reservations about hiring Jepson. In an undated letter to William Maud, William Tuke noted that Jepson had abilities superior to the position of keeper to the men patients, but he was concerned that his experience was not "in the Government and order of a pretty large Family." However, he considered him a "steady religious Friend and in that respect to be fully confided in." Tuke also considered his knowledge of medicine to be an asset. Therefore George Jepson came to the Retreat in 1797 from Edward Long Fox's private asylum, Cleve Hill near Bristol, following his future wife Katherine Allen, who preceded him to the Retreat as matron of the female patients.

Despite his interest in medicine, we see from Tuke's work that Jepson followed common sense. He noticed, for instance, that wild animals were most easily tamed by gentle methods, so he inferred that a person bereft of reason might be similarly influenced. Using judgment and feelings as his guide, Jepson gradually abandoned the use of medicines for treatment of the mentally ill (except where the body was clearly diseased). This approach to moral management became popular and influenced the development of a number of institutions here and abroad. Nonetheless, the approach was not wholly accepted.

In his 1828 *Sketch* of the Retreat, Samuel Tuke summarized the medical experience at the asylum for the previous thirty-two years. He noted that as with Fowler's approach, medical treatment remained experimental and emphasis was placed on observation of particular cases and how each patient responded to various medicines. Perhaps, he implied, with more such research and sharing of information, the "medical treatment of insanity will become better understood, and more successfully practiced" (31). For the moment, however, it was necessary to rely on moral treatment, hoping that the proper arrangement of environment would alleviate symptoms and by interaction of mental and physical, "lessen or remove the physical cause of the disease." While Tuke acknowledged that "derangement of mind may probably in all cases be connected with bodily disease," it was equally true that "proper regulation of the mind" (36) was essential to preventing it. Often the foundation for mental illness was "an injudicious indulgence in early life; by which the ill trained man has been brought into contact with the oppositions and difficulties of the world, without the habits of endurance or self-government" (36).

To support the feelings of satisfaction with regard to moral treatment, Tuke cited statistics showing high rates of recovery or improvement. For instance, of all cases through 1827 from the asylum's opening that included a first attack of not more than three months' duration, fifty-six of seventy patients recovered and three improved, while eight died and three remained at the Retreat. Thus slightly more than 84% recovered or improved. The percentage decreased with cases in which the attack was of longer duration.

By 1846 in a fiftieth anniversary *Report* on the "State of the Retreat," Tuke again stated his view with regard to the efficacy of medical treatment versus the "expectant system" (38) of waiting upon nature. He derided the "cruel quackery" of much of what had earlier passed for medical treatment and noted the benefits of the Retreat's medical and moral regimen. He stressed that the Retreat had not been indifferent to medical advances, especially the study of the brain and the influence of chemical agents on its workings. He noted too that the managers had sent John Kitching to Germany to study the work done there by Dr. Jacobi at Siegburg and Dr. Zeller at Winnenden. He also mentioned that the Retreat always had visiting physicians and surgeons, but not until 1838, with the appointment of Dr. Thurnam, did it have a resident medical officer and then in 1847 its first medical superintendent when Thurnam ascended to that position. It was clear during this period that the doctors were gaining control over the institution, but Tuke still affirmed that medicine cannot cure insanity but merely promotes the general "well-being" of the patient (45). The doctor, he avowed, should not be discouraged to discover "that he had to depend more upon the influence of mind upon matter, than of matter upon mind" (46).

As Digby (1985) convincingly demonstrates, medicine gradually gained ascendancy at the Retreat, and its Quaker character diminished. The latter phenomenon was the result partially of the Separation of Friends through the Hicksite split, especially in America (see the next chapter) and the decreasing number of Quaker patients and administrators. As for medicine replacing moral treatment, this was partially inevitable because of the lack of rigor found in moral treatment and the lack of a clear general theory to be followed. It is also true that the many writings of Samuel Tuke on the Retreat concealed to some degree what was actually taking place. Tuke obviously took relish in the success and renown of the Retreat, and he remained blind to the forces for change in the treatment of the insane that were taking place in both England and America—forces that would, if not undermine them, at least diminish the stature of Quaker efforts with moral treatment. For instance, one significant movement—never mentioned by Tuke—was the effort of some Friends to establish an institution for medical treatment of the insane, the Southern Retreat. A detailed account of this project reveals the currents that would help undermine moral treatment.

The Southern Retreat

Documents at the Library of the Religious Society of Friends in London[6] reveal an attempt in 1839 by prominent Quakers to establish the Southern Retreat as a counterpart to the already famous Tuke-inspired York Retreat. Though unsuccessful, the effort is interesting in several respects, not the least being the close involvement in the project of Thomas Hodgkin and his relationship with Achille-Louis Foville.

The Friends who met at Devonshire House in London on 1 June 1838, the day after yearly meeting, to discuss the "propriety of form-ing an Institution for the Insane, in the South of England" were conscious of a kinship with York Retreat that was more than seman-tic,[7] for those present included men who had contributed to York Retreat and were friendly with that institution's leaders. The main force and paramount figure at this meeting was Thomas Hodgkin (1798–1866). A man of broad interests, ranging from his original investigations of lymph glands while a pathologist at Guy's Hospital in London to his intense antislavery efforts, Hodgkin was a birthright Quaker and member of Westminster Meeting at the time of his attempt to found the Southern Retreat. He had also been a close friend of Samuel Tuke for several years.[8]

Out of this meeting came a special committee consisting of Hodgkin, Dr. Ball, John Sanderson, Joseph Jackson Lister, Samuel Gurney, Jr., and Thomas Bevan. They worked with others to compose a prospectus for the project. At a meeting held on 15 July, those present supported this document, which was henceforth dated 17 July 1839 and distributed to potential supporters under the title "Pro-posals for the establishment of a lunatic asylum under the care of Friends, to be called the Southern Retreat."[9]

The prospectus begins by paying respectful tribute to the work of York Retreat, but repeats a concern first expressed by Friends when William Tuke was seeking support for his venture—namely, the "ex-pensive, painful, and fatiguing travelling" that Friends in Southern England must undergo to reach York. The Southern Retreat would hope to imitate the kind of care for which York Retreat was famous and would continue the practice of receiving wealthy patients, Friends or otherwise, at increased terms by way of subsidizing the reception of poorer patients:

The feasibility of this project is almost demonstrated by the fact that the Managers of the Retreat at York, have within a comparatively short time contemplated the establishment of such an Institution by the employment of their own accumulated funds. Local changes which have induced the Directors to abandon this plan, have not, however, materially diminished the expediency of the measure, which has been approved by competent judges in the Medical Profession, and is called for by the fact that it has repeatedly been found necessary to send Insane Friends to Asylums in no way connected with the Society.

Should enough financial support be given, the prospectus continues, Dr. Foville would be hired as medical director, with high hopes for his success: "The advantages of treatment under his direction would doubtless not be confined to the inmates of the Institution, but a most important reform in the medical and physical treatment of the Insane might reasonably be expected to spread from this Institution to most of the considerable Lunatic Asylums in this country." Of more importance, Foville's presence would signify a radical departure from the heritage of York Retreat: "As the Northern Retreat has had the merit of contributing materially to improve the moral management and personal condition of British Lunatics, so its Southern counterpart might be equally happy in effecting a similar amelioration in the very important but too much neglected branch, to which belongs the medical treatment of mental and cerebral disease."

The prospectus then makes an appeal to raise £20,000 through the sale of 400 shares of £50 each with no individual holding more than twenty shares. The net proceeds of the institution would be divided among shareholders, with a maximum individual gain of seven and one-half percent per year on money invested, any surplus going to "the improvement of the establishment." Also, a guarantee list would enable those who did not wish to buy shares to support the institution by guaranteeing with the shareholders any money lost during the first seven years of operation.

I have already named Thomas Hodgkin as the moving force behind the Southern Retreat. Several facts support this idea, the most important being his relationship to Foville. Achille-Louis Foville (1799–1878) was born at Andelys, studied medicine at the University of Paris, and interned under Esquirol at Salpêtriere.[10] His 1824 medical thesis is dedicated to "mes maîtres Esquirol, Ferrus, Pinel et Rostan," and is entitled "Observations cliniques propres à éclairer certaines questions relatives à l'aliénation mentale." ("Clinical observations for the purpose of clarifying certain questions related to mental illness.")[11] In this work he takes issue with those who feel that madness is incurable and who "attribuent toujours sa terminaison aux bienfaits de la nature, et jamais aux resources de l'art." ("always attribute the cure of mental illness to natural causes and never to science.") Citing the success of the medical approach in a variety of cases, such as the cure of hysterical mania through the use of blisters on the neck and cold water, he concludes that "la folie est curable." ("Madness is curable.")

Following graduation and on Esquirol's recommendation, Foville was appointed medical superintendent in 1825 of the Saint-You Asylum at Rouen, which had just opened, and he later became a professor of physiology at the Rouen medical school. When Esquirol died in 1840, Foville was appointed the chief medical officer at Charenton, a post which he lost in the political revolution of 1848. His major work was *Traité complet de l'anatomie, de la physiologie et de la pathologie du système nerveux cérébro-spinal* (1844), the fruit of his many years of research. Thomas Hodgkin is acknowledged in the preface to this work: "Mon excellent ami le docteur Hodgkin de Londres a trouvé moyen de me seconder malgré la distance qui nous sépare." ("My good friend Dr. Hodgkin from London has always managed to support me despite the distance that separates us.")

Their friendship obviously antedates this work, going back perhaps as far as the period of Hodgkin's Paris studies at the Necker Hospital in 1822.[12] What would have drawn them together, besides Hodgkin's fluent command of the French language, was a mutual interest in pathology. In a speech in 1827[13] on medical education delivered before the Physical Society of Guy's Hospital, Hodgkin paid tribute to French pathologists and may well have had Foville in mind. The Hodgkin papers[14] reveal more certain evidence of their relationship. A letter to Hodgkin from William Stroud dated 6 December 1830 speaks of Foville's stay in England. Stroud asks for an introduction so that he might see Foville's "preparations of the brain." And in Hodgkin's diary entries for summer 1838 there are a number of references to dinner and travel with Foville and William Frederic Edwards, whose work *On the Influence of Physical Agents on Life* (1832) had been translated from the French by Hodgkin in 1838.

One can reasonably speculate that despite the lack of his own writings on the subject of mental illness, Hodgkin's appetite was whetted for the scientific aspects of the study by his close interaction with the experienced Foville and by his own general scientific curiosity. Though he was friendly with and later eulogized James Cowles Prichard, (Kass 1988, 396), the man who coined the phrase "moral insanity," Hodgkin had a greater interest in "chemical physiology" (letter of 1 May 1839) and the physical effects on the brain as seen in pathological investigation. Also, while his many humanitarian ventures—ranging from concern over poor sanitation, chimney sweeps, drunkenness, and bad housing to his antislavery efforts and presidency of the Aborigines Protection Society—consumed much of his time, Hodgkin was preeminently a scientist, one who concurred with his colleague Sir William Withey Gull's remark that "the road to medical knowledge is through the Hunterian [pathological] museum, and not through an apothecary's shop."[15] Hodgkin had little sympathy for those who administered remedies without knowledge of the disease. His humanitarian and scientific impulses coverged admirably in the plan to establish an asylum whose medical emphasis would complement the moral direction of York Retreat.

Hodgkin probably felt that a clearer, more comprehensive medical approach to mental illness, combined no doubt with detailed pathological examinations, would advance both the store of medical knowledge and the reputation of the Southern Retreat, just as over forty years earlier the "Northern Retreat" began making its impact through a moral regimen of religion, sound diet, and useful labor. This is the reason for the sense of optimism conveyed by the prospectus. And for Hodgkin, who could better head such an institution than a close friend, experienced alienist, and noted pathologist?

It should be kept in mind, however, that the dichotomy suggested by the medical-moral approach was not a radical one. Like the mind-body problem, it was more a matter of emphasis. The Southern Retreat would not neglect the moral aspects of care any more than York Retreat neglected the medical. Bleedings, blisters, and evacuants were used at York Retreat, but without success, so as time progressed its leaders felt less confident of the medical approach, excepting perhaps the warm bath. Yet Samuel Tuke often spoke of the "inexplicable sympathy" (1964, 116) between body and mind. In a diary note of 22 January 1817, he speaks of nightmares as the product of indigestion and suggests that bodily disorders are the cause of some cases of insanity. Reason, he says, is

> liable to be eclipsed by the derangement of those organs which we in degree understand, and, [is] perhaps, infinitely more subject to the vicissitudes and diseases of those finer parts of our bodily frame, of which we know no more, than that they baffle our greatest skill to dissect or unravel. Here and here alone is the true source of cheerfulness and confidence—that not one hair of our heads shall fall to the ground without our heavenly Father's knowledge. (1860, 1:291)

Still, moral treatment remained the primary concern of York Retreat. This philosophy challenged a profession based on medical care of the insane and the profitable administration of expensive home-made nostrums. As Andrew Scull notes (1979, 163–70), in the period of York Retreat's success doctors were threatened by the fact that they might have to admit that they could not demonstrate the efficacy of medical treatment; as a result, sympathetic laymen like William Tuke were as capable of heading asylums as physicians. But gradually the medical profession assimilated moral treatment into its plan of treatment and reasserted its primacy and authority to treat mental illness as a medical problem. The Madhouse Act of 1828 reinforced this change.

These alterations no doubt influenced Hodgkin's conception of his asylum. A religious man but also a careful scientist, he wanted more certainty and was more confident of medical solutions. The Southern Retreat, as he envisioned it, would emphasize close bedside observation of physical symptoms combined with cadaveric examinations. The man who confidently proclaimed from a medical viewpoint that "la folie est curable" would head the Southern Retreat. Thus on 12 March 1839 Hodgkin wrote to Foville on a matter he had no doubt broached on earlier visits to Paris: "I have spoken to my friends on the subject of the lunatic asylum which I have proposed to have established and which I have long thought was really wanted but which could be more than doubly important if it could have the advantage of thy medical direction." Hodgkin admits that a particular friend[16] is not sanguine about Hodgkin's prevailing on Foville, but that the "subject is one which has [not] sufficiently come under his consideration for him to be aware of its importance." Yearly meeting, Hodgkin continues, will occur in about two months, and that will be the "time when its practicability may be decided on and steps for its commencement may be taken. . . ." Hodgkin then concludes with a wish that Foville's "cerebral researches" are going well.

As mentioned, it did not take the committee much time after the meeting of 1 June 1839 to do its work. Meetings subsequent to the issuing of the prospectus concentrated on establishing a constitution for the asylum and selecting a housing site. On 18 May 1840 Rickman Godlee, Lister's son-in-law and secretary of the Southern Retreat Committee, asked all subscribers to remit £10 per share on shares subscribed for so that suitable grounds might be leased. By the deadline of 1 June 1840 £1,620 had been collected and by 11 July £2,450 was in hand; since this represented but twenty percent of the total amount committed by the subscribers, £12,250 had already been subscribed for the Southern Retreat. Money was no problem; other obstacles would arise to foil the venture.

The ostensible difficulty was the failure to secure a suitable property. Long negotiations were held with a Dr. Jersey of Wyke House near Brentford, who initially was interested in leasing the committee a property for twenty-one years. Negotiations fell through, however, and in a notice of 13 July 1840 subscribers were urged to recommend other possible sites. The Minute Book records an energetic pursuit and examination of possible locations. Areas in and around London were checked—Leyton, Chelsea, Hampstead, Southgate, Hammersmith—but to no avail. Finally a letter dated 17 May 1841 went out to all subscribers indicating that despite extensive inquiries and their inspection of various houses, the committee had not been successful in acquiring a property they could recommend as suitable.

The letter mentions another problem: "The Committee have recently learned that Dr. Foville, whose services it was proposed to obtain for the medical direction of the Institution, and who, for a long time, held himself at liberty for that purpose, has now, in consequence of an opportunity occurring which did not admit of delay, entered into an engagement with an establishment in France." The post alluded to is that of the medical directorship at Charenton. Foville's decision sealed the fate of the proposed Southern Retreat. In consideration of the failure to find a proper home for the asylum and secure the services of its chosen medical director, the committee decided to return all money to subscribers, less minor expenses,[17] and the entire venture thus came to an end, with its records forgotten. The initial enthusiasm with which the ideas were greeted failed to translate into a visible institution. And what of Hodgkin? No record of his personal reaction to defeat has been found. However, his correspondence for the period between 1839 and 1841 reveals a heavy absorption in the slavery issue and especially the Aborigines Protection Society, which, with Sir Thomas Fowell Buxton, he had founded in 1838. These duties, as the letters and journals indicate, included worldwide correspondence with supporters, the writing of declarations, and numerous personal interviews with the colonial secretary and other officials. No doubt this involvement distracted his attention, causing Rickman Godlee to assume a greater part of the logistical chores, including secretarial duties and recording the minutes of the meetings.

It is worth mentioning one other block to the successful establishment of Southern Retreat, not only to clarify the difficulties besetting Hodgkin and his committee but also to return full circle to the establishment of York Retreat. For some evidence exists to show that Hodgkin, like William Tuke, faced problems emanating from within the Society of Friends itself. Tuke met with much indifference and some suspicion of his efforts. As mentioned earlier, some Quakers questioned the expense involved in building York Retreat, its distant location from London, and the need for a separate Quaker asylum—

the kinds of doubts that ultimately caused Tuke to lament that "all men seem to desert me in maters essential" (Hunt 1937, 15). Hodgkin too had his problems with fellow-Quakers, the most important one being Samuel Tuke.

Samuel Tuke attended Hodgkin's June 1839 meeting at Devonshire House. But since he was clerk of London Yearly Meeting and would be in London anyway and had been connected with York Retreat most directly as its treasurer and author of the influential *Description*, it would have been very odd for him not to have been invited and not to have accepted the invitation, the more so since he and Hodgkin were friends of long standing. Yet because of Tuke's close attachment to York Retreat and its therapy of moral management, it is equally understandable that he might have been lukewarm or even hostile to the idea of a rival Quaker asylum with a different philosophy of care. An important letter of 21 August 1839 from Hodgkin to Tuke touches on this tension:

> Although I am aware that thou hast felt some doubt as to the present necessity for a lunatic asylum in the South of England in some respects resembling your Retreat and destined for the reception of members of the Society of Friends yet I believe that there are few if any persons who will feel more interested in the progress and results of the Institution should it be formed than thyself. That it will be established is now I think scarcely to be doubted as names are given in for shares to the amount of more than 10,000. In its progress I think we may be excused if we occasionally apply to thee for advice and assistance.

After this diplomatic opening, Hodgkin immediately moves to the question of Foville. He says that the "loss will be incalculable" if Foville cannot head the institution. He elaborates on the need for Foville:

> After having visited many asylums and several medical men engaged in the treatment of the insane and of course being somewhat acquainted with the writings of others I certainly know of no one to be compared to the Dr. He is both theoretically and practically very far before his master Esquirol and yet he is looked up to both on the Continent and in this country. I cannot help feeling that if we appoint Dr. F. we rather than the Dr. will be the obliged party. It is therefore rather trying to find that it is said that ours is a job got up by the Drs. The reverse is really the case. . . . And as respecting myself though my means are very limited I intended to subscribe rather than to invest had there been subscribers. As regards Dr. Foville I ought to say that he is leaving very serious prospects in consenting to join us. The state of Esquirol's health is such that the several lucrative appointments which he holds must soon be vacant and to some of these there is the stronger reason to believe that Dr. Foville might be

appointed. His well earned reputation as a cerebral pathologist, as a writer on Insanity and kindred subjects and his proved abilities as exhibited at the Hospice de St. You at Rouen would justly entitle him to any office of the kind which he might seek. . . .

Hodgkin then further details Foville's virtues and experience, re-marking how his attendance on the king of France for a year should place him in a favorable position for future appointments. Why then does Foville wish to come to England? "He is however a highly serious man, by no means avaricious and very anxious correctly to bring up his two children as well as to enjoy quiet for the publication of the materials which [he] has been long collecting. It is this disposi-tion which makes him prefer the prospect of being with us to the chance of having the best post in a Parisian Institution." The defensive tone of these remarks suggests that the Southern Retreat proposal had some under attack from other Friends or perhaps from Tuke himself. In any case, Hodgkin becomes aggressive toward the end of the letter. He says that some are suspicious of Foville because he is a "foreigner." He concludes by asking Tuke to write a letter supporting Foville as medical superintendent. He refers to Dr. Prichard and Caleb Wil-liams, the surgeon at York Retreat, as individuals familiar with the quality of Foville's work.[18]

I have found no record of Tuke's response, if indeed there was one. No doubt if one existed, D. Hack Tuke, the probable editor of *The Memoirs of Samuel Tuke,* would have included it in that work, but he never mentions in this or his many important works either such a letter or the proposed Southern Retreat itself. In fact, without the materials of the Friends Library coming to light, all information on the attempt to found the Southern Retreat would be lost. Since the scheme never came to fruition, one can only speculate as to the kind of research that might have been conducted and its ultimate worth or influence. Perhaps the Southern Retreat might have caused its own kind of revolution in the history of psychiatric care and treatment. As matters stand, however, these documents may be viewed as added testimony to the Quaker tradition of good works and in particular as another chapter in the history of Thomas Hodgkin's human-itarianism.

Summary

Thus it can be seen that moral treatment—the therapeutic bedrock upon which York Retreat had been developed—was questioned on the basis of its approach—and by respected Quaker physicians, no less.

These doubts were a reflection of the changes on a broader front as more and more physicians, aided by the Madhouse Acts and lunacy legislation, began to reassert their leadership as asylum superintendents and healers of the mentally ill. Further, the establishment and growth of York Retreat were interwined with the personalities and values of Quaker society, especially the Tuke family. As the next chapter will demonstrate, York Retreat and Quaker values also played an important part in the founding of Friends Asylum.

George Fox (1624–90), founder of the Society of Friends, as depicted in a London Print of 1822. (Quaker Collection, Haverford College Library)

James Nayler (1618?–60), a former quartermaster in a Puritan regiment, was after Fox the most prominent Quaker leader and preacher. This German print depicts Nayler being led into Bristol in 1656 by two of his emotional disciples (Martha Simmons and Hannah Stranger) in a re-enactment of Jesus's entry into Jerusalem on Palm Sunday. The Presbyterian majority in Parliament accused Nayler of blasphemy; they did so as a way of subverting Cromwell's authority and his reputation as a protector of religious freedom. (Quaker Collection, Haverford College Library)

This 1657 portrait of Nayler identifies him as "The great Impostor & false Messiah King of the Quakers." He holds a paper identifying him as a "Millenarium," i.e., one of the many radical preachers who expected the millennium or reign of Christ on earth based on Old Testament laws. (Quaker Collection, Haverford College Library)

Following his conviction by Parliament on charges of blasphemy, Nayler was whipped, placed in the pillory, had his tongue bored through with a hot iron, and had a "B" branded on his forehead. (Quaker Collection, Haverford College Library)

Hannah or Anna Trapnel was the daughter of a London shipwright and author of *The Cry of a Stone* (1653) and *A Legacy for Saints* (1654). These visionary works resulted from her work as a preacher. (Quaker Collection, Haverford College Library)

This print, similar in design to that of Hannah Trapnel, illustrates the anti-Quaker and anti-feminist identification of female preachers with witchcraft and demonology. The author calls the woman a "Presumptious wretch" for preaching the Light within and suggests that she might better remain at home and "mind hir howsewifery." (Quaker Collection, Haverford College Library)

THOMAS VENNER,
ORATOR CONVENTICULORUM REGNI
MILLENARII ET LIBERTINORUM, SEDUCTOR
et CAPITANEUS SEDITIOSOR. ANABAPTISTARUM
ET QVACKERORUM IN CIVITAT. LONDINENS.
Decollatus in quatuor partes dissectus d. 19. Jan. Anno 1661.

"Thomas Venner, preacher at the conventicles of the Fifth Monarchy men and seducer of libertines and captain of the seditious Anabaptists and Quakers in the City of London. Beheaded and quartered 19 January, 1661." Fifth Monarchy men (after the fifth and final era foretold in Daniel 7) sought through violent means to establish a religious kingdom on earth with the destruction of the ungodly. Venner led a rush from a meeting in Coleman Street with cries supposedly of "King Jesus and their heads upon the gates." The insurrection was suppressed and thousands of Quakers imprisoned. They were absolved on 25 January by the lord mayor as having had no involvement in the plot, but this French print continues the identification of Quakers with such radicals. (Quaker Collection, Haverford College Library)

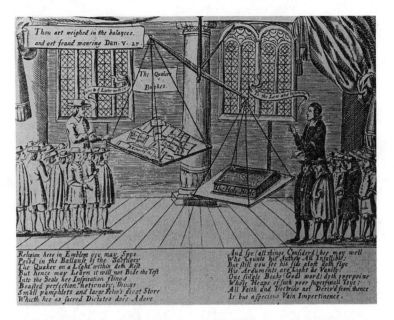

Religion here in Emblem you may Spye
Pois'd in the Ballanse of the Sactuary
The Quaker on a Light within doth Rest
But hence may Learn it will not Bide the Test
Into the Scale hee Inspiration flings
Boasted perfection notionary things
Small pamphletts and large Folio's great Store
Which hee as sacred Dictates does Adore

And see (all things Consider'd) hee may well
Who Counts his Authors All Infallible;
But still you see his side aloft doth flye
His Arguments are Light as Vanity
One single Booke (Gods word) doth overpoize
Whole Heaps of such poor superfinall Toys;
All Faith and Doctrine not Deriv'd from thence
Is but a specious Vain Impertinence.

"Weighting Quaker books against the bible"—an illustration to *The Grand Imposter Discovered*, a poem against Quakers by Benjamin Keach, published in London in 1675. The "Light within" inspiring Quaker books is but "Vain impertinence" when weighed against

In "A Short Examination of the Spirit of Quakerism," the artist captures what he sees as the spirit of Quaker meeting. The text advises Quakers to heed Robert Barclay's warning not to confuse true movings of the Spirit with temptations of the devil. The author says that Quakers are subject to the "Spirit of Enthusiasm" if not the "Convulsions of Demoniacks"; if they are to be saved, they must repent and be baptized. (Quaker Collection, Haverford College Library)

In this 1781 print by Humphrey entitled "The Quakers Meeting," we have the same image as "A Short Examination" but with the women's breasts unclothed. The artist uses nakedness as an additional insult to the already caricatured Friends. Even this late, Friends are still being criticized for allowing women to preach. (Quaker Collection, Haverford College Library)

Flusht with Conceit(which she ý Spirit call)
Upon a Tub see how Dame Silence bawls
Whilst Dunghill Cocks in a most pious strain
Listen to heare the Cackling of the Hen

{ The Quakers
Meeting }

In publick who can beare a Females tattle
Let me in Bed heare my kinde Mistress prattle
For ý their Preaching edifies the Nation
It must be by an use of Application

An engraving by Marcel Lauron from a painting by Egbert van Heemskerk (1645–1704). It satirizes both the Quaker espousal of the Inner Light (here identified with "Conceit") and the notion of a woman preaching: "In publick who can beare a Females tattle / Let me in Bed heare my kinde Mistress prattle." (Quaker Collection, Haverford College Library)

William Penn (1644–1718) in Quaker plain dress but with a wig. George Fox defended Penn against charges of false adornment, noting that Penn was bald and needed the wig for warmth. This 1770 engraving was designed by Du Simitière from an ivory medallion by Silvanus Bevan, a London Quaker who knew Penn. This is the earliest published portrait of Penn and is generally assumed to be an accurate likeness. (Quaker Collection, Haverford College Library)

A woodcut by Robert Spence illustrating an incident from Fox's *Journal*. Feeling despondent, Fox sought counsel from a local priest, but was told only to take tobacco and sing psalms. (Quaker Collection, Haverford College Library)

Fox speaks to people about dreams. He distinguishes among dreams as normal accumulations of images, whisperings of Satan, or whisperings of God. (Quaker Collection, Haverford College Library)

"They are all great men in your country—eh—but I suppose they are like you—not very fond of fighting—Is not that the case, Master Quaker."

"Little man—it is not the case. I myself encourage not fighting—But if thou or any of thy Comrades darest to Cross the great Waters my Countrymen shall make Quakers of ye all"

BONAPARTE and the QUAKER.

This cartoon from the Napoleonic wars reflects increased sympathy for Quakers at a time when their pacifism might have been perceived as disloyalty. (Quaker Collection, Haverford College Library)

William Tuke III (1732–1822), a portrait by Henry Scott Tuke (1858–1929), a member of the Royal Academy. (Quaker Collection, Haverford College Library)

York Retreat, founded by William Tuke, opened in 1796. This sketch was used as the frontispiece for Samuel Tuke's *Description* (1813). (Quaker Collection, Haverford College Library)

DESCRIPTION

OF

THE RETREAT,

AN INSTITUTION NEAR YORK

For Insane Persons

OF THE

SOCIETY OF FRIENDS.

CONTAINING AN ACCOUNT OF ITS

ORIGIN AND PROGRESS,

The Modes of Treatment,

AND

A STATEMENT OF CASES.

◆

By SAMUEL TUKE.

◆

With an Elevation and Plans of the Building.

YORK:

PRINTED FOR W. ALEXANDER, AND SOLD BY HIM;
SOLD ALSO BY M. M. AND E. WEBB, BRISTOL:
AND BY DARTON, HARVEY, AND CO.; WILLIAM PHILLIPS; AND
W. DARTON, LONDON.

1813.

The title page of Samuel Tuke's work. (Quaker Collection, Haverford College Library)

Samuel Tuke (1784–1857), the grandson of William Tuke and author of the *Description,* a work that did much to publicize the moral treatment therapy practiced at York Retreat. (Quaker Collection, Haverford College Library)

Benjamin Rush (1745?–1813), as engraved by J. B. Longacre from a painting by Sully. Rush's *Medical Inquiries and Observations Upon the Diseases of the Mind* (1812) dominated treatment of the insane in nineteenth-century America. (Quaker Collection, Haverford College Library)

Thomas Scattergood (1748–1814), from a pencil sketch by his son-in-law, Stephen Pike. We generally attribute to Scattergood the inspiration for the founding of Friends Asylum. (Quaker Collection, Haverford College Library)

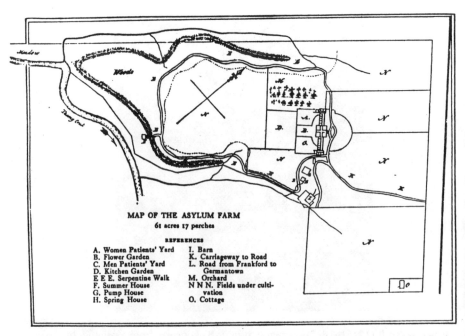

MAP OF THE ASYLUM FARM
61 acres 17 perches

REFERENCES

A. Women Patients' Yard
B. Flower Garden
C. Men Patients' Yard
D. Kitchen Garden
E E E. Serpentine Walk
F. Summer House
G. Pump House
H. Spring House
I. Barn
K. Carriageway to Road
L. Road from Frankford to
   Germantown
M. Orchard
N N N. Fields under culti-
   vation
O. Cottage

A map of the asylum farm. Friends Asylum was planned as a working farm providing both food for the patients and staff as well as useful, therapeutic labor for some of the patients. (Friends Hospital Archives)

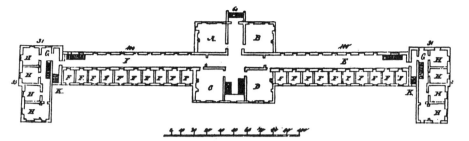

GROUND FLOOR OF THE ASYLUM

A. Manager's Room
B. Superintendent's Parlour
C. Women's Day Room
D. Men's Day Room
E. Men's Wing
F F. Patients' Rooms
G. New Wing for Maniacs
H. Rooms for Maniacs
I. Women's Wing
K. Door into Patients' Yards

Ground floor of Friends Asylum. York Retreat provided the general model for construction, with the major difference being the placement of rooms only on one side of the hall. The windowed corridor thus provided direct light for the patients' rooms. (Friends Hospital Archives)

Friends Asylum around 1835. The circular railway provided both amusement and exercise for the patients. A similar railway was also constructed at the Pennsylvania Hospital for the Insane. (Friends Hospital Archives)

This print shows the original building around 1885 following major architectural changes, including the addition of a third floor and a mansard roof. The building, which housed patients for more than 160 years, is currently used for offices and admissions. (Friends Hospital Archives)

Eastern Penitentiary of Pennsylvania, an 1829 print by C. G. Childs after a drawing by William Mason. (Quaker Collection, Haverford College Library)

Elias Hicks (1748–1830), a Quaker from Long Island whose preaching provoked a split within the Society of Friends into Orthodox and Hicksite. (Quaker Collection, Haverford College Library)

5

FRIENDS ASYLUM AND MORAL TREATMENT

Like most early nineteenth-century Quaker efforts in the field of mental health reform, the roots of Friends Asylum[1] are to be found at York Retreat, its direct model. While not the first asylum in the United States—that honor going to the Public Hospital in Williamsburg, founded in 1773 (though Pennsylvania Hospital, the Quaker-inspired institution that opened in 1751, contained a separate ward for the treatment of insane persons)—it can justifiably call itself the first private, nonprofit mental institution in America. This chapter tracks the development of Friends Asylum from its founding in 1813 to the 1840s. While the Quaker ties between York Retreat and Friends Asylum were strong and the approaches to mental illness were similar, gradually Friends Asylum shifted away from moral treatment as the primary focus of therapy. This shift resulted from changes within the Society of Friends as well as changes in American perceptions and attitudes toward the treatment and curability of the mentally ill.

Roots

Thomas Scattergood was instrumental in the founding of Friends Asylum. Son of Joseph and Rebecca Scattergood, he was born in Burlington, New Jersey on 23 January 1748. His parents were both members of the Society of Friends. His father, apprenticed as a mariner and later a student of the law, died when Thomas was six. Little is known of Thomas's youth, but it is said that even from an early age he was favored "with seasons of serious thoughtfulness."[2] At the same time he resisted the call to the Light and followed his "corrupt will." Eventually the solicitude of his mother and the influence of his meeting led him to become a traveling minister; his ministry was marked by a seriously contemplative, even melancholy manner, of having a mind, as he said, "partly in Egypt and partly in the wilderness." Reading his *Memoirs* (1845), in fact, one is struck by how the rhetoric seems to transcend the usual self-condemnatory, quietist close analysis of past and present imperfections. Scattergood's introspection is almost pathological. He feels "stripped and tried," blown about by the Spirit, and unworthy of any divine favor. For this reason he often resorted to silent tears of resignation in his ministry, "appearing closed up to any public communication" (1845, 27).

He traveled to meetings in New York, New England, Maryland, Virginia, and the Carolinas before deciding in 1794 to visit England. He traveled throughout the United Kingdom, his reputation as a weighty Friend everywhere preceding him. His schedule was an arduous one; he spoke at a variety of formal and informal meetings to a variety of audiences. On 29 March he dined at Lindley Murray's home near York and recorded that he "afterwards visited the Retreat and boarding school; returned to L. Murray's" and lodged (1874, 372). On 24 September 1799 he stayed with Lindley Murray again, then dined with Henry Tuke the next day after attending quarterly meeting. On 26 September he recorded: "To a parting meeting: I had nothing to communicate, and sunk very low after it. I went to the girls' school and dined with W. Tuke, and felt a concern to go to the Retreat, a place where about thirty of our Society are taken in, being disordered in mind. We got most of them together, and after we had sat a little in quiet, and I had vented a few tears, I was engaged in supplication. Returned back to the school and drank tea, and after night to Lindley Murray's" (1874, 404).

Scattergood returned home in 1800, but apparently his experiences at York were not forgotten. Perhaps because of his tendencies toward depression (like William Tuke), he had been deeply stirred by the visit to the Retreat. These feelings were recalled for him by an incident in 1808. Along with several Friends he had traveled to Lancaster, where the Legislature was meeting, in order to testify on a bill that would penalize conscientious objectors. After successfully completing their task, they stopped at the home of a Friend much downcast in spirit because his wife was in despair. Her depression cast a pall over the evening. Next morning Scattergood, feeling deep sympathy for the woman, spoke to her needs, setting "before her peace and happiness, through her laying hold of the hand of deliverance mercifully stretched out even for her."[3]

At yearly meeting the following year, a strange woman accosted him with friendly animation. When he admitted not knowing her, she said, "Why, don't thee know me? I am the Friend that through thy instrumentality was raised *right up* out of the earth" (1874, 465). On further questioning she proved to be the woman at Sadsbury whose gloom and despair had yielded to the message of love and peace that Scattergood had delivered to her.

This particular incident might well have inspired in Scattergood the idea of dealing with mental illness in America as his counterparts had been doing in York: that is, with a creative mixture of love and fraternal religious feeling. In any event, it is part of oral history more than record that Scattergood continued to agitate for the establishment of an institution in Philadelphia that would be similar to York Retreat. No record exists in the minutes of any meetings before 1811 concerning the establishment of an asylum, and it is not until 4 February 1811, in the minutes of Scattergood's home meeting (Burlington, New Jersey) that we read of a concern to be brought to the attention of quarterly meeting. This was done on 26 February, was approved and sent to yearly meeting; at the same time a similar concern was being transmitted by the men's and women's meetings of Western Quarterly Meeting. At Philadelphia Yearly Meeting held 15 April 1811, the following minute was approved: "The subject from the Western and Burlington quarters, respecting a provision for such of our members as may be deprived of the use of their reason, being introduced to the notice of the meeting by reading the reports, it is thought proper to appoint the following friends to take it under further consideration and report to a future sitting. . . ."[4]

The committee actually consisted of forty-four members of yearly meeting, only two of whom (Samuel P. Griffitts and Nathan Harper) would eventually serve on the first board of managers, although two of the committee members (Thomas Wistar and John Moore) eventually joined the asylum's building committee. The committee did its work quickly, holding two meetings and reading a report during the final day of yearly meeting, but consideration was deferred until the following year. Thus the report, dated 18 April 1811 and submitted by John Hoskins and Thomas Wistar, was actually discussed on 20 April 1812 at the next yearly meeting. The committee said that the asylum should be established but should not be under the control of the yearly meeting; instead it should be constructed through direct contributions of the members of yearly meeting. Such an asylum should be built for the "better accommodations" of the insane and the "relief of their families and friends."

They then recommended the establishment of a committee of Friends charged to raise the funds and organize the construction of the asylum. A general plan and solicitation of contributions for the asylum was circulated by a committee consisting of Thomas Scattergood, Jonathan Evans, Ellis Yarnall, Isaac Bonsall, Emmor Kimber, Thomas Wistar, and Samuel Power Griffitts. The plan was to purchase land and construct a facility to accommodate at least fifty persons. The institution should be "in a retired situation, with the necessary medical assistance, and wholly under the care and notice of Friends, for the relief and accommodation of persons thus afflicted; including members and professors with us, of every description, with respect to property." Membership would require a $200 contribution from a meeting and $10 per annum from individuals or $50 at one time. Such amounts would entitle the donor to recommend one poor patient one time, on the lowest terms of admission.

On 14 April 1813 the first meeting of the "Contributors to the Asylum for the Relief of Persons deprived of the use of their Reason" was held. At the next meeting in June a constitution was adopted that stressed both medical and moral treatment for patients and noted the purchase of a fifty-two acre tract of land five miles from Philadelphia and one mile west of Frankford. Then at a March 1814 meeting of the contributors it was recommended that a document be published that would report on progress made in the construction of the asylum and solicit money for the venture. This became the *Account of The Rise and Progress of the Asylum, Proposed to be Established, near Philadelphia, for The Relief of Persons Deprived of the Use of Their Reason, With an Abridged Account of The Retreat, A similar institution near York, in England* (1814). A frontispiece contained a sketch of the proposed building showing the northeast elevation. It also listed the thirty-one meetings and 288 individuals who contributed a total of $24,170.75. Samuel Tuke's account of the Retreat was attached "to convey correct information of the nature of the proposed establishment, the views of both institutions being nearly the same."

The managers, who were elected for one year terms and who were responsible for appointing the physicians, superintendent, and matron, consisted of a treasurer (John Hallowell), a clerk (Isaac Bonsall), and the following twenty individuals who held their first meeting on 11 October 1813:

John Cooke	Abraham L. Pennock
Caleb Cresson, Jr.	Joseph Scattergood
Joseph Paul	Ellis Yarnall
John C. Evans	Samuel P. Griffitts
Nathan Harper	Samuel Bettle
Thomas C. James	Jonas Preston
Joseph Parrish	Solomon Conrad
Edward Randolph	Philip Garrett
Roberts Vaux	William Penrose
John Moore	John Paul

On the same day, the building committee met. Its members were:

Thomas Wistar	John Moore
William Garrigues	George Woolley
Samuel P. Griffitts	Edward Randolph
Nathan Harper	Edward Garrigues
Jonathan Evans	Eden Haydock
Joseph M. Paul	Roberts Vaux
John Cooke	Ellis Yarnall
John C. Evans	

It is clear from the early records that this all-male, all-Quaker committee saw the asylum as designed, like York Retreat, to serve Quaker
patients and perhaps attenders or spouses of Friends. Philadelphia
Monthly Meeting had proposed the establishment of a hospital in the
city as early as 1709—a dream that would not be realized until 1757
with the completion of Pennsylvania Hospital. A wing of this hospital
was used to house the insane, who became the patients of Benjamin
Rush. As mentioned previously, Rush had Quaker roots but was not
himself a Friend. And though Friends such as Israel Pemberton, Jr.,
Edward Pennington, and Thomas Wharton were instrumental in the
founding of the hospital, by the end of the century Friends had ceased
to exert a strong influence on that institution, especially with respect
to treatment of the insane, so they sought to create a hospital environment of their own conducted by their own as much as possible. Thus
the element of religious exclusivity that had motivated the founding of
York Retreat was a similar factor in Philadelphia.

At the same time the Friends Asylum at Frankford was an expression of the Quaker desire to turn inward. Just as they sought to
establish their own schools and to educate their children in "ancient
simplicity" of lifestyle and faith, so too did they wish to avoid consigning their mentally ill to the ministrations of non-Friends. Quakers
had lost much of their political power and influence by refusing to
participate in the revolution. George Washington, for instance, regarded them as Tory spies until their charitable handling of hungry,
sick troops convinced him otherwise. They had, as a Society, with-
drawn unto themselves in much the same way that British Friends had
done following the excesses of the seventeenth century.

Traveling ministers such as Thomas Scattergood reaffirmed the
organizational nature of the Society that kept it strong while at the
same time abjuring members to discipline themselves and forsake
"creaturely activity." The opportunity to perform a good work and
engage in purposeful activity while opening up fellow Friends to

clearer expressions of the Inner Light must have made an appealing combination to those involved in designing and building Friends Asylum. Friends would recognize the moral imperative of removing shackles such as slavery, poverty, or insanity in order to permit the individual the full expression of the God within. So it is easy to understand why the idea for the asylum received immediate approval and money was quickly raised. Of course, these efforts were not impaired by the fact that potential contributors were made aware of the successful model of York Retreat expressed in the book written by Samuel Tuke, which circulated widely throughout Philadelphia Yearly Meeting.

Building Committee

The building committee charged to oversee the actual construction of the asylum was an interesting mix of professionals who provided the element of practical humanitarianism that became synonymous with so many Quaker social reforms. The most important member of the board of managers was Samuel P. Griffitts (1759–1826), who was also a prominent member of the building committee. Educated at the College of Philadelphia, later called the University of Pennsylvania, Griffitts studied Latin and then medicine under Adam Kuhn in Philadelphia. Barred from studying in London or Edinburgh because of the war, he attended the lectures of Barthez at Montpellier in France before finally going to London in 1783 and then on to the center of medical education—Edinburgh, where he studied under the celebrated Cullen. Returning to Philadelphia in 1784, he took up private medical practice and then in 1786, with the help of 320 subscribers, founded the Philadelphia Dispensary for the medical relief of the poor. He was an original member of the College of Physicians (where he helped in the development of a national pharmacopoeia), and like so many Friends, a member of the Pennsylvania Abolition Society, the Society for Alleviating the Miseries of Public Prisons, and the American Philosophical Society (Benjamin Franklin was then its president). He was a professor of materia medica at the University of Pennsylvania from 1792 until 1796 and also distinguished himself during the yellow fever epidemic of 1793 by remaining at his post and treating the sick—he was one of only six physicians left in the city to treat those infected.

Griffitts must have provided invaluable service to the group. Like John Moore, a fellow board member, Griffitts was a physician and thus conversant with medical practice and terminology. A *Biographical*

Memoir by Dr. Emerson[5] says that Griffitts was the author of the original building plan of the asylum. This cannot be verified, but it is certainly clear from the minutes of the building committee that he took an active role in that body's work, especially regarding fine points of construction. For instance, he and Joseph M. Paul were placed on the subcommittee charged with overseeing the construction of iron sashes and seeing to the admission of light and air into the building. The extreme detail that consumed the committee's attention is best illustrated by reference to several of the meetings. For example, at a joint meeting on 11 April 1814 of managers and building committee members, directions were given to the carpenters and masons that

> the mouth of the oven be placed in the Southeast part of the front basement story of the main building, the oven to be under ground outside, with double arches—the floor to be sunk so as to accommodate the oven if necessary. The oven is to be about 8×9 feet in the clear. The alterations in the doors & windows, are marked on the draught, also two arches crosswise separating the cells of the basement story. The Center cell of the basement story of each wing to be arched on 32 inch piers, except the two cells nearest the centre building—which are to be arched crosswise.[6]

On 4 June 1814 they considered whether the windows in the northeast front of the wings were set too high at four feet nine inches from the floor and decided to lower them twelve inches.

This kind of careful, meticulous attention to detail marks the records of the more than one hundred meetings held from 11 October 1813 to 29 November 1817, when the asylum opened after an expenditure of $42,670.74.[7] Other committee members provided valuable skills that aided in the successful completion of the building. Some of their backgrounds serve to illustrate the wealth and diversity of experience on this committee.

Roberts Vaux (1786–1836) was an active Friend with a special interest in education who ultimately became the first president of the board of controllers of the Philadelphia school system. He wrote several essays on prison reform, was a founding member of the Philadelphia Saving Fund Society, the Apprentices' Library Academy of Natural Sciences, and the Historical Society of Pennsylvania. In 1835 he was appointed associate justice of the Court of Common Pleas.

Thomas Wistar (1764–1851) was an elder of the Western District Monthly Meeting who opposed Elias Hicks, the Quaker liberal who provoked the separation of 1827 into evangelical Friends (Orthodox) and Hicksites and who espoused a more progressive sense of divine revelation. He was a member of the Committee of Safety, which remained in Philadelphia during the yellow fever epidemic to minister to the sick. He caught the fever but recovered.

Ellis Yarnall (1757–1847) was a merchant and coppersmith who sold tinware, ironware, and cutlery. An elder of the Twelfth Street Meeting, he was involved in various projects benefiting Negroes and Indians. He was treasurer of yearly meeting and a foe of Elias Hicks.

John Wilson Moore (1789–1865) studied medicine at the University of Pennsylvania, graduating in 1812. An active physician and Friend, after the Separation he helped establish a meeting at Ninth and Spruce Streets in Philadelphia. His second wife was a traveling minister, and he accompanied her on several journeys. In 1859 he established a school in lower Canada for the children of refugee slaves.

Edward Randolph (1753–1837) was a gentlemen merchant and one of the Philadelphia group of elders who signed a letter to Elias Hicks, requesting an interview to clarify Hicks's views on the divinity of Jesus Christ.

Among the building committee members were also a number of individuals with experience in construction. Jonathan Evans (1759–1839) was a carpenter and lumber merchant. He became clerk of Philadelphia Yearly Meeting and vigorously opposed Elias Hicks. The records are unclear, but apparently Edward and William Garrigues (father and son) (n.d.) were involved in the printing or publication trade. Like Thomas Wistar, they were friendly with Thomas Scattergood. Eden Haydock (n.d.) was apparently involved with the plumbing trade, and John C. Evans (n.d.) was apparently an ironmonger. The mix of religious commitment and professional knowledge undoubtedly contributed to the group's effectiveness.

The Building

A detailed look at the main building reveals how deeply influenced the building committee was by the theory and practice of moral treatment. The frontispiece of the 1814 *Account* provides a good sense of how the main building must have appeared in 1817. Architecture was a very important element in a place for treatment, because it was felt that the comfort and care of the insane were materially affected by the construction of the building in which they would be housed. Tuke believed and Charles Evans, attending physician to Friends Asylum, affirmed that the most useful architecture would be one that "combines the most means for introducing well-adapted employment and exercise, with the best arrangement of an extensive classification which can be kept permanently distinct."[8]

The builders of the Friends Asylum of course benefitted from York Retreat. Tuke had devoted an entire chapter of the *Description* to the design of the Retreat. He said that the designers did well considering their lack of experience but that the Retreat had a number of structural problems—problems that no doubt would have been impressed upon Scattergood during his visit. The major lament of Samuel Tuke was the failure to have rooms only on one side of the hall with windows on the other—a detail remedied in Friends Asylum. Tuke showed a consuming interest in the architecture of asylums throughout his life, for he felt that the physical environment was critical to a patient's recovery. He referred in the *Description* (1964, 106) to the "Remarks on the Construction of Public Hospitals" by William Stark, the architect of a new asylum at Glasgow, and to another architect—Robert Reid—and his "Observations on the Treatment of Lunatics." Stark was the first professional architect to write about the construction of asylums. He had visited the Retreat and been impressed by the Quakers' attention to architectural details, even to the elimination of the grating sound made by the bolts on the patients' doors. His discussion contains the summary comment: ". . .however desirable a good system of management may be, no such system can be prosecuted with effect in an ill contrived building."[9]

In 1815 Tuke was asked to help in the design of West Riding Asylum, and he wrote for the building committee "Instructions for the Architects who prepared designs for the West Riding Asylum." Later he expanded his idea into a more detailed work, *Practical Hints in the Construction and Economy of Pauper Lunatic Asylums* (1815). Here he emphasized that the building must be constructed to reflect different classifications of patients (Digby 1985, 245). Tuke's final work on architecture was his introduction to Maximilian Jacobi's *On the Construction and Management of Hospitals for the Insane,* translated into English by John Kitching in 1841. Jacobi, who had translated Tuke's *Description* into German in 1822, was founder and physician superintendent of the asylum at Siegburg near Bonn. His ideas on asylum construction and the treatment of patients owed much to his relationship with Tuke and the Retreat.

The original site of Friends Asylum had been well chosen—52 acres on the outskirts of Philadelphia purchased for $6,764, with six more acres purchased shortly afterwards—with an eye to developing the land as a working farm, thereby affording creative outlets for the patients and a degree of self-sufficiency for the institution. Much of the acreage was under cultivation, with the principal crops being corn, potatoes and wheat. Cows supplied the needed milk and butter, while vegetables and herbs came from gardens on the property. The lovely grounds were also seen as an important environmental therapy (indeed, horticultural therapy became and has remained important). A mile-long serpentine walk, many trees, a duck pond—these and more provided the patients with an atmosphere of quiet serenity intended to evoke the calm of a "retreat." Its privacy and isolation from the city also permitted the patients freedom from the curious and some measure of protection from infection and plague; after all, Philadelphia's devastating yellow fever epidemic of 1793 was not that distant in memory. To further divert the patients and provide a form of exercise, a circular railway of about four-hundred feet in circumference was constructed in 1835 on the front lawn of the building with a car two persons could propel themselves. Also, the nearby Frankford Meeting provided a worship site as well as a spiritual outing for those patients meriting it.

The main building was consciously constructed on the model of York Retreat. An earlier version of Samuel Tuke's *Description* had been circulated to potential contributors and formed a subject of much study for the managers and building committee members. The building came to be regarded as an instrument of treatment, and the "architecture of compassion" demanded that attention be paid to every detail of its construction. For instance, the apparently ordinary fence encircling Friends Asylum was pivoted, so that anyone attempting to climb it from the inside would be gently dropped back upon the hospital grounds. Using an idea adopted at York Retreat, the builders did not place iron bars across the windows; rather, the windows were constructed with iron sashes painted to resemble wood, thus affording both a pleasant, nonintimidating appearance and security.

The main building was a large house designed to evoke the "family" atmosphere considered so critical to the cure of the patients' maladies. All was devised to suggest a pleasant domestic arrangement—well ordered, peaceful, and stable. Stone, quarried for the most part from the farm grounds, was used to construct a large central house with wings extending from both sides. The center portion was occupied by Isaac Bonsall, his wife, and staff members, with male patients in one wing and female patients in the other. Day rooms were strategically placed at the center of the building, thus functioning as parlors where patients could come together for conversation and various activities. Attempts were made to isolate the more disruptive, manic patients, who were housed on the second floor. Special rooms on the fourth floor were also used for especially noisy patients. These were small, dark rooms, not unlike those adopted for solitary confinement in prisons, since the Quakers, influenced in part by the associationist psychology of the eighteenth century, tried to protect the patient from stimulating impressions from the outside while also affording him or her a quiet space in which to reflect and receive the Spirit. Patients' rooms were constructed on only one side of the halls, thus allowing windows to be placed along the entire length of the hall; this lessened the sense of confinement while providing the free passage of air and light. Much committee time went into the choice of locks, in an attempt to find those most secure yet inconspicuous.

The main building fronted but was at some distance from the public road, thus preventing the curious from idle gazing and affording, as one report noted, a "privacy calculated to inspire their troubled minds, on every dawn of intellect, and in every moment of calmness, with consoling evidence, that they were indeed regarded *As Men and Brethren*."[10] The large stone building was three stories high and had two wings. Each wing was two stories high and terminated, as of 1827, in end buildings that projected forward and were three stories high. These end buildings corresponded in height with the front wings and thus offered a pleasing symmetry. Male patients occupied the east wing and female patients the west wing. The end buildings were added to isolate disturbed patients, whose noise continually bothered the calmer patients and (it was felt) checked the progress of their recovery.

The first floor of the central building had four large rooms. One front room was used as a parlor for the superintendent, the other for his office, receiving room, library, and meeting room for the visiting managers. The two rear rooms, which communicated directly with the wings, were used as day rooms for the male and female patients, respectively. The parlors were important to creating a sense of domestic order and regularity. Patients would come together here for conversation and activities, but socializing would undoubtedly be restricted only to those patients capable of rational conduct and self-control. Such restrictions exemplify what the Quakers perceived as therapeutic self-discipline, while to their critics it was a subtle form of manipulation. The tea party, cited by Foucault in his criticism of York Retreat, was also featured here. It was held for many years every fifth-day (Thursday) in the officer's dining room on the second floor of the center building: an occasion, says one anonymous observer, that "partakes in a larger degree than might be supposed of those social qualities called 'a feast of reason and a flow of soul,' by which similar functions in society are described."[11]

The second floor had two large rooms as day rooms for the healthier, more tractable patients and four smaller rooms for the accommodation of Isaac Bonsall and his family. The third story had four large and three smaller rooms. One of the larger rooms was occupied by the resident physician, who had total medical care of the patients but reported to the visiting physician, and another was used as a sitting room for the convalescent female patients. The basement of the center building contained the refectory, kitchen, dining room, and storerooms, with rooms for cooking and washing under the wings, along with the furnaces; furnaces were also located in the end buildings or lodges. Much time and effort was expended by the building committee on the arches dividing the wings; these were used as storerooms for fuel and often goods, and as a smokehouse. The center building was heated by means of stoves and grates, while the wings and lodges had heated air from the furnaces fed into the room by ceiling dampers controlled by the attendants.

As mentioned, Samuel Tuke had felt that one major failing of the York Retreat structure was the placement of rooms on both sides of the hall. While an economical way to build, it created potential problems by increasing the likelihood that patients would annoy each other. Friends Asylum solved this problem by having the rooms only on one side, with windows on the other, allowing for "a cheerful admission of light and air." Each wing had twenty rooms, each ten feet square. Each room, as well as the seven rooms on the third floor, had a window with a stationary cast-iron frame. Each room opened onto a lobby ten feet wide; the lobby was heated in order to permit walking and exercise in cold weather and provide for the free flow of patient-staff relations.

Across from each room was a window corresponding in size to that in the room. A stationary cast-iron sash was over each door and above that a corresponding moveable sash with ten panes of glass that could be opened to permit a free flow of air and light. The iron sashes provided security without giving the appearance of a prison. Small doors were fixed in the door of each room, secured as were the doors themselves with mortise locks so that they could not be opened from within. The small doors allowed attendants to convey food, especially to violent patients, and to check on the condition of the patients without entering the room and disturbing them. Tuke had said earlier that in too many institutions concern for security was paramount to such a degree that it led to a debilitating confinement of the patients and to a prison appearance that was equally debilitating. The Quaker building committees took care to remedy these deficiencies and saw the importance of ample air and light for patients confined by sickness and weather.

Light could also be controlled by shutters, so that "salutary darkness" could be provided those patients who were restless, sleepless, or unmanageable. In fact, "black" or "dark" rooms were frequently used as a form of punishment or control by the superintendent or the attendants. Quakers used a similar approach in their ideas about solitary confinement in the prisons, believing that a place of quiet isolation afforded a better environment for fruitful contemplation and the release of the power of the Inner Light. Its use in the asylum, however, flowed more directly from the Lockean or associationist view that stimulating, invasive external stimuli had the potential to excite further already manic patients. Sheltering them as much as possible was a way to calm them.

In the rear of the wings and lodges were the airing yards for the use of those patients not able by health or temperament to walk in the general gardens and pathways of the property. These yards were surrounded by ten-foot walls and enclosed about half an acre of ground for each sex. Each yard was subdivided by a board fence cutting off about a third of the ground for use by the less controllable patients lest they offend or hamper the movement of those better able to take care of themselves. A door in the wall allowed patients to get to the privies, which were all outside the buildings. Separating each yard was a flower garden and beyond them was the two-acre vegetable garden. At the end of a gravel walk leading directly from the house through the gardens was an ornamental garden house, surrounded by a piazza, that was furnished as a library and reading room with books on natural history, maps, drawings, etc. This afforded another form of relaxation and diversion for some patients.

The design and construction of the asylum also supported and reinforced the classification of patients, for it was felt disadvantageous to mingle individuals of strongly different backgrounds and degrees of recoverability. In his 1825 account of the asylum, Robert Waln, Jr. said that ideally patients should be classified into curable, incurable, and convalescent, according to the plan espoused by Johann Spurzheim, the phrenologist. But the form of the building in 1825 did not easily permit this division, especially the separation of noisy from calmer patients. It was not until 1828 that the lodges were constructed to isolate the particularly manic patients from the others. During the early years of operation, the asylum relied primarily on two divisions: the quiet and convalescent patients were housed on the second floors and the violent and incurable on the lower floors, each with its own day room and sections of the airing yard. The fourth story of the center building had rooms (called by Bonsall the "dark room" or "small room") for containing those patients whose cries were consistently disruptive.

By contrast, York Retreat used an apartment near the day room for such isolation, which was not as convenient an arrangement since the patient's cries could still be heard. Tuke also noted that while the term "superior class" of patient referred to "behaviour, and to capacity of rational enjoyment" (96), distinctions were also made with regard to economic class. Wealthier patients were invited to take their meals with the superintendent and females of the same class. Also, their bedrooms were better situated and had curtains attached to the head of the bed rather than hung on rods; otherwise the furniture was the same. The more democratic Friends Asylum, while it charged different rates, admitted no such differences. Waln says, in fact, that it would be "unjustifiable, and even criminal" (1825, 28) to allow such considerations to interfere with the curative process. Thus no consideration was given to prior social position "except as it relates to a due regard to his feelings, and a proper adaptation of labour" (1825, 29).

Treatment

It is a commonplace to see a distinction made between medical and moral treatment during the late eighteenth and early nineteenth centuries. Tuke devoted a chapter to each approach in his *Description,* although the section on medical approaches amounted to little more than a recitation of those medical treatments that failed. As mentioned in chapter 3, in the eighteenth century, asylum managers began to replace the medical approach to mental illness with a stronger emphasis on moral treatment and then in the nineteenth century circled back when the medical profession gained ascendancy by law at asylums. At Friends Asylum, for example, Isaac Bonsall, the first superintendent, had to defer to the attending physician, who in turn answered to the visiting physicians. Bonsall was not happy with this arrangement and on a number of occasions stated his feelings in his superintendent's day book.

Bonsall was the superintendent for the first six years until he was replaced in 1823 by Dr. Edward Taylor. The first matron was Bonsall's wife, the former Ann Paul. It was appropriate for Bonsall to assume this position since he had been involved with the institution from its inception. A member of the founding committee along with Thomas Scattergood and five other Friends, he was also a member of the constitution committee, the committee on site, and was first clerk of the contributors. He was qualified to become superintendent mainly by virtue of his practical intelligence, interest, and background as a strong Friend. The latter qualification was probably seen as most important by the board of managers, who of course knew Bonsall well from his involvement in Philadelphia Yearly Meeting and other

Quaker religious activities. He was an active minister, often traveling to other meetings. He was also the clerk of the Robeson Meeting in Berks County. Judging from the number of agricultural references in his day book, he apparently also had a farming background.

Bonsall's day book is a daily journal of two volumes kept from 1817 until 1823 and currently housed in the Quaker Collection of the Haverford College Library, which contains most of the asylum records.[12] Many of the notations have to do with domestic arrangements, planting of crops, lists of visitors, the weather, but the more valuable comments have to do with patient care. In this regard it was clear that Bonsall was generally accepting of much medical treatment and reasonable restraint. He often recorded the use of medicines, blistering agents, and emetics as facts without discussing their efficacy. Undoubtedly he was feeling his way; undoubtedly too he must have been somewhat intimidated by the medical professionals over whom he had no direct control or supervision. On 13 June 1817 blisters were used on the ankles of Sarah W. and Hannah J. On 31 July the latter figure also was "cupped and had a Blister applied almost over the top & back part of her head." Bonsall did object, however, to Hannah receiving meat and butter, feeling that "strong food may be best for such violent cases of insanity but I very much doubt it." There was no indication that Bonsall had done much reading on the subject of insanity; rather, like William Tuke, he relied on his practical intelligence, keen sense of observation, and humanitarian instincts to cope with the patients and fulfill the charge of his position. For instance, before it became popular he noticed the value of water therapy. On 23 July 1817, with regard to John H., Bonsall noted that the "Shower Bath may be resorted to either as a punishment for not labouring or as a stimulant in the place of labour."

William Tuke had less patience with medical approaches than Bonsall. In his testimony before the Parliamentary inquiry into madhouses in 1815, he said that very little could be done for the mentally ill with medical treatment. His grandson was similarly ill disposed toward medical treatment. In chapter 5 of his *Description* on "Moral Treatment," Samuel Tuke noted that whatever theory one has about the causes of insanity, moral treatment or management must be considered of primary importance in its cure. If one assumes that the disease is based in the mind, then direct applications to the mind are "most natural" and most likely to meet with success. If, on the other hand, one believes the mind to be immortal and thus free from disease, the body must somehow cause the impairment. Then one must conclude from the reciprocal action of the one against the other that the greatest attention must be paid to influences on the mind.

As noted in chapter 4, Samuel Tuke disparaged most medical approaches to mental illness. Tuke discounted the beneficent effects of fear, arguing that it did not assist but usually harmed either the manic or melancholic patient. Fear also implied that the patient was merely a dumb animal controlled by base emotions. Tuke reminded his reader of man's divine nature and the necessary appeal to that nature of a kind and caring mode of treatment. As for melancholics, it was important to divert their minds. For the men this meant labor appropriate to their station, such as farming or gardening; for the female patients it meant sewing, knitting, or other domestic arts. For Quakers, labor functioned as an important self-discipline as well as a meaningful expression of individual worth. This "desire of esteem" was aided by the cultivation of ways in which patients were induced to exhibit self-restraint.

For Samuel Tuke, one way to achieve this goal was by conversing with the patients, and introducing topics that would interest them and on which they might converse rationally and knowledgeably. Too many people addressed patients as if they were children to be led or dominated. The cultivation of religious sentiments and practices was also a means of promoting self-restraint; thus attendance at meeting and regular Bible readings were two devotional practices utilized. In all these activities the attitude of the attendant was particularly important. He should not expect immediate results, but keep in mind Bacon's dictum that "it is order, pursuit, sequence, and interchange of application, which is mighty in nature; which, although it require more exact knowledge in prescribing, and more precise obedience in observing, yet is recompensed with the magnitude of effects" (1964, 161–162). The attendant should spend the greater part of a patient's stay with him. He must seek at all times to gain the patient's confidence and esteem, to excite the patient's rational side, and to remember that "in the wreck of the intellect, the affections not unfrequently survive" (1964, 162).

Tuke stressed that restraint should be used only to protect the patient. Haslam's views were influential on Tuke and in turn on the managers of Friends Asylum. According to Haslam, patients in violent states of mania should be confined alone in a dark room, so as to prevent their associating ideas that might be transmitted to them through the senses. The use of the strait-waistcoat was urged for those manic patients who were not suicidal since they might walk about freely while wearing it; for those who were suicidal, York Retreat managers used a complicated apparatus of webbed leather straps to secure the patient to his bed. "Judicious kindness," however, was usually of more use in dealing with manic patients or with those who refused to eat. Neither at York Retreat nor Friends Asylum did the superintendents resort to the spouting boat, an instrument frequently used in eighteenth century madhouses to gain entrance to a patient's mouth for force-feeding and that not infrequently caused the loss of the patient's front teeth. Rather, when clever persuasion or kind intervention failed to induce a patient to eat, the attendants resorted to "Haslam's key," which pressed down the tongue and kept the jaw sufficiently open to allow for the introduction of food. Tuke said that this procedure was infrequently used and had never resulted in injury to the patient.

In a summary remark, Tuke noted how important the attendant was in applying the principles of "salutary restraint" and knowing the degree to which the patient may be influenced by "moral and rational inducements." One reason for the success of York Retreat and, later, Friends Asylum can certainly be traced not only to the quality of the attendants but to the fact that many of them were apparently members of the Society of Friends. They were thus sympathetic philosophically and religiously to the principles enunciated in Tuke's book. They helped structure the kind of sympathetic environment so essential to milieu or moral therapy. At both institutions the managers were conscious of the importance of attendants and sought to establish rules with respect to their treatment of the patients.[13]

The final section of the chapter on moral treatment dealt with ways in which to promote the comfort of the patients. Tuke said that all his prior discussion dealt in some way with comfort, but he added a few more details. In addition to attending Mrs. Jepson's tea parties alluded to earlier, patients were also allowed to pay visits to friends in the city and receive visitors, though only after the restoration of their faculties had been greatly advanced. Since indolence is the enemy of recovery, patients were encouraged to read, draw, play ball or chess—whatever would divert their minds from their problems and prevent melancholy and ennui. Tuke added one caution, however: namely, the reading matter must be carefully screened to avoid "works of imagination" and any readings that reinforce the patient's curious notions. It was natural for a Quaker like Tuke to stress readings in mathematics and natural science, since these were the "arts" to which Quakers most often were attracted, i.e., the practical disciplines.

Concluding this chapter, Tuke said that no doubt other avenues of moral treatment would meet with further success. He lamented the fact that too often the calamity of mental illness had been aggravated by those charged to cure it. In reflecting on the management of the insane, he quoted Montesquieu: "Experience continually demonstrates, that men who possess power, are prone to abuse it: they are apt to go to the utmost limits. May it not be said, that the most virtuous require to be limited?" (1964, 187).

Moral Management at Friends Asylum

How then were these principles applied at Friends Asylum? Without explicitly stating the principles of moral management, it was clear that Bonsall had absorbed—either from reading Tuke and others or from natural instincts—many of the principles and that he applied them with care and insight to the patients.[14] In Bonsall's day book one may see the application of the theories discussed by Tuke. Yet although Bonsall contrasted moral with medical treatment and argued that the former was better, he never really defined or theorized about moral treatment. Rather, his views were revealed through action as Bonsall sought to embody Tuke's theories in his relationships to patients and staff.

Of primary importance was the superintendent's personal attitude toward the patients. He seems to espouse the views contained in the 1818 annual report to the contributors: to extend to all patients "treatment the most soothing and gentle" in which "they are indeed *Regarded as Men and Brethren.*" The importance of the concept of "family" not only at York Retreat, but throughout Quaker history, has been discussed. It was a principle of comfortable community and interdependent welfare that sustained early Friends in their trials and continued as a source of consolation and strength, moral and spiritual reinforcement through a number of generations. Bonsall took care to develop the principle of the staff and patients as family, as if the asylum were but a home for troubled individuals cared for by concerned relatives. On 6 July 1817 he spoke of "no obvious difference in the family," and commented that Lydia C. told her sister that "she was pleased with the place, and that the Family took a great deal of pains to interest her by conversation."

Tuke had emphasized conversation as a way of diverting the patient, establishing a dialogue with unreason, and most important, touching the "divine principle" within and letting it shine through. It was clear from his journal that Bonsall took every opportunity to engage patients in conversation. He said: "I try to watch for favorable opportunities to enter into conversation with the patients, individually and sometimes collectively." The results were not always successful and sometimes unsettling. Frances T., for instance, "insists that she has no brains, and that her left hand and arm are dead, and that she does not sleep any." Hannah J. proved to be an incessant, even manic talker (11

December 1817). Samuel M., who died at the asylum, revealed through his conversation an understanding "much shattered" and ideas "very disarranged" (25 July 1819).

Yet Bonsall had his small successes, such as when Hannah J. "was pleasant and said some clever things," and when he noted a favorable experience with John H.: "I had the most rational conversation with John H. that I ever had. He seems quite intelligent, and states many facts relative to his father's business, his father's successes, and his want of it. Most of what he said, I knew to be correct. It was truly a pleasure to discover such rationality." After observing Dr. Charles French Matlack, who had taken over as resident physician from Charles Lukens, Bonsall praised him for "moral treatment," pointing out that Matlack spent much time conversing with the patients.

Bonsall would also eat with the patients. In addition to providing an opportunity for conversation, it was both an expression of familial confidence in the patients and a reward for their "regular" conduct. Those who did not act politely were not allowed to eat with the rest. Hannah L., who was considered sane but troublesome, had "pride of disposition and unwillingness to submit to the order judged necessary to be observed." She roused the other patients and was not allowed to eat with them (29 January 1818). Such banishment, it was hoped, would shame the patients into proper conduct and provide an incentive for self-discipline by way of developing self-esteem. Bonsall mentioned in January 1818 that William H. evacuated and feared that the visiting managers who made weekly visits to the asylum would know that he had dirtied himself: "We were pleased to find so much shame excited and considered it a favourable symptom." Bonsall was disappointed that the visiting managers did not take enough opportunities to converse with the patients when they came to the asylum, but he perceived them as outside authority figures for whom the patients might display a healthy respect and from whom they might seek approval. In February 1818 Bonsall noted that the patients dined with the visiting managers, who were "pleased with their orderly conduct."

The appearance of order and normality, a sort of formalism or external rigor that was demanded in the average Quaker's daily life— these were the qualities stressed and sought at the asylum. Even if sanity was not achieved, "an establishment in habits" was important (26 February 1818). Quakers were exceptionally sensitive, as already noted, to any hint of public scandal and were expected to lead lives beyond reproach or else leave the Society.

How difficult it must have been, then, for a serious, sober Quaker-like Bonsall to witness such eccentric deviations from normal conduct, much less the exacting standards established by Friends. He and his wife were subject not only to physical abuse, but to obscene language, manic activity, exhibitionism, even—in the case of John H.—coprophilia:

> I think I have not stated heretofore in what his "filth" consisted. He would mix his excrement with his urine, and rub this mixture over his body, and other parts of his person. Frequently, his excrement is made into cakes, and placed between papers, and then put either into his pockets, or between his clothes. While he was allowed the use of his trunk, he deposited considerable among his clothes placed therein. (Roby 1982, 15)

That Bonsall recorded this noxious activity with a kind of detached acceptance conveys some idea of his sympathetic, nonjudgmental attitudes toward his patients. Through the journal it is hard to find instances of Bonsall being angry or impatient. He did have some strong views and got upset with the managers or physicians when he disagreed with their approaches, but he remained calmly accepting and was a model for the practice of "regulating desires" that he sought in the patients. When patients broke windows or furniture, he sought to understand why and then tried to have them promise not to do so in the future. He allowed patients to spend time away from the asylum in the city or permitted them to go on errands into Frankford. When they abused these privileges or ran away, he did not indulge in recriminations. In encountering violent patients, he seemed observantly detached rather than fearful or intimidated. One particular case was illustrative of the "moral" way of handling violent patients, of why a patient characterized the Bonsalls as *"firm* but not *cross"* (7 January 1821).

William P. B. was a particularly troublesome patient:

> William P. B. has gotten so loud that we concluded that he must be fastened down on his bedstead. He manifested a most ferocious disposition, by far exceeding anything I have ever conceived any human being capable of. He looked truly terrific. However, when he saw several of us, he was secured without actual attempt to injure us.

Bonsall sought through quiet conversation and a walk in the yard to soothe the patient, but this was not successful, for when the doctor later that day offered William a drink, the patient "bit the tumbler into pieces." Two days later, Bonsall says:

> William P. B. appeared quiet, and so desirous to be released from his confinement. . . . He did not blame us for his confinement in that his conduct had made it necessary. He hoped we would forgive him. I told him I freely forgave him—that we had done what we had done because it

appeared necessary, but as his disposition had now changed, he should be released.

The patient then became affectionate to Bonsall and his wife, so the waistcoat was removed and the patient entered on a "trial of good behavior" before he again became wild and needed to be restrained. He then would alternately be wild and calm, but rather than conveniently keeping him restrained, Bonsall tried another tack: "We however let him have the liberty to go out with the men to their work in the woods. They did not lay him under any particular restraint, intending during this spell to try the effect of liberty with strict watching, but without letting him know that we were apprehensive of a change." Finally after a reasonable period of liberty, William P. B. again had to be restrained: "We had continued his liberty during this period of disease longer than was proper, in hopes it would have a beneficial effect. Now however, we think that an earlier confinement would be best" (Roby 12–13).

Restraint

The episode with William P. B. is also illustrative of the Quaker philosophy of restraint as espoused by Tuke. Restraint was applied in a charitable manner in order to keep the patient from doing injury to himself. It was not until John Conolly became resident physician in 1839 at Middlesex County Lunatic Asylum in Hanwell, then the largest asylum in England with over eight hundred patients, that there was any attempt at total nonrestraint of patients. This courageous act from a man who had never headed an asylum before meant, "no form of strait-waistcoat, no handcuffs, no leg-locks, nor any contrivance confining the trunk, or limbs, or any of the muscles, is now in use. The coercion chairs, about forty in number, have been altogether removed from the wards" (Hunter 1963, 10–31). No doubt Conolly encountered strong resistance against this radical change, especially from the attendants, who had found restraints both necessary and convenient. What he was attempting to do was not only to free the patients but also change the attitude of the attendants. He reasoned that restraints not only excited the patient in a negative way but also encouraged the attendant to perceive the patient as less than human and in this way to subtly influence for the worse the patient's sense of self. Hunter and Macalpine concluded from Conolly's writings that in addition to promoting the concept of nonrestraint he also began the profession of psychiatric nursing (1963, 1032).

As mentioned, restraint was used somewhat sparingly both at York Retreat and Friends Asylum. When used it took the form of straps, the straight waistcoat (or "jackcoat"), the use of the "dark room," and the "chair for tranquility." Anticipating the later development of sedatives and other forms of chemical restraint, there was also the reliance, especially at Friends Asylum, on such things as "salts" and strong emetics, blisters, bleedings, and laudanum (opium dissolved in alcohol) not only to provoke a medical cure but also to weaken and deplete manic patients—those in a state of "excitement"—by way of inducing in them a state of calm. With their education and optimistic personal theology Quakers tended to place great emphasis on self-restraint.

Isaac Bonsall also had a strong personal preference for hydro-therapy, which he used on a variety of occasions and for different reasons. In July after the opening of the asylum, Bonsall had a shower bath installed. As mentioned, Bonsall intended it to be used as a punishment for a patient who refused to labor or as a stimulant in place of labor. The patients were given both warm and cold baths, one apparently to soothe and the other to stimulate or punish. On 27 November 1817 the usually manic Hannah J. was given a shower bath for using "improper language." A. P. W. was "put in bathing tub in cold water as a punishment" for breaking seventeen panes of glass (29 September 1820). The visiting committee minutes indicate that Bonsall's use of the shower bath as a coercive measure was somewhat controversial. When questioned about it, Bonsall spoke strongly for its continuation and said that he had not been informed that its use should be discontinued. It was finally agreed that the visiting physician would have the final say. Bonsall agreed but argued consistently for its use. In his journal for May 1821, when apparently rebuffed for using it for a particularly manic patient, Bonsall said: "We submitted to his opinion as it is a Medical as well as in our view as essential part of the Moral system proper to be pursued. It has been in time past productive of more benefit to the Patients than any other thing in use."

When Dr. Edward Taylor and his wife Sarah—Friends from Upper Freehold, New Jersey—took over from the Bonsalls in May 1823, they continued the use of hydrotherapy, particularly the pouring of cold water on the the head while the patient rested in a warm bath. In 1787, when first in charge of the insane patients at Pennsylvania Hospital, this had been the mode of treatment stressed by Benjamin Rush; only later, around 1795, did he begin to emphasize the copious bleeding now associated with his name and from which he acquired the title the "lancet-loving surgeon." The new superintendents no doubt referred to Rush's *Medical Inquiries and Observations Upon the Diseases of the Mind,* published in 1812, and although their use of water treatment appeared to have a moral rather than the medical goal of cooling the inflammation of the brain, they nonetheless found it helpful.

Occupation

The chief means of both occupying and diverting the mind was productive labor. Since the asylum was a working farm, this primarily meant work outdoors for the men planting and cultivating the crops, milking the cows, cleaning the stables, clearing the land, etc. Patients were not only urged but, in some cases, forced to contribute their assistance. The case of John H. is relevant here. He was a patient, Bonsall says, so lazy that he could not even be encouraged to watch other patients work. One of the attendants (Samuel Raleigh) used the shower to stimulate John H. to labor, but it proved ineffective. So Raleigh, after trying to coax John H. to carry some sticks, finally tied them on his back and made him walk up the stairs with them. He did this several times until John H. finally agreed to carry sticks and bricks on his own, gradually finding that he enjoyed the effort. Bonsall's comment: "John H. is now one of our best workers, and in other respects improves much" (Roby 1982, 14).

Those patients who by background or economic circumstances had no experience with manual labor were nonetheless encouraged to find something to do; tending the flowers—a precursor of the horticultural therapy program established later in a more formal way—was one solution to this problem. In addition to the livestock, the managers introduced to the grounds deer, lambs, chickens, rabbits, and pigeons for the diversion of the patients. Carriage rides and use of the circular railway were other sources of amusement. The women were encouraged to sew, knit, or quilt and during the colder months, like the men, were occupied in the making of whisk brooms.

This concept of recreation and diversion was later expanded. In 1838 a library and reading pavilion was constructed on the rear lawn, where it housed reading matter, maps, scientific instruments, and a collection of stuffed birds and animals. In 1889 a gymnasium was donated by Friends for patients' activities. On the top floor was the gym itself, filled with weights, mats, ring, vaults, medicine balls, and Indian clubs, while the bottom floor housed rooms and studios for classes in drawing and other arts and crafts. The rooms were also used for lectures, readings, stereopticon and moving picture shows.

In 1879 a greenhouse and in 1905 a large conservatory were built to support the patients' interest in the cultivation of flowers and to provide flowers and plants for the houses and grounds. As has been suggested, from the outset the managers and superintendents re-garded the beauty of the grounds as an important component in the curative process of the patients. Bonsall several times commented on the beauty of the grounds and called patients' attention to them both to divert and literally to impress on their minds the positive beauty and soothing quietness of the setting. This use of the environment was a natural outgrowth of the associationist philosophy.

Religious Oversight

Although Bonsall did not dwell on the matter, the importance and influence of Quakerism on the curative process was always implied. The 1813 "Constitution of the Contributors of the Asylum for the Relief of Persons Deprived of the Use of their Reason" stated ex-plicitly that the asylum was established in order to "furnish, besides the requisite medical aid, such tender sympathetic attention and reli-gious oversight, as may soothe their agitated minds, and, thereby, under the Divine blessing, facilitate their restoration to the enjoyment of this inestimable gift." It was required that contributors be members of Philadelphia Yearly Meeting. Any contributor disowned by the Society would lose all rights unless reinstated.

The feelings of a common religious bond among members of the "family" undoubtedly contributed to the high rates of cure and feeling of community. Only Quakers or those professing the doctrines of Quakerism were admitted as patients until 1834, and this kind of screening had the beneficial effect of eliminating from the "family" the criminally insane and others who might disrupt the organization and upset the other patients. The founders of the asylum felt that the "indiscriminate mixture of persons of opposite religious sentiments and practices; of the profligate and the virtuous; the profane and the serious; would very probably check the progress of returning reason" (Waln 1825, 3). Some individuals apparently criticized Friends for the sectarian spirit of the asylum; Robert Waln, Jr. felt it important to raise this matter in his 1825 account of Friends Asylum. He men-tioned that fifteen of the thirty-seven patients currently in the asylum were in fact not members of the Society of Friends, though presum-ably they professed its doctrine (i.e., they were attenders at meeting or were married to Friends). He added that by establishing an institution to treat their own, Friends relieved the public at large by diminishing the poor-rates of caring for the indigent insane, just as they saved the public money through the establishment of the Friends Alms House on Walnut Street. Waln said that Friends were willing to admit patients of other sects if vacancies arose, but such patients would need to be removed in order to make room for Friends.

In actual treatment it was the religious ambience and the feeling of religious homogeneity more than direct use of religion that was important in the treatment of the insane at Friends Asylum. The Bible was read in the day rooms following supper on Sunday evenings, but Bonsall did not usually permit preachers to come to the asylum since he felt that they might be disruptive or did not know how to preach to the insane. The other major Quaker religious outlet was attendance at the nearby Frankford Meeting, sometimes twice a week. Not all patients were routinely allowed to go to meeting for fear of their becoming disruptive, so it became a reward for regular conduct. It often produced positive results, as noted by Bonsall: "Hannah J. mentioned that the first time she went from here to meeting, it was very mortifying. She was humbled to be looked upon as one of the insane riding in the crazy carriage. But after getting to the meeting, she felt sweet peace, and from that period, she desired to attend whenever possible" (Roby 1982, 5). Patients who failed to conduct themselves properly during meeting for worship at Frankford or during the Sunday services were punished by ostracism.

In discussing the religious dimension of treatment, it is important to note that the asylum was not left untouched by the serious religious rift that occurred in 1827–29. Each year from the inception of the asylum, the contributors met, as demanded by the constitution, to hear the report from the board of managers and appoint board members for the coming year. As William Cadbury notes, however, instead of a record of minutes for the March 1828 meeting, there was only a loose sheet of paper with rough minutes, probably written by Clement Biddle, clerk to the contributors at that time. The clerk's statement reads:

> The minutes for the Board of Managers for the past year were read as well as the following summary report of their proceedings during that time, which claiming the deliberate consideration of the present meeting, a considerable diversity of sentiment was expressed as to the course pursued by the managers, particularly relating to their declining acknowledging the right of membership of two of their number, their proceedings are therefore neither approved nor disapproved. Before any conclusion on the foregoing minute was come to, the meeting got into a state of great confusion, and not being in situation to go on, it is evidently out of question to proceed, this meeting is therefore adjourned.[15]

The eleventh annual report on the asylum for 1828 discussed this conflict in detail. Under the constitution, every monthly meeting that contributed $200 to the asylum had the right to appoint an agent to attend the yearly meeting of contributors held every year on the Wednesday preceding the third Saturday in March; every member who contributed fifty dollars and continued as a member of the Society of Friends could recommend one poor patient on the lowest terms of admission. However, with the Separation and the division of individual meetings, each meeting claimed the right to appoint an agent for the asylum. Also, testimonies of disownment had been issued against forty of the contributors, yet they still claimed the right to recommend a poor patient. Finally, two of the managers had been disowned and lost their seats on the board. These and other matters were hotly debated, and the board of managers finally decided to seek legal counsel for answers.

As the annual report noted, eight specific questions were submitted to a lawyer, Horace Binney, for his ruling. These included questions about which agents should be seated, how could it be determined that a person was disunited from the Society (e.g., can Philadelphia Quarterly Meeting dissolve Green Street Monthly Meeting?), could disowned Friends be on the board of managers, were the rights of a contributor affected by disownment, could members of other yearly meetings be on the board of managers? Binney's decisions focused on the fact that at the time of the establishment of Friends Asylum and the writing of the Constitution, the only true yearly meeting was Philadelphia's Arch Street Yearly Meeting (the Hicksites had established Green Street as its Philadelphia Yearly Meeting); therefore, only agents and contributors approved by that yearly meeting were eligible to serve. Any member disowned by a meeting not holding itself in subordination to the old Philadelphia Yearly Meeting was not really disowned and was eligible to serve on the board of managers. Also, members from yearly meetings other than Philadelphia could serve on the board as long as that yearly meeting was recognized by the old Philadelphia Yearly Meeting.

The controversy referred to concerned the conflict in the Society between the followers of Elias Hicks, who espoused a liberal progressive sense of revelation that they felt to be in accord with primitive Quakerism, and the Orthodox Friends, who had been touched by the evangelical spirit and thus emphasized what they felt were such absolute truths as the divinity, death, and resurrection of Jesus Christ. The worsening relations between these two groups reached a breaking point at the 1827 Philadelphia Yearly Meeting when the dissenters moved to Green Street Meeting House while the Orthodox Friends established as a base of operations Arch Street Meeting. The board of managers at Friends Asylum was basically Orthodox, having in its background and current leadership such important Orthodox Friends as Thomas Wistar, Jonathan Evans and Samuel Bettle. The membership question thus arose over the association of liberal Friends with what the Orthodox perceived to be dissenting meetings. The Binney rulings were a total victory for Orthodox members. Consequently, future admissions, appointments of staff, and election to the board of managers had to be considered in light of whether or not the individual was Orthodox or Hicksite. Only in 1945 was the breach formally healed when at the annual meeting of what was now called Friends Hospital the following motion was passed:

> Whereas it has been the practice of this Corporation . . . to restrict its membership to individuals who are members of meetings belonging to Philadelphia Yearly Meeting, now held at 4th and Arch Streets, and Whereas the Board of Managers now recommends the abandonment of this practice, therefore be it resolved that hereafter all members of the Religious Society of Friends shall be considered eligible for membership in the Corporation, any of whom may be elected as provided in the By-laws of the Corporation (Cadbury 1946, 69–70).

One can appreciate how stormy this 1828 meeting must have been when one considers the situation the next year at the Western District Burial Ground, a plot purchased in 1817 by five city monthly meetings. Orthodox members, believing that Green Street Meeting no longer had burial rights as Friends, attempted to lock them out of the grounds. Green Street members in turn came with ladders and axes to break the locks, climb the walls, and build their own gates. While this occurred an Orthodox Friend who approached was told "in the perfect manner of Friends . . . thee had better go away; thee will get dust on thee." Finally, the matter was settled in the courts with the Green Street members proving their claims of access.[16]

How remarkable that Friends who for so many years had sought to avoid public scandal and avoid any actions that might call attention to the Society were now caught up in such unseemly acts as public brawls, courtroom fights, and ideological contests that spilled over into the view of their fellow citizens not only in Philadelphia but wherever large groups of Friends had settled. The fact that the Society of Friends had become a society of enemies was troubling, but that it had engaged in a public feud that brought both ridicule and criticism to the Society compounded the problem. These activities would in one sense prepare public opinion for the Warder Cresson and Morgan Hinchman trials that will be discussed in the next chapter.

Rates of Cure

The Quaker penchant for maintaining detailed records makes it easier to evaluate the rates of cure at Friends Asylum. In his account of the asylum published in 1839, Charles Evans provided a useful summary of statistics on patients from the first admission in 1817 through the end of 1838, from the eighteen patients admitted in 1818 to the sixty-three admitted in 1838. The total number of admissions during this period was 634, 127 of whom were readmissions, leaving a total of 507 patients who received care at the asylum—almost evenly divided into men and women. Evans indicates the duration of treatment in a tabular format (see table 5.1).

As he noted, the proportion of cures was 42.21 out of every 100, but if one deducted the sixty-one cases where the patients had been ill for more than ten years (including twenty who had been idiots from birth) and thus unlikely to benefit from treatment and the ten cases where epilepsy or paralysis was involved, then there is an improvement rate of forty-nine per one hundred. The percentage of cures for those cases of less than a year's duration was 58.23. These statistics reinforced the strong sense at Friends Asylum and at York Retreat that it was important for patients to receive treatment as quickly as possible once the first signs of disease had been detected; the longer the disease endured before treatment, the less likely the cure.

Both institutions also had to confront whether or not Quakers were more subject to mental illness than the general population. The high rate of intermarriage was generally given as the reason for this charge. Evans grappled with this problem and concluded that the evidence was too spotty for the rest of society to indict the Quakers. A later article by Maximilian Jacobi in *The Lancet* made similar charges. Jacobi felt Quakers were prone to insanity because of a "greater liveliness of conscience" leading to despair and because of "inward feelings of discrepancy" provoked by their being limited in vocational choices to business life. He also thought that marrying late caused them to feel lonely and depressed, and that too often they intermarried. Tuke defended Friends against these charges, pointing out that at the Retreat few Friends were patients who suffered from common causes of insanity—religious madness, alcoholism, or poverty. Quakers who did suffer from mental illness were admitted chiefly for

Table 5.1

Duration	No.	Restored	Much Imp.	Imp.	Stationary	Remaining	Died
Less than 1 year	261	152	26	27	18	4	34
From 1 to 2 years	57	18	8	8	9	7	7
From 2 to 3 years	36	17	3	3	4	5	4
From 3 to 5 years	45	14	7	6	9	3	6
From 5 to 10 years	47	13	7	3	8	11	5
Over 10 years	61	0	7	5	22	13	14
Aggregate	507	214	58	52	70	43	70

"disappointment of the affections, domestic affliction, or failure in business."[17]

In his 1828 *A Sketch of the Origin, Progress, and Present State of the Retreat, An Institution Near York, for the Reception of Persons Afflicted with Disorders of the Mind, Among the Society of Friends,* Samuel Tuke nicely summarized the medical versus moral approach to mental illness. He believed that the medical arts were still in their "infancy" and, like Lord Bacon, one still seeks to know "how and how far the humours of the body act upon the mind, and how and how far the affections of the mind act upon the body." He went on to say: "We are still obliged to confess, that in some cases bodily symptoms afford but an uncertain clue to the seat of the disease, and consequently to its medical treatment; as regards human means, on that arrangement of external circumstances, which constitutes moral treatment; and which, tending primarily to the alleviation of *symptoms,* may ultimately, from the influence of mental emotions on the body, lessen or remove the physical cause of the disease" (1828, 32).

The source of mental illness, he maintained, "may probably in all cases be connected with bodily disease," yet its origin in "numerous" cases may be traced to "mental affections" that can be prevented by "proper regulation of the mind." Individuals have often encountered difficulties in life while being armed with the "habits of endurance or self-government." Thus these must be provided in the Retreat's environment by reinforcing or recreating the moral atmosphere necessary for mental health. The earlier the patient is removed to the asylum after the onslaught of the disease, however, the more likelihood there is of a cure. Tuke pointed out that of the 379 cases admitted between 1796 and 1828, only seventy were of three months duration or less since the first attack. The odds of completely restoring people of this class are nine to one, whereas patients of the fourth class—in whom the disease has been of more than twelve months duration—are less likely to be completely restored.

Similar claims were made by others. Thomas S. Kirkbride, resident physician at Friends Asylum from 1832 to 1833 and then superintendent of Pennsylvania Hospital, writing in the 1846 *Report of the Pennsylvania Hospital for the Insane,* said that "insanity is curable in proportion to the early period at which a [patient] is placed under treatment, and a prompt removal from familiar scenes is commonly desired." If prompt treatment is provided, Kirkbride says, "at least eighty percent will probably recover. . . ." In his 1839 report, Charles Evans noted the dramatic cure rates of patients at Friends Asylum whose disease was less than a year's duration. He stated that the cure rate during the twenty-two years since the asylum opened was 58.23 percent, while the last six years saw a discharge of "much improved" of 66 percent of the patients. The improvement would have been even more radical, claims Evans, had the patients not often been prematurely removed by their relatives. Indeed, a total of eighty-one patients had to be readmitted, thirty-nine of whom had suffered from the disease for less than one year. Whereas Tuke would argue that the patient had too quickly been taken from the Retreat's positive milieu, Evans attributed the relapse to the "organs not having been restored to perfect soundness after the original attack" (1839, 13). Diseased organs, especially the brain, were thought to be subject to relapses affected by other bodily organs as well as by "moral feelings and emotions of the mind" unless they had been fully strengthened by the seclusion and "regular habits" of the asylum.

The creation of a "surrogate home and family in which to resocialize the patient" (Digby 1985, 34) was the primary mode of treatment throughout the early years of both the Retreat and Friends Asylum. A sincere if artificial milieu peopled by caring fellow members of the Society of Friends designed to remedy the defects of the patient's natural family or environment was mirrored in the penal system's attempts to create an orderly—indeed strongly regimented—environment to correct the disorders and deficiencies of the milieu that contributed to the criminal's poor choices. This led to an emphasis on prison architecture as much as asylum architecture, one designed to reinforce the principles of milieu training. It was most important, prison reformers felt, to isolate the prisoners from all corrupting influences and to establish patterns of order and regularity during their prison stay. The Reverend James B. Finley, chaplain at the Ohio penitentiary, put the matter forcefully. Christianity will only triumph, he asserted, when the "daily habits of mankind shall undergo a thorough revolution." This can best be accomplished by placing two or three generations in a prison, an advantageous environment in which to inculcate habits of "regularity, and temperance, and sobriety" (Rothman 1971, 84–85).

Similar optimism prevailed with respect to the "moral architecture" of asylums and the emphasis placed on setting. Just as Quakers had argued for the "family" setting as an important corrective to the moral deficiencies of patients' upbringings, so too did many superintendents during the Jacksonian period see the necessity of an ordered environment as a corrective for the "exceptionally open and fluid quality of American society" (Rothman 1971, 133). What began with the Quakers as an informal re-creation of a colonial, agrarian community eventually became a methodized, regimented system more akin to an urban, industrial order. Order and setting became ends in themselves as the interpersonal and spiritual values of the Quakers began to be bypassed in the interests of efficiency and economy (see Rothman 1971, 153–54). As will be seen later, Thomas Eddy's career was interesting in this regard.

Essentially, as Rothman noted, modes of treatment amounted to a question of philosophy. Does one sin or go mad because of socially deviant behavior or internal corruption (or "character" or heredity as it was later to be called)? For Quakers in eighteenth- and early nineteenth-century Philadelphia, there was a strong communal self-policing that acted as a corrective to defective conduct—a mix of church, family, and community that became mirrored in the asylum. Yet as the Society became fractured by the Separation and Quakers began to move away from each other, there was both less governance in the Quaker community and an increasing sense of despair at the asylum that the moral milieu was adequate to achieve a high rate of cure. Because of their optimistic philosophy of man, Quakers saw the potential for reform in both the asylum and prison, unlike the Puritans, for instance, who saw isolation and the lash as the best correctives. That optimism, however, began to diminish. There was a general sense in America in the 1830s that insanity was not only increasing, it was not being cured (Rothman 1971, 110).

Increasingly, as is reflected in the Evans report, cure rates became associated more with medical than moral treatment. The former was gradually replacing the latter as the primary focus of care. Plans to build the Southern Retreat were presumably hindered by Samuel Tuke's commitment to moral treatment. By 1833 the report of Friends Asylum advocated a more vigorous medical approach to insanity, partially in response to the failure of Friends Asylum to achieve the same rates of cure being experienced at other institutions.

Unlike Friends Asylum, York Retreat did not even have a resident medical officer until the appointment in 1838 of a young Quaker who had trained at Westminster Hospital and who was a member of the Royal College of Surgeons—John Thurnam. Tension between this young professional and Thomas Allis, the hosier and dairyman who had succeeded George Jepson as superintendent in 1823, eventually caused Allis's resignation in 1841. Thurnam then became the first medical superintendent in the Retreat's history in 1847, shortly after receiving his medical degree from King's College, Aberdeen in 1846. In part his appointment was a response to the Lunacy Act of 1845, which dictated that any institution with over one hundred patients should have a superintendent with medical qualifications.

The increasing ascendancy of medical over moral treatment was also felt at Friends Asylum. Andrew Scull has suggested that moral treatment was too generalized and too dependent on the character and personality of the superintendent; it lacked a coherent and durable theoretical base to make it last.[18] Also, the study of phrenology was now important; it suggested an organic basis of personality aberrations and reinforced the concept of medical knowledge preceding moral treatment.

While the Tukes had the greatest influence on the establishment of private mental asylums in America in the nineteenth century and while moral treatment and general humanitarian therapy continued to be emphasized, the adoption of medical approaches took hold much faster in the United States than in England. There were several reasons for this difference. One was the heritage of Benjamin Rush, the father of American psychiatry whose *Medical Inquiries and Observations Upon the Diseases of the Mind* (1812) established the medical approaches for treatment of "inflammation of the brain" and whose work remained the dominant psychiatric text in the nineteenth century (Shryock 1960, 130). Another was the failure of the various Quaker hospitals, like those in England, to provide their brand of psychological medicine with any kind of theoretical base. Another reason, perhaps, was the American impatience with theory and the desire for results. Thus the Americans could tolerate the well-meaning aspects of moral therapy while seeking higher cure rates by the more direct intervention of medical care. Whatever the specific reason, it was certainly true that by the late 1830s not only Friends Asylum but several of the other Quaker institutions had increased their emphasis on medical approaches to insanity.

By way of advancing the medical approach, Friends Asylum managers decided in 1832 to hire two doctors (Robert Morton and Charles Evans) to be attending physicians; Thomas Story Kirkbride reported to them as the resident physician. This was at variance with what was being practiced at the Retreat, where the superintendent had control both of medical and moral treatment; George Jepson was the model for such a lay practitioner and, as was noted earlier, was a figure akin to the Dissenting healer epitomized in George Fox. Friends Asylum broke from this pattern by investing the superintendent with responsibility for all dimensions of moral treatment but allowing the resident physician (subject to the attending physicians coordinated by the board of consulting physicians established in March 1818) to dictate all matters related to medical treatment, including those areas, such as hydrotherapy, where there appeared to be an intersection of the medical and moral approach (see the superintendent's journal for 29 May 1832). Friends Asylum differed in another respect from any contemporary institutions by not having a medical superintendent charged with total care of the patients, as was the case at both the McLean Asylum (1818) and the Hartford Retreat (1824). It also became the case at both the Bloomingdale Asylum and the Pennsylvania Hospital (Tomes 1984, 64). It was not until 1850 that Friends Asylum had a medical superintendent. It is true that Edward Taylor, a physician, was superintendent and resident physician from 1823 to 1832, but he had to answer in medical matters to the attending physician, Samuel W. Pickering. The two superintendents from 1832 to 1850—John C. Redmond and Philip Garrett—were both laymen; from 1850 until the present, beginning with Joshua H. Worthington, all superintendents have been medical doctors.

The 1833 annual report of Friends Asylum, reflecting the personnel changes begun in 1832, had a decidedly different tone from the earlier reports. Drs. Morton and Evans filed their own physicians' report, which as extracts or in entirety became regular parts of the annual reports. In 1833 they stated the need to pursue a "judicious system of medical treatment," that moral treatment was a "necessary consequence" of medical remedies, and that in fact the two were parts of the same system. "After what are called medical means have been successfully resorted to, to remove obvious physical disease, moral treatment will then be found very efficient in restoring and strengthening the functions of the diseased organ" (5). The doctors were careful to affirm that medical care must be united with moral treatment, but there was a decided shift of emphasis to the primacy of the medical approach.

This trend continued in later reports. In 1835 the report affirmed that medicine can cure the mind as well as the body if treatment is given early enough, and the 1836 report provided the following definition of insanity: "a morbid state of some of the physical organs, and the deranged manifestations of mind merely the symptoms of that state." Insanity is not, the writers hastened to add, "an unintelligible malady of the immaterial existence itself" (9), though moral treatment, with its reaction of the mental upon the material, was as proper a treatment as "calomel, opium, or the lancet." It is interesting too that in the list of officers in the 1836 report, Charles Evans as attending physician was placed higher than the superintendents. In the 1837 report, additional clarification as to the nature and cause of insanity is given. Evans said that its origin was to be found in "some disturbance of the brain, either structural or functional—which disturbance may spring from either a moral or physical source." No matter how it arose, however, the "proximate cause" was always centered in the brain and was comparable to any physical ailment. Treatment of such was best left not to the "mysticism of metaphysics" but to careful medical care assisted by moral treatment (9).

During this period the managers expressed concern over the increased costs of the medical approach. In addition to the two attending physicians and a resident physician in 1832, there was the cost of the superintendents (John and Laetitia Redmond from New York), and the use as well of at least four consulting physicians. The managers sought to compensate for these expenses and the additional debt incurred by the construction in 1838 of new wings for manic patients by increasing the number of patients. They did so by soliciting new patients both within Philadelphia Yearly Meeting and beyond (stressing that better roads made travel to the hospital easier). Through 1831 the total number of patients never exceeded twenty-eight, even though there was then room for eighty, but by 1838 Dr. Charles Evans noted in his report that the total number of patients had reached sixty-three. He also pointed out that the percentage of cures since 1832 (the year he became with Morton the attending physician) had reached sixty-six percent, compared to an overall rate earlier of forty-two percent. Thus he and presumably the managers felt vindicated by the new emphasis on medical treatment.

The changes in treatment beginning in 1832 with this change of leadership were pronounced: more bleeding and cupping was done to reduce the inflammation of the brain, and the use of emetics and shower baths to stir dull patients was increased. Yet the lay superintendent did continue to exercise control over the moral treatment of the patients, and his occasional successes left a solid impression on Thomas Story Kirkbride—the young resident physician and Quaker who eventually achieved fame as head of Pennsylvania Hospital for the Insane. In one of his cases, a patient who had through "most filthy habits" continually dirtied her room and her person was transferred by the superintendent to a finer room and provided decent clothes and the use of pen, ink, and paper. Kirkbride noted that she reacted positively to these changes and experienced a turn for the better (Tomes 1984, 66).

Chapter 3 provided a broad outline of the theory and practice of asylum medicine that prevailed not only at Friends Asylum but throughout most asylums until the 1880s. The essential concept of the mind-body relationship as it was viewed at the time was that the immediate cause of mental illness was a physical disorder with psychological problems acting as predisposing or remote causes of the disorder (such causes act on the body, which in turn affects the mind). Most of the medical superintendents who in 1844 formed the Association of Medical Superintendents of American Institutions for the Insane (AMSAII) were comfortable with this concept. As active Christians, they eschewed any concept of mental illness that would suggest that the immaterial mind was subject to disease, and they also were concerned that such a primary emphasis would embroil medical doctors in theological controversies such as demonic possession. Thus they were never truly comfortable with Pinel's emphasis on psychological factors that act directly on the mind with the result often being physical disorders, e.g., grief causing anxiety that would result in a rapid pulse.

Pinel also emphasized the emotional or moral cause of mental illness. Medical superintendents incorporated this notion into their treatment by arguing that mental illness was a nervous disease caused in part by patients living in a more frenetic age. These nervous problems in turn affected the workings of the brain and, if left untreated, could result in serious brain damange. Physical and moral factors could thus cause mental illness, and any valid therapy should thus combine both medical and moral means. Gentler depletions and the use of narcotics such as morphine and opium to calm the nerves became therapies of choice at many asylums. Kindly isolation and quiet were also instrumental in dealing with nervous disorders. Interesting too was a new emphasis on religious enthusiasm as a pernicious cause of much mental illness. This was a reaction to the Great Awakening with its enthusiastic "New Light" practices and the development of new sects. For example, Dr. Woodward noted that twenty-eight of 220 cases at the Worcester Asylum were a consequence of Millerism, a sect that developed from William Miller's conviction that the second coming of Christ would occur some time between 21 March 1843 and 21 March 1844. Followers withdrew from their own religions to form a group taking the name Adventist, the forerunner of the Seventh Day Adventists formed in 1860 in Battle Creek, Michigan. Kirkbride mentioned in the 1844–45 report of the Pennsylvania Hospital that four cases of insanity could be attributed to Millerism and four to fright during the summer riots.[19]

No matter what the attribution, more medical superintendents were convinced that social, economic, and political factors were the most important ingredients in causing mental illness. In his *Mental Institutions in America: Social Policy to 1875* (1973), Gerald Grob nicely summarized these attitudes:

> In the absence of demonstrable etiological concepts or a germ theory of disease, American physicians and laymen interpreted health as a consequence of a proper and orderly relationship between nature, society, and the individual. Disease followed the violation of the natural laws that governed human behavior and was indissolubly linked with filth, immorality, and improper living conditions. Health, on the other hand, was synonymous with virtue and order. (88)

We also see developing a kind of romantic primitivism with a sense that civilization is the major culprit and that simpler cultures experience a lesser degree of mental illness. In *Causes of Insanity* (1851), Edward Jarvis contrasted the hectic pace and intensity of Jacksonian democracy with the less ambitious, more socially stable and hierarchical society of an earlier period and goes on to note: "In an uneducated community, or where people are overborne by despotic government or inflexible customs, where men are born in castes and die without overstepping their native condition, where the child is content with the pursuit and the fortune of his father . . . there these undue mental excitements and struggles do not happen" (Rothman 1971, 115). In this view, the very fluidity of American society endangered the mental health of its citizens. Thus citizens must exert degrees of self-control to avert their moving into insanity. Asylums were structured to aid in that control.

Influences

Other Quaker-related hospitals directly touched by York Retreat included Bloomingdale Asylum (1821), McLean Asylum (1818), Hartford Retreat (1824), and Sheppard-Pratt Hospital (1891). Of the thirteen founding members of The Association of Medical Superintendents of American Institutions for the Insane (AMSAII) which eventually became the American Psychiatric Association, six had connections with at least one of these asylums and Friends Asylum: 1)

Amariah Brigham (1798–1849), the superintendent at Hartford Retreat from 1840 to 1842 and founder of the *American Journal of Insanity;* 2) John S. Butler (1803–90), superintendent at Hartford Retreat from 1843 to 1883; 3) Pliny Earle (1809–92), resident physician at Friends Asylum from 1840 to 1842, then attending physician at Bloomingdale beginning in 1844; 4) Thomas Story Kirkbride (1809 to 1893), resident physician at Friends Asylum in 1832 and then head of Pennsylvania Hospital; 5) Luther Bell (1806–62), at McLean Asylum from 1826 to 1846; 6) Samuel B. Woodward (1787–1850), active in founding Hartford Retreat and later superintendent of Worcester State Hospital. Other AMSAII founders included John M. Galt, William M. Awl, Isaac Ray, Samuel White, Nehemiah Cutter, Francis Stribling, and Charles Harrison Stedman.

The Quaker merchant Thomas Eddy was the prime mover in the establishment of New York Hospital's Bloomingdale Asylum, having been directly influenced by Lindley Murray, with whom he had corresponded concerning York Retreat, and more importantly by Samuel Tuke's *Description.* On 4 April 1815, Eddy read before his fellow governors of New York Hospital a pamphlet entitled "Hints for Introducing an Improved Mode of Treating the Insane in an Asylum." In it he asserted that the "radical defect" in the treatment of the insane had been the false assumption that mental illness was a bodily or physical disease when in fact it had moral causes and should often be dealt with by moral therapy. He mentioned being influenced in these ideas by Creighton, Arnold, and Rush but especially by Samuel Tuke, who had been induced to write in 1814 "A Letter to Thomas Eddy of New York on Pauper Lunatic Asylums." Eddy proposed the purchase of land on which to erect an asylum for fifty patients. On 3 June the board of governors charged Eddy to chair a committee to do so, and they reported back on 1 August 1815 that they had purchased thirty-eight acres at Bloomingdale for $246 an acre.

It is significant, too, that Eddy as a major figure in penal reform was a strong advocate of the Auburn Method. This prison system emphasized labor and silence. Prisoners were isolated in their own cells, were not allowed to converse with each other, and were even hooded when being moved from one location to another. This was done to prevent corrupting contact but also to emphasize the potential through silent contemplation of opening up oneself to the Inner Light and communion with God. It was a method of religious reform and renewal that had many advocates and was advanced with the same sense of optimism and humanitarian impulse as was moral treatment of the insane. The fact that both approaches ultimately proved to be less than totally successful did not prevent their enduring. In fact, in the same year that Bloomingdale Asylum opened (1821), architect John Haviland won the commission to construct Eastern State Penitentiary in Philadelphia. The structure was the result of a reform movement begun primarily by Quakers in the 1787 establishment of the "Members of the Society for Alleviating the Miseries of Public Prisons." This building became one of the most famous structures of its kind in America; when Charles Dickens visited America in 1842 he asked explicitly to be shown Niagara and the penitentiary at Philadelphia.

Following the Auburn Method (the state prison in New York that had a modified single-cell plan permitting prisoners to work in groups), Eastern fully implemented Eddy's sense of how a prison should be constructed and organized. It had 252 cells in seven corridors radiating from a central rotunda. Each cell was eight by twelve feet accompanied by a yard eight by eighteen feet. Such isolation permitted the prisoners to work by themselves and reflect on past misconduct, and in doing so to begin the process of reformation. By analogy with the moral treatment of the insane, Eddy conceived of this penal system as a Lockean scheme to correct failings in early moral and religious instruction. According to him, its advantages were that it "affords an opportunity alternately for silent and solitary reflection, for the salutary action of the mind upon itself; and for that mental activity upon other objects, and that relaxation from the severer task of thinking, which is at once necessary to preserve the healthy state of the mind and body, and to give efficacy to the meditation which is thus encouraged." In the silence and darkness "the voice of religious instruction is heard and the prisoner discovers his spiritual nature" (Knapp 1834, 71).

Pliny Earle (1809–92) also provided a direct connection between Friends Asylum and Bloomingdale Asylum. Born in Leicester near Worcester, Massachusetts of Quaker parents, he attended the Medical College at Philadelphia while broadening his education with a series of visits to England and the Continent. He was resident physician at Friends Asylum from 1840 to 1842 before becoming head of Bloomingdale in 1844 and staying there for five years. Conditioned by his experiences at Friends Asylum, he came to reject the "heroic treatment" espoused by Benjamin Rush, which was still so influential in the medical schools. He came to believe that the cupping, blistering, and bleeding emphasized by Rush were approaches "consigning hundreds prematurely to the grave, and hundreds more to premature insanity" (Earle 1898, 145).

His other important contribution, one leading to a changed attitude about the curability of insanity, was to perform more precise statistical studies of cure rates at various asylums. In his *The Curability of Insanity* (1877),[20] he demonstrated the failure in many of the records to distinguish between persons and cases and to equate recovery with discharge. Thus at Bloomingdale one patient was discharged as cured six times in one year and another one at Worcester Hospital seven times in one year. These kinds of statistical methods thus led Dr. Galt at the Williamsburg, Virginia Asylum to claim a cure rate of 92.3 percent and Dr. Woodward at Worcester Hospital to claim rates at different years of 90 percent and 91.42 percent. The failure to sustain these rates or prove their accuracy led the public to distrust such care. Earle's own studies of over thirty-nine American asylums with 33,318 cases was that the recovery rate was 29.15 percent. This referred to all recoveries calculated on all admissions. The recovery rate increased significantly in cases where the duration of the disease had been short before admission to an institution. The growing lack of confidence in the cure rates led eventually to the warehousing of patients and the tendency to care for them, not cure them.

McLean Asylum, founded in 1818, was built as a complementary structure to Massachusetts General Hospital; the latter was built in imitation of New York Hospital and Pennsylvania Hospital. McLean's first superintendent was a physician—Dr. Morrill Wyman. Dr. Wyman spent some time studying the treatment of the mentally ill at Pennsylvania Hospital, New York Hospital and Friends Asylum. Though not a Quaker he felt that moral treatment should receive primacy, even in cases where there was obvious organic disease. He ably used the resources of Boston in treating the patients, taking them for country rides, rowing on the Charles River, and even to events at the Boston Atheneum (Eaton 1977, 135–37).

The Hartford Retreat had a unique history. Dr. Eli Todd, a physician with a history of mental illness in his family, decided out of self-interest to familiarize himself with the work at York Retreat. Although he was a political radical and religious skeptic, he was impressed enough with the layman's approach to mental illness to advocate its duplication in Connecticut. To that end he organized in 1822 a Society for the Relief of the Insane and lobbied through the Connecticut Medical Society for the construction of an asylum. The Hartford Retreat opened in 1824 with Todd as its first director. Its primary emphasis was on moral treatment with a great sensitivity to the individual patient. According to Dr. Charles W. Page, the system "was not a code of rules for subordinates to enforce, no austere, remote authority, but personal devotion and painstaking labor with his patients—that method of true leadership in a good cause which always commands respect and insures success."[21]

At the same time, influenced as much by Pinel as by Tuke, Todd did indeed take notice of medical treatment and in doing so followed a pattern established at Friends Asylum. Though Bonsall cringed at times when the physicians used what he felt to be too much medicine, he nonetheless saw its benefit and combined it with moral treatment. So too with Todd and the leaders of the major asylums established in the 1820s and 1830s. In retrospect, it is striking that these physician-superintendents were strongly influenced by Quaker laymen and continued to avow the necessity of moral treatment.

Dr. Samuel B. Woodward, who had aided Todd in promoting the building of Hartford Retreat and who himself became the first super-intendent in 1833 of Worcester State Hospital, the first state institution for the mentally ill in New England, saw Worcester state hospital as a "proving ground for moral treatment" (Bockoven 1963, 14). In 1841 he articulated the philosophy of moral treatment used at Worcester State: "By our whole moral treatment, as well as our religious services, we inculcate all the habits and obligations of rational society. We think the insane should never be deceived. . . . They may be held responsible for their conduct so far as they are capable of regulating it. By encouraging self-control and respect for themselves we make them better men" (Digby 1985, 253). This approach, combined with medical treatment, resulted in a claimed recovery rate, from 1833 to 1842, of 82.3 percent (Bockoven 1963, 15), a statistic later challenged by Pliny Earle, who though he agreed with the therapy cast doubts on it by his own statistical work.

The Sheppard and Enoch Pratt Hospital in Baltimore, chartered in 1853 but not opened for patients until 1891, was established by Moses Sheppard, a Quaker businessman who started as an errand boy with John Mitchell, a provision merchant, and who eventually became a partner in the firm. He then accumulated a major fortune through this firm and astute investments in real estate. He oversaw the early planning of the asylum and then at his death in 1857 left over $571,000 for its construction. The asylum was not completed until 1891, however, because Sheppard stipulated in his will that only the income, not the principal, could be used to sustain the institution. Following the tradition of religious exclusivity, he asserted that the asylum was for the care "first, for the poor of the Society of Friends; secondly, for such of the Society as are able to pay; and then for the poor indiscriminately; afterwards the Trustees will use their discretion" (Forbush 1971, 18).

By the time of its opening, organizers of the asylum could rely on the benefit of more than seventy years of experience at Friends Asylum and elsewhere. For example, the principles of its construction were those articulated by Kirkbride as published in the *American Journal of*

Insanity. The hospital had the advantage as well of able leadership by Edward N. Brush (1891–1920) and Ross McLure Chapman (1920–48), who became presidents of the American Psychiatric Association, and the pioneering work with male schizophrenics by Harry Stack Sullivan in the 1920s.[22] One is struck, however, by how little the science of treating the mentally ill had advanced during this period. Mustard and salt baths, tonics, and morphine were still employed, with occasional use being made of some of the newer drugs such as chloral hydrate, sodium amytal, stramonium, and digitalis. What had changed, however, was the classification or taxonomy of patients. No longer was the cause of insanity identified as religious enthusiasm or self-pollution. During the first ten years of the asylum's operations 874 patients were admitted, and the diagnoses provided were considerably more sophisticated than those given in the early Quaker asylums. Mania, for example, was divided into acute and chronic varieties, with these further subdivided into ten categories, including puerperal, subacute, chronic delusional, and paranoia. The bequest in 1896 of Enoch Pratt's estate, amounting to $1,631,493, enabled the hospital, however, to engage in numerous avenues of original research that would advance the study and treatment of mental illness.

Summary

The nineteenth century was an exciting time for many of these asylums. Their work reflected a generally optimistic sense during the period from 1817 until the 1840s that individuals could regenerate themselves and learn through environment and example the degree of self-restraint needed to become useful, productive citizens and to correct the deficiencies of early education or family weakness. An Emersonian sense of self-reliance, in combination with a movement of moral rearmament, led concerned citizens to combat madness, slavery, crime, and poverty through a variety of humane societies and institutions. Only later, as the number of cures and conversions appeared to dwindle, did a sense of frustration and futility take over and lead, at least in the case of mental illness, to a strongly different regimen in the asylums, especially the state institutions.

David Rothman (1971) argues that a period of Jacksonian democracy, with its destructive breakup of traditional communities and the movement to the cities, contributed to an increase in mental illness and at the same time to a call for a more ordered regimen to cope with this increase. The development of asylums in America thus arose primarily out of various traits in the American character and society. Andrew Scull (1981) disputes such "parochial theories" and emphasizes the importance to American asylums and their founders of the preceding work of Tuke, Pinel, and others in the philosophy of care and architecture in eighteenth- and especially nineteenth-century American treatment of the insane. In his article entitled "The Discovery of the Asylum Revisited: Lunacy Reform in the New American Republic" (1981), Scull provides a brief overview of the earliest corporate asylums, i.e., those built with private appeals to the public. These were the Quaker-founded or influenced institutions such as Friends Asylum, Hartford Retreat, McLean Asylum, and Bloomingdale Asylum (and later, Sheppard-Pratt Hospital). As Scull suggests (and I have tried to show), the efficacy of treatment at these institutions—especially in their early years when their approach was in such marked contrast to what had gone before and when they were dealing primarily with a prosperous, homogenous clientele—helped shape American attitudes toward the curability of insanity and the merits of institutionalization. It also helped advance the establishment of public hospitals, and the corporate asylums often supplied them with their early administrators.[23]

The Quaker character of these asylums, especially Friends Asylum, is noteworthy, while Quaker attitudes and ideas contributed to their development in a distinctive manner. Moral treatment was doomed for a variety of reasons not so much to fail as to be replaced. Its basic tenets endured but primarily at the private hospitals ministering to patients able to afford the pleasant environment, the smaller attendant-patient ratio, the better diet, and the provision of a wide range of diversions and services. The concept of moral treatment—to the extent that it basically involved treating human beings with respect and kindness—was not suddenly extinguished by the emphasis on medical treatment. Yet the fact that a physician's article in 1963 (Bockoven) called for its return suggests that as an overriding philosophy of care it had fallen perhaps into disuse if not disrepute. Some of the reasons for moral treatment being overtaken by the medical approach have already been suggested. The next chapter will examine several specific events that directly touched on Quaker ideas and institutions and, along with the Separation discussed previously, contributed to a lessening of Quaker influence, particularly in the field of mental illness.

6

QUAKERS AND MORAL TREATMENT IN AMERICA

Just as York Retreat had inspired the founding of Friends Asylum, so too did the latter institution influence the establishment of and treatment at a variety of American asylums. In addition to being a model for moral treatment, it provided valuable experience for those who would become the leaders in nineteenth-century asylum care—individuals such as Thomas Story Kirkbride and Pliny Earle. Its failure to lead the way in developing other approaches to the treatment of mental illness was the result of several factors. Some of these had to do with the limited theoretical application of moral treatment, some with its Quaker sense of understatement with regard to its achievements and the desire to remain a private, sectarian institution. Other influences included external attacks on the asylum and the debate over the idea of moral insanity. Particularly important was the Hinchman case.

Mind-Body Relationship

An inchoate but nonetheless well-intentioned effort to bring scientific understanding to the problem of mental illness marked the liberal humanitarianism of the eighteenth century. As we have seen, theorists groped for an understanding of the physical causes of mental illness and a formulation of an appropriate pharmacopoeia or physical regimen to treat the disease while other practitioners, without totally dismissing the benefits to be gained from medicine, instinctively treated patients with a mix of compassion and kindness. The early reformers had a modified somatic view of mental illness. That is, they conceived of its arising from inflammations of the brain due to physical causes as well as to such psychological bases as disappointment, religious enthusiasm, business failures, and a deficient education.

As we have seen from his remarks in his *Description* (1964), *Sketch* (1828), and *Memoirs* (1860), Samuel Tuke felt instinctively that moral treatment—the proper arrangement of external circumstances to alleviate symptoms and perhaps in the process lessen or remove the physical cause—was the surest way to cure mental illness. He retreated, however, from assured pronouncements on the exact relationship between mind and body, between physical and mental illness. He felt that medical treatment of the insane was still in its infancy and that Lord Bacon's question as to the effect of the humors upon the mind and the affections of the mind upon the body remained to be answered. Like Samuel Johnson, he feared the uncertain continuance of reason, believing that one could be shunted into madness for no clearly discernible reason. He lamented that reason could be "eclipsed by the derangement of those organs which we in degree understand" and that it was "subject to the vicissitudes and diseases of those finer parts of our bodily frame, of which we know no more, than that they baffle our greatest skill to dissect or unravel" (1860 1:291). Ultimately Tuke found the only true source of consolation to be divine providence.

The Tukes and Pinel drifted into moral treatment out of a humanitarian impulse rather than any well-defined therapeutic model. Basically they saw the need for an ordered, kind environment as a way of countering the disorder and unkindness that had permeated the lives of their patients. The rudimentary theories of disease that existed were tested at York Retreat and found wanting, so the practical Friends developed their own amalgam of kindness, good food, useful work, distraction, and religious inspiration—an environment of respect—to heal the injuries of the mind. Some eighteenth-century theorists stressed damage to the central nervous system as the root cause of mental illness, while others, such as Benjamin Rush, said that insanity was rooted in the blood vessels of the brain. Gradually ideas about insanity became firm and toward the middle of the nineteenth century unanimity developed.

In the twentieth report (1837) of Friends Asylum, the attending physician (Dr. Charles Evans) spoke with more assurance of the precise definition of insanity: "Insanity, in its various forms and degrees, has its origin in some disturbance of the brain, either structural or functional—which disturbance may spring from either a moral or physical source" (1837, 9). No matter how it arises, however, the "proximate cause producing the deranged manifestation of the mind, is always located in the brain—and the disease should be viewed in the same light as any other malady to which the human system is obnoxious." This meant a full range of "judicious" medical treatment while the patient rested in an environment full of useful and pleasant distractions. These "moral circumstances" diverted the patient's mind from "that train of thought, which, if it has not been the means of goading him to madness, is yet so productive of irritation and excitement, as to destroy the efficacy of the remedial means employed, and almost preclude the hope of recovery" (1837, 10).

Although not directly involved with the 1844 initial meeting of the Association of Medical Superintendents of American Institutions for the Insane (AMSAII), Evans and his colleagues would have been very comfortable with the theory of mental illness and the practice adopted toward its cure as articulated by this body. These men felt similarly confident of their ability to define insanity. Basically they were influenced by a combination of Lockean associationism and a religious sense of the separation of body and soul. They posited the importance of the environment and the effect of sensations upon the surface of the brain. These sensations are the basis of all thought. Interference in the reception or structuring of such impressions can lead to disordered judgment or delusions. One treats the brain to correct such disorders. Most alienists, as orthodox believers, felt that the mind is a spiritual power that could not become diseased and that it acted through the medium of the brain. The mind would be unable to act if the brain were diseased. As a malleable organ subject to the impressions upon its surface, the brain was vulnerable to a host of environmental and bodily stimuli and could be aided or injured by a variety of influences. Sudden shocks, fevers, poor early education, masturbation, abstract studies, Gothic novels—any or all of these had the potential to mar the brain's physiological structure with "lesions." At the same time, the brain's malleability made re-formation and healing possible. In an 1851 report, Evans said that by "restored" he meant that the disorder causing the derangement "whether of the brain directly, or by sympathy with some other organ," had been removed, and the mind "has consequently returned to the condition natural to it in a healthy state of the system" (12).

All AMSAII members adhered to the Pinel-Tuke tradition of moral treatment and stressed the need for a positive "family" atmosphere as an appropriately "moral" environment in which to retrain and nourish the psyche while as a side effect diminishing somatic damage and restoring the patient to good physical and mental health. York Retreat became famous because, in part, it formalized such instincts into an institutional setting and promoted its effectiveness through publications and the testimonies of famous visitors, but similar efforts took place in Italy, Germany, and America through the leadership of Chiarugi, Reil, and Rush. Through the fourth decade of the nineteenth century, in fact, there was an explosive period of construction in which a number of "retreats" were built to implement the principles stated in Tuke's *Description*. In America alone there were Friends Asylum for the Insane (1817), McLean Asylum for the Insane (1818), Bloomingdale Asylum (1821), Connecticut (Hartford) Retreat for the Insane (1824), Kentucky Eastern Lunatic Asylum (1824), Virginia Western Lunatic Asylum (1828), South Carolina Lunatic Asylum (1828), Worcester State Lunatic Hospital (1833), Maryland Hospital for the Insane (1834), Central Ohio Lunatic Asylum 1838), the New York City Lunatic Asylum, Blackwell's Island (1839), and Boston Lunatic Asylum (1839).

These public and private asylums all initially shared the optimism that mental illness was indeed curable and that moral treatment was the primary therapy. These views were gradually to change, especially at large public asylums. Some of the reasons for the breakdown of moral treatment at these institutions have already been explored. Moral treatment is a therapy of scale; that is, it demands individualized treatment. One cannot prescribe generally for all of the patients. In an 1841 report on Friends Asylum, the physicians noted that careful analysis of each situation was required:

> The same principles which regulate the application of medical agents in disease unaccompanied by mental aberration, must be called in to requisition here; each symptom must be interpreted until the whole case is analyzed; and success can be rationally anticipated, only, as each lesion obtains due notice, and receives its appropriate remedy. (16)

This demanded that the physician structure proper experiences, either to dispel hallucinations in some patients or "to arouse the slumbering energies of others, and awaken in them new hopes, desires and affections" (1838, 12). At Friends Asylum, a range of therapies was possible: horticultural therapy; workshop labor for the manufacture of baskets and brooms; manual labor in the fields; attendance at lectures on such topics as chemistry, zoology, pneumatics, optics and electricity; time spent in the library reading or examining the collection of shells and minerals. Such resources were simply not available at many of the large public asylums, nor could such institutions afford the small staff-patient ratio needed for moral treatment.

The more superintendents advocated the curability of insanity and announced their success, the more patients they attracted. The result was that the average annual admission to American mental institutions rose from thirty-one in 1820 to 182 in 1870, while the average total number of patients treated went from fifty-seven in 1820 to 473 in 1870 (Grob 1973, 371). Without a corresponding increase in staff, it became difficult if not impossible to treat individuals and to resist the temptation merely to house rather than cure the patients. Also, a latent if not overt racism began to affect a number of such institutions. There was a sense that the immigrants who were committed were not as capable of neatness, order, and cleanliness as native citizens and thus were not worth a significant investment of resources. In his 1854 *Report on Insanity and Idiocy in Massachusetts,* for instance, Edward Jarvis argued for the construction of separate asylums for native-born Americans and for immigrants (Jarvis 1971, 149).

Other problems compounded this situation and led to the mere warehousing of patients. One was Pliny Earle's questioning of curability statistics, which cast doubt upon the claims made by superintendents and must have aroused suspicion in the public mind. The public became disillusioned with the institutions, and the alienists themselves, not seeing positive results, "abandoned what we might now regard as progressive therapeutic ventures and contact with the community," retiring to such attainable goals as "good administration" (Caplan 1969, 49). The failure to provide a lasting theory of moral treatment that had a predictable rigor, one in which cures could be traced to concrete and documentable cause-effect relationships, dampened the enthusiasm of earlier years. Furthermore, most asylums failed to provide for programs of scientific research to justify or advance the philosophy of treatment. This lack of support remained a constant problem: in 1911 Bayard Holmes decried the fact that of the $25 million spent annually on the care of the insane, not even one-thousandth of that amount went to research for cures (1911, 99). Yet another problem was the death or resignation of such prominent superintendents as Brigham, Woodward, Bell, Awl, Butler, and Galt. Finally, as Caplan notes, the ultimate victory of a medical model of the insane meant the exclusion of lay practitioners—the tradition of the Tukes and men like George Jepson and Isaac Bonsall—and the separation of the general community from the increasingly esoteric work of a restricted group of alienists (1969, 49).

In this movement, then, from moral treatment to custodial care, what happened to the small private hospitals with the resources and patient selection enabling them to continue moral treatment? Scull says that they became "resorts for the upper classes" (1981, 159). It is true that their private character enabled them to avoid the influx of pauper lunatics the state institutions experienced. It is true as well that their wealth protected them from change and that they faded into a sort of genteel obscurity. A variety of forces for change were at work, including the growing pressure for more medical treatment. At York Retreat there was an attempt to establish the Southern Retreat and a gradual movement to a more professional regimen of therapy that included but did not emphasize moral treatment. This occurred as well at Friends Asylum as the medical staff was increased and the annual reports placed more emphasis on medical approaches. These institutions also began to lose their Quaker character, as more non-Friends, both patients and staff, joined them. Such modifications of shared value systems thus inevitably aided in the transformation of both York Retreat and Friends Asylum from "refuge to institution" (Digby 1985, 105).

But it is also true with respect to Friends Asylum that it went through turbulent experiences in the 1840s which not only indirectly hurt the moral treatment approach to insanity but also placed the Quakers in some disrepute. I touch on these events and the climate of ideas preceding them in order to show the marked change in attitude toward moral treatment from the opening of Friends Asylum in 1817 to around 1850. I pay particular attention to the concept of moral insanity and the Morgan Hinchman case, by way of tracing the story of Quakers and moral treatment in America until 1850. These events, though peculiar to Friends Asylum, would have repercussions throughout the nineteenth century on patient care.

Hinchman Case

It is ironic that Friends Asylum, often called the most progressive and enlightened asylum in early nineteenth-century America, should become involved in the celebrated forced commitment case of Morgan Hinchman, a case that not only generated intense public interest but also revealed the medical, legal, and social complications implicit in the term "moral insanity."

Morgan Hinchman, a member of the North Meeting of Friends in Philadelphia, was committed by family and friends to Friends Asylum on 7 January 1847 and left on 6 July of the same year.[1] According to asylum records he was a thirty-year-old farmer suffering from "mania," which had first become evident in 1841. Some time after his discharge, Hinchman charged that he had been forcibly committed as part of a conspiracy to deprive him of his property; he sought $40,000 in damages. Those assuming a major role in the commitment and who were formally charged in Hinchman's suit were Samuel S. Richie and Edward Richie, brothers who played the major role in conveying Hinchman to the asylum; John M. Whitall; George M. Elkinton and John Lippincott, who assisted the Richies; John D. Griscom, Hinchman's family physician who encouraged him to go; Anna Webb Hinchman, Morgan's sister; John L. Kite, a physician who issued the certificate of insanity; Elizabeth Robeson Shoemaker

Taylor, the sister of Hinchman's wife, Margaretta Shoemaker Hinchman; Benjamin H. Warder, a manager of Friends Asylum who gave the order of admission; Philip Garrett, superintendent of Friends Asylum; Charles Evans, attending physician of Friends Asylum; William Biddle, a member of the sheriff's jury that examined the question of Morgan's insanity after his being committed; Thomas Wistar, Jr., charged with having been criminally involved in the sale of Morgan's property.

The defendants seemed to have had a strong case for proving both the lack of conspiracy and need for commitment. Testimony regarding Hinchman's strange conduct came from individuals who knew him well: William J. Allinson, later editor of *Friends' Review*[2] and husband of Morgan's sister (Rebecca Webb Hinchman) spoke of Morgan's erratic, manic-depressive conduct on his wedding day; Joseph B. Matlack, who had known him for twelve years, spoke of Hinchman's troubled, paranoid attitude toward the Shoemaker family; James R. Garrigues, a clerk in Penn Township Bank, spoke of his "excitement of mind" and believed Morgan to be insane when he stole money from the bank (a sin that Morgan felt compelled to confess publicly out of fear of losing his firstborn); his sister Rebecca also spoke about his unpredictable behavior. William Hawkins described Morgan's beating Hawkins's son in 1844 without provocation; Hannah Hicks, a servant in the Hinchman home in 1844, mentioned his undressing before her preparatory to taking a bath; Dr. Evans related Morgan's strange beliefs about himself and his family: that he had syphilis, that at Friends Asylum he was on a ward for syphilitics, that he had committed unpardonable sins, and that his wife and sister-in-law were insane and in need of medical treatment.

Morgan's wife, Margaretta Shoemaker Hinchman, was unable to testify, but her views can perhaps be reconstructed from two sources: Shoemaker family correspondence[3] and the physician's records. Margaretta's own letters to family and friends touch but never dwell on the matter of both the trial itself and the conduct that led to Hinchman's being committed. It is almost as if the entire affair were an unhappy interlude in a life taken up with Quaker services, domestic duties, concern for relations, and visits from friends. Margaretta's letters do suggest the tension and burdens of enduring such a scandal without being totally absorbed by it, but her sister Elizabeth's letters are ultimately more informative, perhaps because she had more distance and could speak more freely.

On 2 January 1847, just five days before Morgan's commitment, Elizabeth wrote her brother Isaac that Morgan was "more decidedly deranged than ever before." Eliza Hinchman, Morgan's mother, had even come to discuss "means of preserving Morgan's property (if there be any) and placing him in an institution for the insane." Elizabeth also mentioned meeting Dr. Griscom, who had always felt that Morgan should not be at large. Elizabeth was more specific in these remarks from the same letter:

> One of his hallucinations is that his mother has a right to half of the ground on which the town of Wilkesbarre stands, but it has been swindled from her—another that brother J[ohn] is a gentleman of wealth retired to live upon his means in the refined and literary society of the great *Metropolis* of Chicago! and proposes to sue him for the loss he M[organ] has sustained by parting himself after John had delivered all unto his hands, with some of Margaretta's stock for 1/9 of its present value: and has warned C. Bosler that he has a heavy claim upon the estate—

In a letter written after the commitment (17 January) Elizabeth took care to mention that "nothing has been done without consulting a lawyer, and *I suppose* in this respect we are safe, yet there are so many turns in the law, that we may get difficulty, and some seem disposed to make it if they can. . . ." She went on to praise the Richies, adding that it was "E[liza] Hinchman, and the friends of North meeting who are responsible for placing M[organ] out of the way. . . ."

Earlier correspondence suggests that problems had arisen before. Writing Isaac Shoemaker on 4 April 1844, Elizabeth was cryptically ominous: "The house [the Hinchmans had moved a week earlier to a Doylestown farm in Bucks county; Elizabeth was visiting at this time since she felt that Margaretta needed "kin"] is good and if its inmates would only *do as well as they know how, how happy we might be, but if we had no alloys,* how easy it would be to forget that this world is not an abiding place." In a note appended to the same letter, Elizabeth commented on the farm and said that while its beauty should have promoted happiness, all was not well: "Morgan is already uneasy and dissatisfied, poor unsettled being that he is. . . ." She implied that he lacked "contentment" and thus her heart "ache[d]" for her sister. Letters to Isaac from Elizabeth in Roxborough (23 May 1844) and Philadelphia (9 November 1844) spoke about a "dark" future and Margaretta's "trials."

Several other letters are relevant. On 20 May 1847 Elizabeth, writing from Germantown, said that Morgan was doing well at Frankford (Friends Asylum) and "controls himself with great art," according to Dr. Evans, who adds that the "moral faculties rather than mental are diseased." Writing her brother Isaac on 2 July 1847, Elizabeth said that measures had been taken by "course of law" to remove Morgan from Friends Asylum. Although she anticipated his being pronounced recovered, Elizabeth, who had seen him, felt he was no better and feared "he is in a disposition to give us a good deal of trouble. . . ." Her fears proved warranted, as Morgan initiated his suit soon thereafter. Thus her letters from September 1847 on dealt intermittently with the impending trial and the mounting anxiety. She said that Morgan had five lawyers paid for by his uncle, Benjamin Hinchman, "a man who has scarcely known him thro' his life—" (7 November 1847). Finally on 19 December 1847 Margaretta wondered if they had done the right thing in having Morgan committed. The lawyers informed her that the case might take two years; thus she felt that it was "no easy matter at all times to maintain a quiet spirit" (10 September 1848).

The Journal of Cases at Friends Asylum, probably kept by Dr. Evans, the attending physician, has a number of remarks covering Hinchman's stay at the Asylum. The following excerpt is relevant:

> From a child has been in the habit of giving way to violent fits of passion which have increased, with a disposition to cross every person with whom he has anything to do particularly his wife. This was manifested almost immediately after his marriage. It was impossible for her to please him in her domestic arrangements. If he came home and found his dinner such as he did not choose to fancy he would throw himself on the floor in a paroxysm of anger. He was generally kind to her in the presence of strangers—at least apparently so though sometimes he would take advantage of their presence to vex her when she could have no redress. In some of these fits he has cruelly abused his wife as well as his mother. He has lately manifested Insanity on other subjects by making foolish bargains, by forgetfulness and by staying out at his work the greater part of the night. . . .[4]

Probably the doctor received this background on the patient from prejudiced sources, perhaps Morgan's mother since she was one of the sureties along with Samuel Richie for Morgan's stay at the hospital, but it does shed more light on the tension suggested by the Shoemaker letters.

Three other facts were relevant to the case for the defense. Morgan had apparently struck his mother and dragged her about his apple orchard when she irritated him in some way. As a result, the Bucks County Meeting at Buckingham returned his certificate from the North Meeting, which in turn convened a committee to look into this matter. Dr. Kite, named in Hinchman's suit, was a member of this committee that ruled "in consequence of the unsoundness of his mental or moral or intellectual faculties, Morgan Hinchman was not a person with whom that meeting should deal" (Anon. 1849c, 110). The meeting did not discipline him because the committee felt him to be mentally unbalanced. Morgan did not appeal the decision. Second, Dr. Evans was acquitted early in the trial, an odd decision since if there were a conspiracy to commit Morgan and divest him of his property, the physician who decided on the discharge of patients would have been an important component of it. It is equally odd that all members of the Friends Asylum staff were later acquitted. Finally, Hinchman's worth when he was taken to the asylum was only a little more than $5,000, a figure apparently not disputed by Hinchman's counsel. That amount divided among the fifteen presumed members of the conspiracy would yield shares that, if not trifling, would hardly be worth the trouble, especially, since a number of defendants were people of property.

Nonetheless, the court ruled in Hinchman's favor. Guilty as charged were the Richies, Whitall, Lippincott, Kite, Elkinton, and Elizabeth Shoemaker, with damages assessed at $10,000. Acquitted were Anna Hinchman, Warder, Biddle, Wistar, Worthington, Garrett, and Griscom. An appeal of the decision was denied. Thus ended a trail that began on 9 March in the Common Pleas Court in Philadelphia before Judge Burnside and lasted until the jury's verdict of 13 April. Eighty witnesses were called for the plaintiff, seventy for the defendants. Sessions lasted from 10 A.M. until evening with interested crowds packing the courtroom.

The science of the mind is a science susceptible to nonmedical, philosophical conceptions—in brief, it reflects the zeitgeist in which it is practiced. The success of Hinchman's suit is to be explained more by these factors than the strength of his lawyers' arguments or the testimony of numerous individuals (mostly nodding acquaintances and distant relatives) who affirmed his sanity. Ultimately important are such disparate influences as phrenology, moral insanity, the development of medical jurisprudence, and the American character. An investigation of these influences gives an idea of the attitudes of the physicians, lawyers, and laymen involved in the case and clarifies the implicit legal and philosophical problems. It also reflects on the perception by the general public of Friends Asylum.

Phrenology

The Enlightenment emphasis on reason and the conception of the mind-body relationship provided by philosophes and commonsense philosophers laid the foundations for eighteenth- and nineteenth-century faculty psychology and thus influenced in an important way the embryonic science of the mind. Contemporary psychology posited the existence of three faculties—reason, emotion, and will. Most eighteenth-century writers on mental illness concentrated on the first of these and regarded mental illness as a flight from reason. Even Tuke's *Description,* for all of its humanitarian impulses and revolutionary break with past therapies, remains preeminently a document of the Age of Reason. Though written at the height of the Romantic revolt in literature, its appeal is not to William Blake's "tygers of wrath," a symbol of romantic energy, but to the rationalists' "horses of instruction." Tuke stressed order and reason and would agree with Benjamin Rush that insanity is "a false perception of truth; with conversation and actions contrary to right reason, established maxim, and order" (Dain 1964, 6).

Yet what of those seemingly rational but sick men who do not publicly assume the tattered mantle of folly like that worn by Shakespeare's Tom of Bedlam? What happens to standard classifications when the presence or absence of reason is no longer the standard criterion in determining sanity? This question was posed by the Hinchman case. Morgan Hinchman, the defendants agreed, did run a sound farm, was shrewd, and kept accurate accounts. He was usually a calm, reasonable man, but counsel contended that his commitment was justified because he suffered from "moral insanity." Not his rational but his emotional faculties were impaired, so that he became seriously estranged from those closest to him.

In using this term and describing its symptoms, defense lawyers could and did draw on a clear tradition. While the majority of medical texts continued confidently to define madness as "a most dreadful kind of delirium, without a fever," as did the *Encyclopaedia Britannica* in 1771, investigators beginning with Pinel noticed that individuals could be insane without being irrationally delirious. Pinel called such a condition *manie sans délire* (mania without delirium) and in his *Treatise* (1806) said that he was "not a little surprised to find many maniacs who at no period gave any evidence of any lesion of the understanding, but who were under the dominion of instinctive and abstract fury, as if the active faculties alone sustained the injury" (150). Others, such as Benjamin Rush, noticed this phenomenon, but it remained for James Cowles Prichard, a British physician, to give these observations a name and a definition:

> Moral Insanity, or madness consisting in a morbid perversion of the
> natural feelings, affections, inclinations, temper, habits, moral disposi
> tions, and natural impulses, without any remarkable disorder or defect of
> the intellect or knowing and reasoning faculties, and particularly without
> any insane illusion or hallucination. (1835, 12)

Prichard's contention that insanity "consists, in certain cases, in a morbid perversion of the affections and moral feelings exclusively, and without any perceptible lesion of the intellectual faculties" (5) was a potentially troublesome concept because it overtly suggested a materialistic, even phrenological, psychology: that particular faculties of the mind have specific locations in the brain.

The basic elements of phrenology were captured in the following poem composed by a patient at the Insane Asylum in Utica and reprinted from the *American Journal of Insanity* in volume 3 of the 1846 issue of the *Friends Weekly Intelligencer:*

> Insanity
> If understood the truth is this,
> The mind has many faculties,
> And one distinct may be deranged,
> And from its proper order changed,
> Whilst all the rest do sound remain,
> In that alone the man's insane.
> Imagination thus diseased,
> Whenever violently seized,
> Produces things within the mind,
> Which are not easily defined. . . . (236)

Late in the eighteenth century Franz Joseph Gall (1758–1828) theorized that the brain was not a single organ but a collection of thirty-seven discernible faculties with such functions as language, benevolence, destructiveness, and time.[5] Working with a former student, Johann Gaspar Spurzheim (1776–1832), he developed a theory of the body that was more credible and sophisticated than its later vulgarization into the reading of head bumps at county fairs. Basically, all human behavior was reduced to a logical construct of brain activity that could be measured and studied. Phrenology was widely accepted, so much so that when Spurzheim died in Boston during a crosscountry speaking tour, the entire Boston Medical Society turned out for the funeral.

Phrenology's basic materialism was troubling to American alienists, however, because they were religious men with strong, self-assured value systems that colored their approaches to therapy. Most of the founding members of AMSAII were optimists influenced by both the Enlightenment sense of man's perfectibility and the Second Great Awakening, that nationwide revival of evangelical religion that counted among its leaders men like Timothy Dwight, Nathaniel W. Taylor, Charles Grandison Finney, and Lyman Beecher. Dwight and Taylor especially, as proponents of a commonsense approach to theology, sought to correct what they saw as errors inherited from the First Great Awakening, in particular the denial of free will insisted upon by Jonathan Edwards. Early nineteenth-century humanitarians accepted man's ability through reason and will to correct not only his sinful ways but build a better person and consequently a better society.

The majority of asylum superintendents believed in organized religion and were, in fact, probably more certain of their religious beliefs than their medical theories. For this reason they were never comfortable with the "moral insanity" concept, for it blurred the mind-brain distinction. As men of orthodox religious views, they felt compelled to assert the physical basis of disease without appearing materialistic. To state that mental illness was purely somatic demanded practical demonstrations that were unavailable to buttress such a view. On the other hand, to remove mental illness from the physical realm would surrender the field once again to the priests. Also, to suggest that mental illness had an immaterial basis would, to the orthodox mind, imply the possibility of the soul having defects. Evans's 1837 definition of insanity as a disturbance of the brain eliminated, he felt, the basis of that "vulgar prejudice which shrouded insanity in the mysticism of metaphysics" (9). Emotional or moral problems might cause "irritations" of the physical brain to produce "lesions" or diseases of the mind. Moral treatment helped structure an environment to calm the mind, remove the irritations, and (if the disease is caught in time) restore the brain to working order. Thus, at Hinchman's trial Evans said that "moral insanity cannot exist without malformation or disease of the brain. All insanity originates from either organic disease or functional disturbance of the brain" (Anon. 1849c, 82).

One founding member of AMSAII who agreed with Evans's testimony and whose strong advocacy of both phrenology and moral insanity played an important role at both the Hinchman trial and the development of medical jurisprudence was Isaac Ray (1807–81), who was medical superintendent at the State Hospital for Insane in Augusta, Maine (1841–45), at Butler Hospital in Providence, Rhode Island (1847–67), and President of AMSAII (1855–59). Phrenology's scientific nature appealed strongly to Ray since it seemed to rescue studies of mental activity from the abstract, nonempirical metaphysicians. His notion of moral insanity owed much to phrenology, though he had the good sense not to use the often-ridiculed term in his major publication, *A Treatise on the Medical Jurisprudence of Insanity* ([1838] 1962). Basically, Ray's sense of moral insanity (later called by him "partial moral mania") was the *manie raisonnante* of Pinel, the derangement of the affective faculties with "the rest of the moral and intellectual constitution preserving its ordinary integrity"

(1962, 237). Thus an individual, by an "instinctive irresistibility" (238), or what might today be called irresistible impulse, may commit an improper or criminal act while being perfectly conscious that it is wrong. Benjamin Rush had verified this observation and recorded examples, such as the moral woman with one uncontrollable vice—a tendency to steal. Ray argued that the law's failure to take such aberrations into account when trying individuals for criminal acts consigned the courts to serve as systems of injustice and inhumanity.

In his review of the case, Isaac Ray had no doubt that Morgan Hinchman suffered from moral insanity and should have been committed (Deutsch 1949, 423), and several physicians at the trial corroborated Evans's testimony. However, the mention of "moral insanity" was simply not palatable or understandable to the average jury member. The latter probably regarded much of the medical testimony as so much jargonistic palaver by pretentious "medico-metaphysicians," a phrase coined by a London physician unsympathetic to the abstract speculation of many of his colleagues.[6] Hinchman's attorney, David Paul Brown, was easily able to hold this concept up to ridicule. Ironically, Brown took a concept favored by Isaac Ray for its seeming scientific objectivity and inverted it; he said that moral insanity was "nothing more than a division formed by metaphysicians, of intellectual insanity" (1849, 19). No doubt Brown's plain words elicited a more positive response from the jury when he continued his attack in hyperbolic terms:

> It is a new theory—who understands it—emotional insanity! Has not your Honor been astonished by this doctrine? Why it is like some of the French dancing;—it is like what Addison calls a "regular confusion"; it is like the polka; it is like all the frippery, sir, of the French schools—though I am an admirer of them—full of phantastic inventions! They are full of jimcrackery—moral insanity! Our friends are plain citizens, grave men—they ought to look before they leap, or they will fall into mazes, from which even Ariadne's clue could never extricate them. Why it's neither fish, flesh, nor red herring! but is—it is that corruption of the moral faculties which is the result of long continued crime; becoming by habit too strong for rational or conscientious control. That's what it is; and that is not a matter which puts a man in the mad house, it puts him in the penitentiary. (1849, 19).

Also, in an editorial published on Saturday, 14 April 1849, just prior to the jury's decision, the *Public Ledger* expressed what it felt to be the public's shock and resentment of the abuse suffered by Hinchman. It particularly derided the conception of "moral insanity," noting that at best it is an academic term that augurs ill for the poor unfortunate accused of it. The malady is too vague, too "equivocal and fluctuating in its symptoms" to justify the deprivation of individual liberty and property. In a ringing climax, the paper stated that only total insanity should justify commitment:

> Partial insanity is the disease of mankind, not of an individual. Hence the absurdity of the doctrine, and the injustice of the treatment, which, in some cases, it has received. Technical insanity, in the medical schools, will not do to bring into the active concerns of life, consigning to a mad-house every man who has one delusion, who speaks too fast, or liquidates the charge of a *shilling*, by the payment of a *dime*. Upon this rule, every man in society may at sometime in his life be deemed insane.

And articles in *The Friend* (22:379–380; 385–86) for 18 and 25 August 1849, while otherwise sympathetic to the defendants' position, questioned the use of the "moral insanity" plea. The articles mentioned resentment of this phrase: "It is supposed to confound the distinctions between depravity and disease, and to yield a misplaced indulgence to vicious propensities and habits. . . . It is useless to say that the obnoxious phrase expresses a scientific fact well observed and authenticated, and consequently can be denied with as little propriety as the prismatic division of the solar ray" (386). These remarks specify the religious as opposed to philosophical or commonsensical objections to the idea of moral insanity. Many orthodox thinkers saw immorality based in conscious evil, not in an illness that freed one from moral responsibility. The possibility of the moral faculty apart from reason becoming diseased is an idea to provoke not only religious doubt but also legal confusion, for it appeared to "leave the court without any moral basis of punishing crime" (Dain 1964, 49).

These facts resonate in the concluding lines of the poem, "Insanity," quoted earlier:

> By searching we shall plainly find,
> 'Tis THUS with ev'ry human mind,
> Let but its powers be truly swung,
> Whilst on their proper pivot hung,
> Then in the mind we weigh things right,
> Which brings us joy and great delight.
> But let their proper balance fall,
> Involuntary fears anon
> With quickest pace come hastening on,
> And spread such terrors through the soul,
> O'er which the will has no control
> That all as lost to us may seem,
> Which makes hope sudden kick the beam.

The poem stresses an important element raised at the trial with respect to moral insanity—the question of the will and moral responsibility. It was always a dimension in moral treatment that the patient's will must be aroused in order that he or she might wage a personal struggle against insanity. The art of self-government replaced an older sense of the need for physical restraint of the patient. Thus Bucknill defined sanity as a "condition of the mind in which the emotions and the instincts are in such a state of subordination to the will, that the latter can direct and control their manifestations; in which moreover the intellectual faculties are capable of submitting to the will sound reasons for its actions" (Skultans 1979, 14). The Quaker stress on management arose out of their history and of a strong sense of self-monitoring and community control of conduct. So it is sadly ironic at the trial to see an important element in the Quaker reform of moral treatment turned upside down. Evans and his colleagues at Friends Asylum were attacked by Brown for somehow in their stress on moral insanity setting up conditions in which patients might be relieved of moral responsibility.

This was clearly a distortion of Quaker intent. As the major theorist on moral management, Tuke stressed self-control: "Insane persons generally possess a degree of control over their wayward propensities" (1964, 133). While he expressed concern about the sense of madness as an uncontrollable malady that could threaten to strike at any time, Tuke basically believed in the emotional and intellectual forces of the individual—manifestations, so to speak, of the Inner Light—to correct imbalances and stabilize the mind.

There is evidence at this trial of a subtle shift in this attitude toward the insane, a shift that would become more pronounced and affect the quality and kind of care, especially at the large public asylums. To use Skultans's phrase, there was a movement from "psychiatric Romanticism," with its stress on individualized care and respect for and reliance on the patient's conscience and will to combat insanity, to a greater emphasis on a more deterministic sense of heredity and flawed character. Some doctors felt that insanity could not be cured because too many of the insane were incurable. They lacked the proper character and breeding that would enable them to practice the arts of self-government emphasized by Tuke. Henry Maudsley, in his *Responsibility in Mental Disease* (1874), focused on the inability of large numbers of human beings to monitor their own behavior. He said they cannot do so because they lack training and education: "A man can no more will than he can speak without having learned to do so, nor can he be taught volition any more than he can be taught speech except by practice" (quoted in Skultans 1979, 132). Maudsley concluded that for a large number of people, moral treatment is impossible. Only more selective breeding to produce a better species can provide hope. The insane may be controlled, but their characters can not be changed. Thus it was neither fruitful nor helpful to indulge in moral treatment for many people.

Commitment Legislation

Another factor important to the Hinchman trial was the nature of commitment law in the United States and the tangential issue of basic liberty. Influenced in part by the new theories of the mind, courts in both England and America immediately prior to the Hinchman trial were establishing important legal precedents in civil and criminal law.[7] Previous legal practice subscribed to Matthew Hale's seventeenth-century requirement that the courts should absolve a person of legal responsibility for his actions only if he could be shown to be totally deranged and without any use of reason. This "wild beast" standard prevailed in common law until successfully challenged by Thomas Erskine, counsel for James Hadfield, who tried to assassinate George III in 1800 at the Theatre Royal in Drury Lane. Hadfield was reasonable on some points but was convinced that he was a messiah and should be martyred like Jesus Christ. This delusion test, successful in Hadfield's case, did not save John Bellingham in his murder of Spencer Percival, the chancellor of the exchequer. Bellingham insisted that he was not insane, though he did have a paranoid delusion that a cabal of officials was out to destroy his business.

Isaac Ray believed that the courts needed the testimony of respected physicians to help them distinguish between crime and disease, and he wanted the courts to adopt the simple rule that no act done by an insane person could be punished as a crime. The determination of sanity and insanity, he felt, should be left to expert testimony, not legal formulas created in prior centuries that took no account of contemporary science. Even though Ray could not offer objective proof for his contentions about the brain, his ideas had their effect. Alexander Cockburn based much of his defense of Daniel McNaghten on Ray's *Treatise*. McNaghten, who like Bellingham believed that a group of politicans was following and persecuting him, shot and killed Edward Drummond in 1843 believing him to be the prime minister, Robert Peel. Cockburn used Ray's book and the expert testimony of eight physicians to establish that McNaghten suffered from delusions. The jury agreed, and McNaghten was committed to Bethlem Hospital. The public outcry at what was perceived to be a miscarriage of justice resulted in the establishment of a commission headed by chief justice Nicholas Tindal and his colleagues on the Queen's Bench to provide a formula to determine legal insanity. This led to the McNaghten Rules: the test of insanity would be whether a person knew the act to be right or wrong. One could suffer delusion but act lawfully within the limits of that delusion. Granted that Peel and the Tories, according to McNaghten, were persecuting him, murder was not a lawful response within that delusion.

In another case alluded to by defense counsel at the Hinchman trial, a man named M'Elroy sued for release from a mental hospital in 1843 charging through his lawyers that to prove insanity there must be "entire unsoundness of mind" (Watts & Sergeant 1867, 451). Judge Huston, speaking for the Pennsylvania Supreme Court, declared that madness applied not just to idiots but also to those "who are perfectly rational upon several subjects, but labour under a permanent delusion as to one or more." The court thus expanded the traditional insanity test of "delusion" to embrace partial as well as total delusion. Relevant to the Hinchman case were further statements of the court:

> There are no delusions which more fully stamp the mind with the character of unsoundness, than those which are attended with an insensibility to or a perversion of the paramount feelings and dictates of our nature. Delusion manifests itself in a callousness to a just sense of affection. Strong traces of its inroads on the intellect are found, where a man hates without cause those who were formerly most dear to him . . . when a man conceives something extravagant to exist, which has in fact no foundation or existence. . . . (Watts and Sergeant 1867, 455–56)

This definition is clearly related to "moral insanity," a term that appears consistently in the courts throughout the nineteenth century.[8]

While cited by defense counsel to bolster the argument of partial or moral insanity, the M'Elroy decision does not clarify matters. M'Elroy was a man who developed an open hatred for close friends, beat his wife and accused her of incest and harlotry, accused his family physician of giving him poison pills made from a dead woman's womb, and sued a young woman to reveal the location of buried treasure. Hinchman may have been under some delusion, but it did not express itself so forcibly as to seriously endanger himself or others. Also, Judge Huston expressed the vagueness of medical terminology and the need ultimately to look to outward effects of the individual's mental state:

It is hardly possible to express in words the nice distinctions that mark the
boundaries of reason and insanity. However much may have been written
on the subject as a matter of science, the common sense of mankind is the
best guide in deciding the question of sanity or insanity when presented in
a practical form; and it is justly asserted that its decision can receive no
great degree of aid from metaphysical speculations. (1867, 456)

This points out the weakness of the defense in the Hinchman case,
which stressed—excessively, in the jury's mind—the legitimacy of a
medical theory rather than considering the logical and emotional facts
of the man's erratic conduct.

Two years later (1845), Chief Justice Shaw of the Massachusetts
Supreme Court made an epochal ruling that was forcefully cited by
the defense counsel in the Hinchman case. Josiah Oakes, who had
been committed to the McLean Hospital for the Insane in December
1844, sued for a writ of habeas corpus. The court, assuming the
admissions procedure to have been regular, ruled that "the burden
was upon the petitioner to make out a sufficient case for his discharge." First stressing that Mr. Oakes was placed in a respected
institution, Shaw went on to affirm the right of restraint:

The right to restrain an insane person of his liberty, is found in that great
law of humanity, which makes it necessary to confine those whose going at
large would be dangerous to themselves or others. . . . Private institutions
for the insane have been in use, and sanctioned by the courts; not established by any positive law, but by the great law of necessity and humanity.
Their existence was known and acknowledged at the time the constitution
was adopted. . . . Besides, it is a principle of law that an insane person has
no will of his own. In that case it becomes the duty of others to provide for
his safety and their own.[9]

Shaw was careful to distinguish between judicial rulings on insanity in
criminal and noncriminal cases. He also showed great respect for
medical expertise and displayed a knowledge of contemporary thinking on moral insanity.[10] He said:

We must not fall into the general notion, that a person is not to be
considered insane, merely because he does not always show wildness of
conduct in his every-day appearance. Since the subject has been scientifically investigated, we know that a person may show shrewdness and
sagacity in his business, but still be decidedly insane on some one subject
(Chandler 1864, 125).

Shaw emphasized the necessity for relying on the testimony of the
physician, in this instance Dr. Fox, the asylum doctor: "If we cannot
rely upon the opinion of those who have the charge of the institution,

and there is no law to restrain the persons confined, we must set all the insane at large who are confined in the McLean Asylum" (Chandler 1864, 127).

In both the Oakes and M'Elroy cases, then, there were judicial affirmations of the doctrine of partial insanity and the power to commit individuals even when there was not total delusion. While the McNaghten case followed the legal trend "to reduce the concept of mental disease to merely a symptom called 'delusion,' just as the *mens rea* had been reduced to merely its cognitive elements" (Levy 1957, 214), there was beginning to appear in American jurisprudence a sometimes confused but sincere attempt to draw into court decisions the more sophisticated faculty psychology enunciated in the first half of the nineteenth century. But it is understandable that the jury in the Hinchman case was confused more than convinced by nebulous medical theorizing and vague legal allusions. That the precedents for the use of the "moral insanity" plea in civil and criminal cases were not firm or precise was more a psychological than a legal problem. Also, the public and many lawyers in both America and England were loathe to accept such rulings.[11] In criminal cases insanity pleas could enable a man to escape punishment by confusing iniquity with insanity; in civil cases there was the fear of mere eccentricity resulting in unjust commitment and a conspiratorial denial of civil liberties, an egregious danger in the minds of democratic Americans.

Issue of Liberty

The debate over "moral insanity" and commitment legislation spawned the third related extralegal, extramedical factor involved in the Hinchman case that resulted in his victory. This was the basic issue of civil liberty. The pleas of the defense, attempting to establish the legal and medical validity of "moral insanity," fell on deaf, democratic ears. The theories *were* vague and suspect, so we can not attribute the jury's reluctance to accept them to simple anti-intellectualism. If an average jury during this period was hesitant to declare one innocent of a crime because one was not a free agent, it was equally if not more reluctant to institutionalize someone who generally was rational. A later quotation from *The Times* (London) for 22 July, 1853 (quoted in Skultans 1975, 9) would probably summarize the jury's view: "In strictness, we are all mad when we give way to passion, to prejudice, to vice, to vanity; but if all the passionate, prejudiced, vicious and vain people in this world are to be locked up as lunatics, who is to keep the key of the asylum?" And, in the words of Hinchman's attorney, if such heinous acts as the forced commitment of his client are countenanced, the Bill of Rights is a "dead letter" (*PL* 3 April 1849; 1:7).

Indeed, such later exposés of mental treatment and asylums as the respected *A Mind that Found Itself* (1908) by Clifford W. Beers, the more sensational "Ten Days in a Mad House," an 1887 serialized investigation done by Nelly Bly for the *New York World,* and the 1873 accounts by Mrs. E. P. W. Packard of her forced commitment in *Modern Persecution or Insane Asylums Unveiled* (Deutsch 1949, 307; 424–25) had their just precedents not in the Hinchman case but in the parliamentary investigations of asylums in England and critical descriptions such as that given of the New York asylum on Blackwell's Island by Charles Dickens in his *American Notes for General Circulation* (1842). Hinchman's counsel played on those fears by describing Friends Hospital as a "private mad-house" unsanctioned by the state and subject to no supervision (*PL,* 3 April 1849). Such attacks, combined with the ignorance of asylums themselves, most of which were located in distant rural settings, shaped the natural suspicions and misgivings of the public about both the insane and complicated theories of insanity. A public whose reading matter consisted of the Bible and perhaps some Gothic fiction can be excused from agreeing with Polonius that "to define true madness / What is't but to be nothing else but mad?" Thus the *Public Ledger* undoubtedly spoke for the jury and the majority of its readers when it described Hinchman's commitment as "one of the most flagrant wrongs and cruel oppressions that one man ever suffered from the combined power of secret conspiracy, put in motion by unquenchable hate and inordinate avarice" (*PL,* 23 April 1849).

Attacks on Quakers

As portrayed by David Paul Brown, who delivered his summation on Good Friday, Morgan Hinchman was a Christ figure betrayed by a host of Judases who forced him into the "Quaker Bastille" against his will and kept him there for six months while they looted his property. Brown kept stressing the wrongs done by Quakers and by Friends Asylum. Since the lawyers for the defense had emphasized the tradition of moral treatment at Friends Asylum, the beauty of its grounds, and the kind treatment afforded the patient, Brown feld compelled to counter these ideas in the mind of the jury. Brown alluded to the "Frankford Mad House," the "cage being of gold," with its "golden bars" preventing Hinchman as a "fluttering bird" from securing his liberty, to the "inquisition" that admitted him into the asylum, and to the asylum as a beautiful peacock with "odious and abhorrent legs"—a "beautiful Paradise" enclosing poisoned fruit. The place is charming, "but, do you see the dragon beneath it? Do you look into the cells and see the wreck and ruin of the Human Mind? Do you see the course of treatment or confinement calculated to produce results with any man who is sane, as terrifying as those produced by a visitation of Providence?" (1849, 47).

Overseeing such a prison are greedy men anxious to steal the confined man's property. While disavowing a general attack on all Quakers, Brown does question the motives and conduct of the Friends at Frankford Asylum: *"why the Pope's a fool to a Quaker overseer!"* Brown says Quakers violate human rights and dignity; they usurp a person's freedom and pay no honor to democratic principles. As proof, Brown cites the Quaker discipline of decision in which (in his account) the overseers or weighty Friends outvote the majority: "147 vote one way, the three overseers vote the other way—the clerk has nothing to do but put down, that the *weight* of the meeting is against the *majority*—a perfect autocracy, if it was not for its number—it is a divided though reserved power possessing great and illimitable authority" (1849, 15).

Even the king of England would not attempt to do what "our puritanical and peaceful friends have done" by way of trampling upon constitutional protections. Brown is astonished that the "descendants of Penn," the "peaceful—the pious—the professed lovers of the meek and lowly Saviour," would perpetrate such a forced commitment. They are not Good Samaritans so much as the highwaymen who wounded him and dragged him to his "melancholy cell" (1849, 28–29).

How painful it must have been for Friends and asylum officials to hear such attacks in the courtroom and to read them along with the alleged 280,000 readers of the *Public Ledger*. Perhaps part of the open acerbity of Brown's attacks could be attributed to the fact that Friends no longer enjoyed the power or prestige they once had. As leaders of the abolitionist movement, they were not popular in a city that routinely had race riots against blacks and where in an 1838 riot the city's Pennsylvania Hall, in which an abolitionist meeting led by Quakers was then being held, was burned down. But perhaps more than anything the verdict revealed the basic fear of insanity and especially the ease with which an individual could be deprived of his freedom, even in America.

Morgan Hinchman was apparently a sick man, though the defense did not convincingly demonstrate that he was so sick as to need confinement for six months. His counsel did convincingly demon-

strate that it was absurdly easy to confine Hinchman and that it would
be similarly easy to do so to others. As for motivation and possible
conspiracy, perhaps Hinchman's mother and sister-in-law disliked him
and were concerned that he would mismanage and lose his property.
In fact, Hinchman's property was held in trust and returned to him
when he was discharged from Friends Asylum. None of those involved in his confinement appear to have profited from it. Eliza W.
Hinchman's will (dated 25 May 1868), in fact, said: ". . . my omission
to make any provision for my eldest son is in consequence of his
having already received more than a full proportion of my estate [she
paid $3500 of the settlement], I have lost much by the unjust lawsuit
into which we were forced by the delusion of my poor mistaken
child. . . ." Despite this, she feels "only a mother's affection and
earnest solicitude for his welfare." And in a letter to Rebecca
Hinchman Allinson dated 14 February 1871, William Biddle said that
"although the part I took in the trial brought by thy poor misguided
brother brought us all into much obloquy and mental suffering I
never regretted the part I took in it" (Allinson Collection).

The case was important in its effects and along with subsequent
events had an impact both on Friends Asylum and the concept of
moral treatment. Quakers found themselves involved in another celebrated case when family members and his wife lodged a charge of
lunacy against Warder Cresson on 15 May 1849.[12] The family
charged that Cresson, a convert from Quakerism to Judaism, was
deranged and could no longer handle his business affairs. A sheriff's
jury of six men issued a verdict of insanity. Cresson appealed, and his
trial took place beginning 13 May 1851. Ironically, Elizabeth
Cresson's lawyer was David Paul Brown. Cresson's attorney was able
to show that anti-Semitism motivated the action for lunacy and
Cresson was found innocent of all charges on 19 May. The *Public
Ledger*, which had been so vigilant in attacking Friends Asylum and
the defendants in the Hinchman case, applauded the verdict and said
that it helped in "settling forever the principle that man's religious
opinions never can be made a test of his sanity." Commentators also
linked the Cresson and Hinchman trials as showing the need for
habeas corpus actions with regard to asylum patients and for better
commitment procedures.

In 1868 and into the 1870s, several patients at Kirkbride's Pennsylvania Hospital sued for release or sued those who had incarcerated
them (Bond 1947, 122–39). In these habeas corpus proceedings,
Kirkbride—then considered one of the most respected figures in
asylum care—was ridiculed as an evil prison-keeper who forced people

into a snakepit against their wills. These attacks on Kirkbride were mentioned in an 1868 article in *The Atlantic Monthly* entitled "A Modern Lettre de Cachet" (cited in Applebaum and Kemp 1982, 346). The anonymous author speaks of how easy it was in 1847 for Hinchman to be sequestered behind Frankford Asylum's "strong walls" and forbidden to communicate with the outside world. He was kept a prisoner because, like the *lettre* of France which consigned its victim to the Bastille, someone had merely signed a certificate alleging that he was insane and in need of confinement. As an aside, the author also mentions that since the trial Hinchman had worked as a conveyancer: "a profession requiring not only sound, unclouded intellect, but especial talents of a high order. In and out of his vocation, he is justly esteemed as well for his culture and refined intelligence and his moral worth" (1868, 594). Even where patients are free of delusions, have an unimpaired memory, and talk sensibly on ordinary subjects, an alienist may say that the person has "emotional insanity." The author remarks: "By such subtleties as these the liberty of any citizen may be frittered away" (1868, 602).

And what were the immediate effects of the trial on Friends Asylum? Neither "The Minutes of the Managers of Friends Asylum" (vol. 3) for 1849–50 and "The Director's Diary" for the same period discuss the Hinchman case. The only indirect allusions, in fact, come in a diary notation by Philip Garrett, then superintendent, for 5 May 1849 mentioning the receipt of a letter threatening the demolition of the asylum and freedom for its inmates (a threat perhaps motivated by the Hinchman trial); and a diary reference from 11 July 1851 by Dr. Worthington to a letter received accompanied by a statement from the *Delaware Journal* "founded upon the 'Hinchman Case'—strongly reflecting upon the management of this Institution.

Yet in more subtle ways the effect was apparent. The classification of patients was influenced. Friends Asylum did not begin the published classification of patients until their twentieth annual report (1837). The general classifications during this period were not terribly sophisticated. Such terms as "melancholia" or "mania" generally referred to degrees or stages of madness rather than separate conditions. "Mania," for instance, implied violent behavior, while "monomania" indicated that the illness was confined to a particular issue or what Isaac Ray called the "predominant idea" (1962, 203). In 1837, Dr. Evans indicated that 103 cases had been treated: twenty-four patients were categorized as having "moral insanity," while forty-five had "partial insanity." The following range of causes was given for moral insanity: constitutional, intemperance, pecuniary difficulties, domestic diffi-

culties, religion, defective education, paralysis, opium eating, disappointment, masturbation, disappointed love, head injury, intense
study, ill-requited love.

Subsequent reports listed "moral insanity" as one of the classifications; then in 1850 the category was dropped. The only categories
used for several years thereafter were mania, melancholia, dementia,
imbecility, and monomania. Clearly stung and chastened by the trial,
the asylum avoided the term. Joshua Worthington, the resident physician from 1842 to 1850 and then superintendent from 1850 until
1877, testified at the Hinchman trial that he had examined Hinchman
and agreed with Evans that he suffered from moral insanity. But in his
1857 annual report, he disavowed the term "moral insanity" because
the term had "been so greatly misunderstood and perverted, that it
would perhaps have been better had it never been invented" (10). He
went on to say that while there are instances of insanity in which
immoral conduct is more conspicuous than signs of derangement, one
cannot simply call any evidence of such conduct insanity. "Indulgence
of bad passions" may lead to insanity but of itself does not constitute
insanity.

Worthington's commitment to moral treatment also began to wane.
Along with other superintendents, he began to feel that many patients, for reasons of heredity, could not be cured and that the stress
should perhaps be on the care of the chronically ill rather than on cure
rates. Such a tendency gradually became more pronounced. While
asylums continued to acknowledge the tradition of moral treatment,
the rapid decline in recovery rates and the influence of somaticism on a
new generation of psychiatrists had their effect. Dain says that "by
1900 moral treatment was reduced to a minor form of therapy in the
corporate asylums," including Friends Asylum (1964, 132).

These reasons, along with those mentioned earlier—including the
economics of care, greater attention to administration, and lack of
research into mental illness—also concealed a subtle shift in the conception of individuals, even among Friends charged with the care of
the mentally ill. There was less tolerance for the insane person's
inability to control his or her antisocial or wayward impulses. Madness came to be perceived either as an unavoidable hereditary disease
or a weak-willed evasion of responsibility. The notion of the Inner
Light, the sense that the individual (though weakened) could still
control and shape his or her destiny, and could recover and become a
functioning member of civil society—these concepts which had under-
girded so much of the Quaker reform movement with the mentally ill,
began to weaken. By 1850, lip service was still accorded these notions,
but the reality was less forceful and less convincing.

7
SUMMARY AND CONCLUSION

The development of moral treatment at York Retreat as an important therapy for the treatment of the mentally ill was an outgrowth of many factors: sensitivity to the historical identification of Quakers as mad enthusiasts and the persecution and ridicule that followed from such an identification; a knowledge of and reaction to contemporary medical practices in the treatment of the insane; a sense of religious exclusivity; access to resources needed to construct and maintain private or corporate asylums espousing a common set of ideals and beliefs; a strong community of practical humanitarians to volunteer their time and talents in reinforcing and forwarding those beliefs. The work of the Tukes and George Jepson both validated and helped promote the concept of moral treatment at other institutions, especially Friends Asylum. Moral treatment became famous not because it was a marked contrast to much that had passed for therapy in previous years but because it appeared to be more successful in restoring patients to sanity.

The individuals who led the establishment of both York Retreat and Friends Asylum were different from the Friends of George Fox's generation. While both would agree on the concept of the Inner Light and seek to remove the illness that clouded or concealed the expression of that Light, late eighteenth- and early nineteenth-century Friends were more rational than mystical, more humanitarian than evangelical. They did not seek to proselytize but to redeem their own kind. Stung and somewhat chastened by years of persecution, they had become more separate, more insular, and more guarded. Children of the Enlightenment in their acceptance of Lockean epistemology and associationist psychology, they were also heirs to an esthetic that rejected an enhanced conception of the imagination; like Samuel Johnson, they saw reason and order as the counter to mental riot and imbalance. They saw irrational persons as flawed yet capable through moral treatment of asserting their will and achieving reason and balance once again.

As the "first practical effort made to provide systematic and responsible care for an appreciable number of the mentally ill" (Bockoven 1963, 13), moral treatment was developed by Friends and promoted by Tuke's *Description* as a way to help and rouse the patient to regain control of his or her own life. It was an emotional or psychological way to arouse dormant faculties of the mind. No single or common method was devised to achieve this. Rather, close personal attention to each patient was required in order to identify specific therapeutic possibilities, such as manual labor, intellectual diversion, or religious worship. Health was achieved in a family or communal setting where every staff member and attendant was sensitive to the patient's needs.

York Retreat became justly famous, even mythical in the tales of William Tuke's heroic efforts to build the asylum and then, along with George Jepson, use a bedrock of kindness and compassion to make individuals "useful" again. The two men tested contemporary science and traditional approaches to treating the mentally ill with a view to formulating the kind of treatment that was widely publicized by the *Description,* an outlook that was to become so influential in the establishment and care at a variety of other institutions, including Friends Asylum.

The Quaker asylums prospered and influenced other asylums during the first three decades of the nineteenth century. Moral treatment had no theoretical foci other than the need for a pleasant milieu peopled by caring individuals who shared a certain value system with most of their patients, but the appeal of this approach was so deeply held that somatic theories of disease were adjusted to allow for its primacy. The strong conviction that all mental disease could be traced to lesions or inflammation of the brain did not preclude the possibility that moral treatment could diminish the lesions and restore the patient to sanity. Quakers could justifiably take pride in the growth of asylums modeled on their care and in the quality of leaders, many of whom were Quakers or Quaker-influenced, who eventually established in 1844 the Association of Medical Superintendents of American Institutions for the Insane.

However, even at this time forces were at work that would accelerate so that "by 1900 moral treatment was reduced to a minor form of therapy in the corporate asylums" (Dain 1964, 132). It became less effective even more quickly at the large public institutions. In addition to the death of leaders in the psychiatric profession committed to moral treatment—and their failure to influence a new generation of such leaders—other factors intruded. One was the increase in the number of patients, attracted by the publicized success of cure rates at so many institutions and Dorothea Dix's successful efforts to promote the growth of institutions to accommodate the influx of patients from jails and almshouses. The number of pauper lunatics, for instance, meant a population of patients that the state did not wish to support and doctors did not wish to treat. The result was often a warehousing of patients, and custodial rather than curative care became more prevalent.

Also, the new generation of doctors/alienists stressed bodily illness over the moral or psychological needs of the patients. They made clear distinctions between mind and brain, believing that the former could not be diseased; as a result, they dismissed such behavior as kleptomania or moral insanity as character deformations, not illnesses. They were bothered as well by the failure to sustain cure rates. As a result, subtle changes occurred, which affected even the Quaker corporate asylums. Insanity was felt to be incurable in some cases because of heredity or senility; the Friends Asylum Report of 1862 attributed the increase in intemperance or the nervous disorders to the "highly civilized state of society" (Friends Asylum Report, 1862, 15). As a result of these new emphases, according to Bockoven, "scientific psychiatry eliminated moral treatment as a definitive therapy and retained it in diluted form as a diversionary adjunct to medical treatment pursued in the empty climate of custodial care" (1963, 43).

York Retreat and Friends Asylum were largely immune from many of these dramatic changes and continued to emphasize in their annual reports the value and primacy of moral treatment. Yet as has been noted, a number of events, while not perhaps directly acknowledged by the Quaker leadership, were impinging on the asylums and leading them belatedly to change. These included the direct assault by Quaker doctors in their desire to establish a medically-oriented Southern Retreat, the greater medical emphasis at Friends Asylum in the 1830s led by Dr. Charles Evans, the ridicule heaped on Quakers and Friends Asylum by the Hinchman episode, and the similar abuse suffered by the leader of the old school of moral treatment, Thomas Story Kirkbride. Also, one source of success at both institutions—the religious homogeneity of the patients as well as the staff—began to erode. Non-Friends were not admitted to Friends Asylum until 1834 or to York Retreat until 1820, and while the growth in unconnected patients was not dramatic, changes in the religious composition of patients and staff were significant by the end of the century.

Still, while up to 1850 seeds for change can be seen, both asylums kept their basic character and paid reverence, as is the case even to this day, to the "climate of caring concern" of the Quaker tradition. Their very isolation allowed them as "resorts for the upper classes" (Scull 1981, 159) to remove themselves as much as possible from the problems as well as the possibilities occurring in the field. At York

Retreat the presence of Samuel Tuke as an active overseer (he died in 1858) undoubtedly must have inhibited experimentation with new approaches, while at Friends Asylum the long tenure of Dr. Joshua Worthington (1850–77) as superintendent—with his continued discussion of the seventy percent cure rates and his typically Quaker commitment to statistics—was probably equally inhibiting; his successor (Dr. John C. Hall, 1877–93) wrote annual reports dealing mostly with maintenance and repairs rather than with speculation about the nature and causes of insanity.

On a positive note, both asylums sustained a therapy that proved of use and once again attracts renewed attention today. In 1963 J. Sanbourne Bockoven, in his *Moral Treatment in American Psychiatry*, decried the absence of moral treatment and called it a "forgotten success in the history of psychiatry." He called for its renewal at contemporary mental institutions and saw its renaissance in "resocialization" therapies; Dain says it has been revived today and expanded with such names as "milieu therapy, therapeutic community, total-push therapy, open hospital" (209). Thus while the direct Quaker influence was somewhat dissipated, the climate of concern created in a tradition beginning with George Fox was sustained in subtle ways at both institutions and through them in others.

APPENDIX

Proposals
for the establishment of a
lunatic asylum under the care of Friends,
to be called
the Southern Retreat

To those who are acquainted with the merits of the lunatic asylum, under the care of the Society of Friends near York, called the retreat, it is presumed that little need be said, either to set forth the benefits which that Institution has conferred, and still continues to confer, or to produce conviction as to the further benefits which might yet be obtained, by the establishment of a similar Institution within a moderate distance from London.

Although there are already numerous Lunatic Asylums in the neighbourhood of the Metropolis, which enjoy a well merited reputation, in consequence of the general care and management of their Directors, yet it is certain that a strong preference exists in the minds of Friends, in favour of sending such members of the Society as may be affected with mental alienation to York, where their religious peculiarities are not likely to subject them to any annoyance or inconvenience, rather than to allow them to be exposed to some trials, which in their particular state, would not be unlikely to occasion an increase or moral and physical suffering. In the case of the persons in low circumstances, these difficulties would probably be felt in the greatest degree—but those in affluence cannot be always exempt from them.

An institution such as is here suggested, would therefore not merely be a saving of much expensive, painful, and fatiguing travelling, but would enable many, to whom the advantages of the Retreat are necessarily denied, to enjoy precisely similar advantages, with, very probably, the addition of some others which will be presently noticed.

It has been the practice at the Retreat not merely to receive on higher terms Patients from the wealthier class of Friends, but also Patients belonging to other Religious Professions, whose relatives repose confidence in the management of the Institution, and who are willing to pay on such liberal terms as contribute greatly to benefit the funds of the establishment. A similar course might doubtless be adopted by the Managers of a Lunatic Asylum under the care of the Society of Friends, situated in the vicinity of London. The advantage would be reciprocal, for the higher class of Patients, whilst aiding the funds of the Establishment, might be so distinct from the poorer class as to be subject to no degree of annoyance from them, but they would derive great benefit from the superior medical and other treatment which the Superintendent and Medical Director would, as experienced practical men, be ever ready to suggest.

The feasibility of this project is almost demonstrated by the fact that the Managers of the Retreat at York, have within a comparatively short time contemplated the establishment of such an Institution by the employment of their own accumulated funds. Local changes which have induced the Directors to abandon the plan, have not, however, materially diminished the expediency of the measure, which has been approved by competent judges in the Medical Profession, and is called for by the fact that it has repeatedly been found necessary to send Insane Friends to Asylums in no way connected with the Society.

Should the foregoing proposal obtain the concurrence of a sufficient number of supporters, the present time would be peculiarly favourable to its adoption, since there is an opportunity of obtaining for the medical direction of the proposed institution, the services of Dr. Foville, whose intimate theoretical and practical acquaintance with this branch of medicine, justly entitles him to the very highest place in this department.

The advantages of treatment under his direction would doubtless not be confined to the inmates of the Institution, but a most important reform in the medical and physical treatment of the Insane might reasonably be expected to spread from this Institution to most of the considerable Lunatic Asylums in this country.

As the Northern Retreat has had the merit of contributing materially to improve the moral management and personal condition of British Lunatics, so its Southern counterpart might be equally happy in effecting a similar amelioration in the very important but too much neglected branch, to which belongs the medical treatment of mental and cerebral disease.

On the first of the sixth month, being the day following the Yearly Meeting, several Friends from different parts of the Country, met at Devonshire House, and took into consideration the preceding proposal, and a Committee was formed, consisting of Dr. Ball,—John Sanderson,—Joseph Jackson Lister,—Samuel Gurney, Jun.—Thomas

Bevan, and Dr. Hodgkin, who were requested to digest and prepare a plan for further consideration.

After repeated meetings of the Committee, assisted by many other friends, the following plan has been agreed to, as the basis of the proposed establishment.

1.—That an institution be formed, to be under the care of a Committee, consisting of members of the society of Friends, and that it be called "THE SOUTHERN RETREAT".

2.—That capital to the amount of £20,000 be raised, in 400 shares of £50 each, and that the shares be transferable, but that no individual be allowed to hold more than 20 shares.

3.—That an estimate of the property and liabilities of the institution be taken annually, and that the net proceeds be divided among the Shareholders, in proportion to the amount of capital subscribed; but that they be not entitled to receive more than 7½ percent, per annum, from the commencement of the Institution, and that the surplus, if any, be appropriated to the improvement of the establishment.

4.—That a Guarantee-list be opened, in order to afford to individuals who may not be desirous of taking share, an opportunity of supporting the institution, by undertaking, in case a loss of capital should be incurred during the first seven years, to participate with the Shareholders therein, in such proportion as the sums for which they may subscribe, the Guarantee-list bear to the whole capital advanced.

5.—That the managing Committee be appointed annually, at a general meeting of the Shareholders and Guarantees.

Members of the Society of Friends, and other persons who are desirous of aiding in the formation of the proposed institution, either as Shareholders or Guarantees, are requested to transmit their names, with the number of shares they are willing to hold, or the sums for which they are willing to become Guarantees, previously to the meeting to be held as under, to

JOHN SANDERSON, Old Jewry,
EDWARD HARRIS, New Broad Street,
Dr. HODGKIN, 9, Brook Street, Grosvenor Square,
THOMAS BEVAN, 20, Finsbury Circus,
WILLIAM MANLEY, 86, Houndsditch; or
THOMAS FOWLER, (DREWETT & FOWLER,), Princess Street, Bank.

THE NEXT GENERAL MEETING

Will be held at Friends' Meeting House, Houndsditch, on the twenty-ninth of the present month, at THREE O'CLOCK in the afternoon, for the purpose of adopting measures for carrying the plan into effect; on which occasion, it is particularly desirable that the Friends to the undertaking should be generally present.

LONDON, 17th of 7th Month, 1839.

NOTES

Chapter 1. Quakers and Asylum Reform

1. While noting Foucault's challenge to the medical Whig tradition, H. C. Erik Midelfort takes issue with a number of Foucault's assertions. He notes, for instance, that no serious researchers have found evidence of real ships of fools; that Foucault underestimates the "force of sin" as a source of madness and thus "grossly exaggerates the Renaissance dialogue with madness"; that the great confinement was not a seventeenth-century innovation but a hearkening back to the monastic tradition of harboring many forms of misery under one roof. Midelfort concludes that Foucault's importance rests not on general philosophy but on his attempt "to explore the deepest meanings of madness and the underlying structures of knowledge within a given period" (1980, 254–59).

Chapter 2. Quakers and Enthusiasm

1. Fox dictated his journal in 1673–74, and an edition of these original manu-scripts has been published by Norman Penney as *The Journal of George Fox* (1911); Penney has also edited the *Short Journal and Itinerary Journals* (1925). Most editions of Fox's *Journal,* however, are reprints, often abridged, of Ellwood's 1694 first edition. I am using John L. Nickalls's revised edition of *The Journal of George Fox* (1975), 42.

2. Samuel Tuke, *Selections from the Epistles, &c. of George Fox* (1825), 192, and the 5 May 1671 instructions from Six Weeks Meeting to London Yearly Meeting; see Issac Sharp, 1901, 714–15. Cadbury mentions (1948, 70) that this epistle, no. 264, is dated 1669, and the first part of it was widely circulated in manuscript.

3. See Jorns 1931, 154. See also Beck and Ball 1869.

4. *The Minute Book of the Monthly Meeting of the Society of Friends for the Upperside of Buckinghamshire 1669–90,* transcribed with introduction and notes by Beatrice Saxon Snell (1937), xiv. These minutes, kept by Thomas Ellwood as clerk, convey the sense of communal feeling and ostracism from the community for violating mores, mostly for marriage to non-Quakers and for scandal of any kind that would bring disrepute on Quakers. For instance, William Eburne was accused of stealing a neighbor's wood: "Whereby ye mouth of ye world was opened in reproach not only agt. them, but also agt. Truth & Friends" (165). Or the case of Andrew Brothers, who was in despair, and the meeting recommended he use physical means to restore health; eventually the meeting disowned him in May 1690 for "giving way to a careless & loose mind" and spending too much time drinking.

5. Crump 1900, 170 ff. Ellwood also mentions Solomon Eccles, who was said to have gone naked to the waist while carrying on his head a chafing dish of coals and

burning brimstone. Crump remarks that "Sewel says he was not mad, but a man of strange zeal" (243).

6. See Hill (1972) and Barbour (1964) for a general discussion of these acts. Barbour indicates that Quakers suffered the most from this punitive legislation. "Of 1240 dissenters convicted in London in 1664 about 850 were Friends, and they totaled 859 out of 909 imprisoned in the rest of Middlesex, though these were puritan strongholds." Barbour also says: "In 1683 there were exchequer suits of 33,300 £ pending against Quakers in Suffolk alone; and the total of fines levied against puritans and Quakers was estimated as between two and fourteen million pounds" (225–28).

7. Three excellent works on the subject of possession, witchcraft, and madness are Walker 1982; Thomas 1971; and MacDonald 1982. In different ways, these books show how skepticism about magical causes of madness (such as demonic possession and witchcraft) led both to a more rational religion and medical approaches to mental problems, especially among the upper classes.

8. Richard Vann's *Social Development of English Quakerism 1655–1755* (1969) challenges the conventional labeling of Quakers as "mechanick preachers" by showing that in fact many were yeomen, traders, and in the case of men like Audland, Hubberthorne, and Howgill, substantial landowners. See also Huntington, 1982, 69–88.

9. Barclay, 1967. See 16–45 for Barclay's Proposition 2, "Inward and Unmediated Revelation." See also Flood 1963.

10. William Penn, *The Witness of William Penn*, ed. Frederick B. Tolles and E. Gordon Alderfer (1957), 191. See Barbour 1964, 234–56 for a discussion of changes in Quaker attitudes after 1662.

11. In fact, says Joseph Wyeth, a priest tried to bleed Fox to cure him of his ailment; Fox did not try to cure it with physic. See *Anguis Flagellatus: or, A Switch for the Snake. Being an Answer to the Third and Last Edition of the Snake in the Grass. Wherein that Author's Injustice Falsehood, both in Quotation and Story, are discover'd and obviated, and the truth doctrinally deliver'd by us, stated and Maintained in opposition to his misrepresentation and Perversion* (1699).

12. See especially sect. 9, "A Digression on Madness" (162–80).

13. Theophilus Evans quotes this passage in *The History of Modern Enthusiasm, from the Reformation to the Present Times* (1752).

14. For discussions of enthusiasm and madness from a more literary perspective, see Byrd 1974; DePorte 1974. See also Davis 1943, 301–19.

15. In his discussion of enthusiasm in *An Essay* (1975) Locke distinguishes between immediate revelation and the labors of strict reasoning. Internal light, he affirms, can not be followed unless it is in accord with reason and scriptural authority. See book 4, chapter 19, 697–706.

16. Coole seeks unity from "the Sword of the Spirit, not of the Magistrate" and stresses the universal principle of "Light and Life" (1712, 20).

17. See also his *Plain Truth: Or, Quakerism Unmask'd* (1756), Dove's supplement to the *Essay* and an equally strong attack on Quakers.

18. In *The Quaker Family*, Frost also comments on these paradoxes: "Quakers could be intellectuals and yet antiintellectual, social activists and mystics, evangelical and quietistic, complacent and insecure, intent on making money and anxious to avoid being wealthy, dogmatic and nontheological, tolerant and strict. Friends were a sect and a church, a chosen people and a mixed multitude" (1973, 217). Margaret H. Bacon in *The Quiet Rebels: The Story of the Quakers in America* (1969), says some Quaker psychologists "have noted a tendency among Friends to refuse to face their own anger, or to turn it inward" (204).

Chapter 3. Eighteenth-Century Intellectual Background

1. In his review of James Douglas's *On the Philosophy of the Mind* (1839), which appeared in the January 1840 edition of the *Edinburgh Review,* Alexander Smith noted that "the light thrown by Shakespeare on the human mind, is much the same sort of substitute for metaphysical knowledge that a landscape in perspective is for a land-surveyor's plan" (1840, 199–200). We could discuss mind-body splits and aberrant conduct by resorting to literature: to William Blake's equation of energy with delight and his mythologizing of psychic disintegration in such epics as *Milton, Jerusalem,* and *The Four Zoas;* to Coleridge's exploration of the fragility of mind in such works as "Kubla Khan" and "Dejection: An Ode"; to Swift's evocation of pride and religious zeal as paradigms of folly; to the literary school of sensibility of Chatterton, Smart, Cowper, and later of Lloyd and Lamb—poets who experienced directly or through family members the particular joys and agonies of mental illness and who felt in their own ways the wrath of a savage god; to Keats's *Lamia,* with its conflict between rational and imaginative faculties and clear implication that to attempt total union with imagination is to die; to Wordsworth for his efforts to animate an increasingly mechanical universe with the energy and moral sensibility of his active inner world. In a period where the physician and the poet/philosopher were concurrently exploring the nature of mental activity and the possibility of inner change affecting social change, much can be learned from such analogies.

2. It is ironic that Locke imposed his own sort of intellectual waistcoat on eighteenth-century medical practitioners when it came to examining insanity. He dominates them both as a philosophical guide and in the influence of his assertion that insanity arises from incorrect reasoning. It is as if he forgot his training under Thomas Sydenham, who concentrated on healing and clinical observation rather than spec-ulating about the true nature of disease. Syndeham was an arch empiricist, aided by Locke, who charged the medical profession of his day with being more interested in favorite hypotheses than in advancing medical knowledge through objective bedside observation.

3. It is interesting to consider Coleridge's "Kubla Khan" with regard to this impulse. If his *Biographia Literaria* is important as a philosophical statement of the elements of imagination, then "Kubla Khan" is equally important as a poetic con-densation of its principles. A magic chemistry of the poet's psyche and perhaps the milk of paradise unleashes the river of the secondary imagination. As a primordial, superhuman force, its threatens a positive upset of the neoclassical balance implied by the rational dome imposed by the Khan onto the world of process. Frequently variants of this approach are found. However, when read in the context of Coleridge's many prose statements on imagination, this Romantic touchstone piece may be interpreted not as the statement of awed respect for the power of imagination but the obverse: the fear of its power, the fear of forces that can move the mind into a dark irrationality. In this respect, Coleridge is not unlike neoclassical writers against whom the Romantic movement supposedly reacts. Just as such figures as Johnson and Swift attempted to stabilize their lives in order to control the aberrant, so too does the Khan-Coleridge construct a secure world of art to transcend and circumvent the world of process. Yet Coleridge is aware of its fragile balance. No such construct is safe from ultimately cracking or crumbling. Thus the river's force embodies not merely Romantic energy but the potentially frightening anarchy of the uncontrolled and uncontrollable. As seen in the previous chapter, closely allied to the fear of imagination is the fear of enthusiasm, a recurrent theme throughout the period.

Chapter 4. York Retreat and Moral Treatment

1. Pinel 1806, 4. For useful overviews of the reformation of eighteenth-century care of the mentally ill, see Jones 1972; Parry-Jones 1972; Donnelly 1983.

2. The Tuke Papers and the Archives of York Retreat may be found at the University of New York's Borthwick Institute of Historical Research in York, England. All references to minute books, case books, visitors' records, retreat correspondence, and Tuke's personal correspondence are to these archives. The materials are generally identified by date. For a version of Hunt's life of Tuke, see Hunt 1937, 3–18.

3. Both broadsides may be found in the Quaker Collection of the Haverford College Library.

4. See also Henry Tuke 1823. This work by Samuel Tuke's father could be found in most Quaker homes. Rufus Jones said that it "became one of the greatest evangelical influences." Quoted in E. E. Taylor, "The Tukes: Tea Dealers and Reformers," *Friends Quarterly Examiner* 80 (1946): 6.

5. See *The York Herald* for 7 May 1892 for an account of the York Retreat centenary celebration at which Elizabeth Pumphrey gave her recollections of the Retreat as it was fifty years earlier. *The Yorkshire Herald* for 22–23 July 1892 gives an account of the British Medico-Psychological Association meeting in York. Reprints of newspaper articles and the "Notes" for Elizabeth Pumphrey's talk are found in the Retreat archives at the Borthwick Institute.

6. The brief history of the Southern Retreat is recorded in two vellum books from Manuscript Box H-13 in the Library of the Religious Society of Friends, London. One, a small lined ledger book, lists the names and amounts of the various investors in this project. On its cover are the names of the three trustees of these funds: John Sanderson, John Pryor, and Joseph Jackson Lister. The second, an unlined journal, contains a copy of the prospectus and the rough minutes of the fifteen recorded meetings held from 1 June 1839 to around May 1841. I wish to thank Malcolm Thomas, Librarian, for bringing these materials to my attention.

7. See Bickford and Bickford 1976. The name "Retreat" was suggested by Mary Maria, Henry Tuke's wife. Hartford Retreat, now the Institute of Living, continued the Quaker semantic tradition in the United States.

8. Hunter, 1966, 263–67. Hunter points out that Hodgkin was consulted by Tuke on his daughter Sarah's illness, and that Hodgkin introduced Tuke to Conolly at Edinburgh in May 1821 while Tuke was in the area visiting New Lanark. William Allen, a Quaker and lecturer on chemistry at Guy's Hospital, was a part-owner of the mills.

9. See the appendix for the complete text of the prospectus.

10. A slim outline of facts about Foville may be found in an obituary article in *Gazette Hebdomadaire de Médecine et de Chirurgie* 15 (1878): 499–500. This article was adapted for publication in *The Medical Times and Gazette* 2 (1878): 232. His son, Achille-Louis Foville fils (d. 1887), was editor-director of *Annales Médico-Psychologiques* and at various times medical director or superintendent of asylums at Dole, Chalons-sur-Marne, and Quatres Mares. See the *American Journal of Insanity* 44 (1888): 573.

11. *Collection de thèses soutenues à la Facultè de Médecine de Paris en (1824)* vol. 4. Foville's thesis is no. 138.

12. E. H. Kass notes that Hodgkin helped to introduce the use of the stethoscope to England after observing Laennec at this time (1966, 272).

13. *An Essay on Medical Education, Read Before the Physical Society of Guy's Hospital, at the First Meeting of the Session 1827–28* (1828) 20.

14. The bulk of Hodgkin's papers, many unpublished, are still held by the family. The author is grateful to Mr. Thomas Hodgkin for permission to quote from the microfilm copy of these papers available at the Library of the Religious Society of Friends, London.

15. Wilks and Bettany, 1892, 264. Under a provision of Guy's will the hospital was to care for up to twenty incurable lunatics. Hodgkin's probable contact with these patients presumably increased his interest in mental illness.

16. See Fry 1847 2:261–333. The friend referred to is Josiah Forster, a member of the Anti-Slavery Society, who was traveling in Paris at this time with Elizabeth Fry, her husband and daughter on one of Mrs. Fry's many excursions to jail and hospitals. Hodgkin had written a letter of introduction on their behalf to Foville. Other letters suggest that Foville had a part in the French publication of the works of Elizabeth Fry's brother, Joseph John Gurney.

17. Hodgkin, for example, having pledged five shares and paid £50 on account, received back £49 13s. 2d—thus suffering a slight financial loss.

18. Though his name does not come up, Hodgkin might also have mentioned John Kitching. Kitching, who pledged five shares to the Southern Retreat, was at the time translating Maximilian Jacobi's *On the Construction and Management of Hospitals for the Insane* (1834), for which Tuke supplied an introduction Kitching eventually became medical superintendent of York Retreat from 1849 to 1874. He is mentioned in the Devonshire House minutes of 9 July 1841 as having applied for the post of superintendent of the Southern Retreat. He requested £200 per annum, plus a home and board.

Chapter 5. Friends Asylum and Moral Treatment

1. Throughout its early history, the asylum was called Friends Asylum or the Frankford Asylum (from its geographical location). Only later in the century, with the emphasis on medical treatment, did it become known as Friends Hospital. The archives of Friends Asylum—including managers' minutes, superintendents' journal, minutes of contributors, visiting committee minutes, minutes of corporation, annual reports and related documents—are at the Quaker Collection of the Haverford College Library. Patients' medical records are at Friends Hospital.

See also Catherine Higgins's Ph.D. dissertation (1986) for a useful compilation of statistics on Friends Asylum, Pennsylvania Hospital, and Blockley Almshouse.

2. Scattergood, 1845, 1.

3. Scattergood, 1874, 463.

4. A microfilm record of the Philadelphia Yearly Meeting minutes may be found in the Quaker Collection of Haverford College Library. The minutes of Western Quarterly Meeting are at Friends Historical Library of Swarthmore College.

5. Emerson, 1827, 17. See also Coutes, 1830, 281–82.

6. The minutes of the building committee are contained in a volume entitled "Minutes of Building Committee Roberts Vaux Clerk Friends Asylum 1813–1817." The handwritten minutes have been transcribed for Edward Teitelman, M.D. by Kathryn W. Jones. I am grateful to Dr. Teitelman for the loan of the transcription and a reproduction of the original minutes.

7. The first "Annual Report on the State of the Asylum for the Relief of Persons Deprived of the Use of Their Reason" (1818) indicated that the Asylum had a debt of

$14,933 and had admitted nineteen patients between 30 March 1817 and 6 February 1818. The Annual Report also had a report from the building committee with its final account of expenditures.

Masons and brick layers	$10,126.94
Carpenters	15,186.79
Plasterers	4,720.94
Ironmongery	2,347.72
Cast iron sashes for 99 windows and 43 transoms	1,309.74
Roof slating and spouts	3,586.49
Paint and glazing	2,138.82
Digging wells and foundation	1,744.14
Warming wing	494.94
Fencing	1,014.22
	$42,670.74

8. Evans, 1839, 3.
9. Quoted in Samuel Tuke, 1964, 26.
10. Waln, 1825, 4. Waln's account and that by Evans are most useful for their discussions of the building's design.
11. *Friends Asylum for the Insane 1813–1913: A Descriptive Account* (n.d.).
12. Excerpts from the journal may be found in David S. Roby, M.D., "Pioneer of Moral Treatment: Isaac Bonsall & the Early Years of Friends Asylum as Recorded in Bonsall's Diaries 1817–1823", (1982). The hospital has also published two other useful booklets. One is a listing of "Managers and Other Key People: Friends Asylum and Friends Hospital 1812–1982," published in 1982 and, like the booklet above, published on the occasion of the dedication of the hospital's new Isaac Bonsall Building. The other is Events Surrounding the Origin of Friends Hospital and a Brief Description of the Early Years of Friends Asylum, 1817–20," by Kim Van Atta, with David S. Roby, M.D. and R. Ross Roby, M.D. (1976).
13. See *Rules for the Observance of the Attendants Upon the Patients at Friends' Asylum, near Frankford. Adopted by the Managers Sixth Month 12, 1843* (1843). The managers stressed that in all their interactions with patients, attendants should display "mildness, firmness and self-control."
14. For a helpful overview see Dain and Carlson, 1960, 277–90.
15. Quoted in Cadbury 1946, 69.
16. See Forbush 1956, 249. Also see Doherty 1967.
17. See an account of this exchange in Forbush, 1968, 215–16. Forbush says that Sheppard could not judge between Tuke and Jacobi: "It has been stated in England, that more of the Society of Friends became insane, in proportion, than of any other Society or Class. I don't know if this is so or not, but there are several here; and more of us half-crazy" (216).
18. Scull 1981: "Moral Treatment Reconsidered." Scull notes as well the case for environmental manipulation to correct deviant behavior and develop self-restraint. See as well Scull's essay in the same volume entitled "The Discovery of the Asylum Revisited: Lunacy Reform in the New Republic," where he charges Rothman with failing to see the heavy dependence in American asylums on ideas and influences from abroad. My own essay stresses the English Quaker influence on American institutions, which Scull also notes. For a discussion of how the Retreat moved from lay therapist to medical superintendent, see Digby 1985, 105–117.
19. See *Friends Weekly Intelligencer* 1 (1844–45): 20 and 389 for accounts of superintendents' reports at Worcester Asylum and Pennsylvania Hospital.
20. The 1877 date refers to the first form of this work in a pamphlet issued by the

New England Psychological Society, which was later published by J. P. Lippincott in 1887 as *The Curability of Insanity: A Series of Studies,* but Earle actually did a first paper on this topic in 1843, and in 1848 published the works which helped reform the keeping of insanity statistics. These were the *History, Description and Statistics of the Bloomingdale Asylum for The Insane* and *Four Annual Reports of the Bloomingdale Asylum for the Insane.* See Sanborn, 317–20.

21. Page, 1912–13, 782. For an overview of the Retreat, see Braceland 1972.

22. See Mullahy 1970, and Perry 1981.

23. My only quibble with Scull's piece is what I regard as his overemphasis on the medical treatment at Hartford and the implication that the medical approach was not used at asylums like Friends. As we have seen, this was not the case.

Chapter 6. Quakers and Moral Treatment in America

1. Philadelphia newspapers gave extensive coverage to the trial. See, for instance, *Public Ledger,* 9 March 1849 to 23 April 1849. This Philadelphia paper (cited as *PL*) gave front page coverage of all testimony in the trial and weighted its coverage in favor of Hinchman. *The Pennsylvania Freeman* (19 April 1849): "Seldom, if ever has there been in this community a case of civil suit which has excited so general an interest and strong feelings among all classes of society." *Pennsylvania Inquirer and National Gazette* (16 April 1849): ". . . a trial that has excited more attention than any civil suit in Phildelphia for many years."

Proof of the widespread general interest in the trial may be seen in the variety of publications following the trial. The reporting of all testimony may be found in *Paper Book,* 1850. Records also include *Speeches* 1849 and *Brown* 1849. A pointed defense of Quakers and Friends Asylum by an "American Citizen" may also be found in *Hinchman* 1849.

Albert Deutsch (1949) has also discussed the importance of this case, noting that it "served to emphasize the necessity for legislation clarifying and extending the common law to conform more closely to the requirements of an increasingly complex social order" (423).

2. Mentioned in *Biographical Sketch of Charles S. Hinchman From Records and Recollections by Lydia S. Hinchman* (1930, n.p.). This account of Morgan Hinchman's son makes no reference to the case.

3. See the Taylor Collection (1848–71) in the Quaker Collection of the Haverford College Library. Elizabeth Robeson Shoemaker later married Abraham Merritt Taylor of Burlington, New Jersey. Other relevant letters are in the Allinson Collection (1832–83), also at the Haverford College Library.

4. "A Journal of Cases, treated in Friends Asylum for the relief of persons deprived of the use of their reason. near Frankford Pa. vol. 6th" (28 December 1846– 28 October 1851), 10–11. Friends Hospital Archives.

5. For a discussion of phrenology, see Dain 1964, 61–63, 87–88, 162–63; Caplan and Caplan, 1969, 120–22. For a useful discussion of the influence of phrenology on Isaac Ray see John Starrett Hughes 1986, esp. 17–34.

6. David Uwins, *A Treatise on Those Disorders of the Brain and Nervous System, which are Usually Considered and Called Mental* (1833), quoted in Hunter and Macalpine 1963, 833.

7. For general discussions of both commitment law and the insanity defense, consult Applebaum and Kemp 1982, 343–354; Gleuck 1962; and Maeder 1985. Hughes (1986, 77–96) is especially helpful on the moral insanity issue.

8. As used, "Moral insanity" denotes a disease of the moral or emotional faculties

that usually results in alienation from loved ones. The Hinchman trial often confusingly joins this term to "Partial insanity," which technically is monomania or a depressed absorption with one topic. See Hinsie and Campbell 1960, 389–90.

Like many physicians, lawyers were hesitant to accept the term "moral insanity." Summarizing past views, Burrill (1851) said that "delusion is said to be the true test of sanity" (622). John Bouvier used Prichard in defining "moral insanity," but said that this is "a term used by medical men, which has not yet acquired much reputation in the courts" (1857, 188). Toward the end of the nineteenth century the term became more common but no more acceptable. In a footnote to his discussion of the term, John Huston Merrill, the editor of *The American and English Encyclopaedia of Law* 11 (1890) said that "the weight of modern authority is, that moral insanity is of itself insufficient to invalidate a civil act or excuse a criminal act" (112). The courts were obviously reluctant to accept a broad correlation between criminal character and insanity. A more modern writer on medical jurisprudence dismisses the term, saying, "It is fallacious to separate the purely intellectual mode of mental life from the conative-affective, and claim that the latter alone, operating in the ethical sphere, are diseased. . . ." (Glueck 1925, 337). Today, instead of "moral insanity" we might use terms like manic-depressive psychosis or psychopathic personality or even sociopathic personality. We discount a faculty psychology and see any disorder as symptomatic of a larger problem, yet the field of medical jurisprudence remains a confused one.

9. Chandler 1864, 124. In British law under the *parens patriae* power the king could act as guardian for lunatics. Following the American Revolution, this power passed to state legislatures and provided the basis of laws for involuntary commitment. The use of the *parens patriae* power, commonly traced to Shaw's Oakes decision, did not, however, negate due process. For a full discussion of these matters see "Developments in the Law. Civil Commitment of the Mentally Ill," *Harvard Law Review* 87 (1974): 1190–1406.

10. Levy 1957, 214. In forming his opinion, Shaw relied especially on the testimony of Isaac Ray. In remarks prophetic of the Hinchman case, Ray discussed the problems of trials involving individuals accused of being morally insane: "And so intimately connected are the ideas of insanity and delusion in the common mind, that it requires no little courage and confidence . . . to declare the existence of the former independently of the latter. The consequence of these erroneous views are often strikingly and painfully exhibited when a person thus affected becomes the object of a legal procedure. While he may be described by one as acute and methodical in his business and rational in his discourse, and believed to be perfectly sane; another will testify to the strangest freaks that ever a madman played and thus deduce the conviction of his insanity; while one represents him as social and kindly in his disposition, ready to assist and oblige and to accommodate himself to the varying humors of those about him, it will be testified by another that in his domestic relations his former cheerfulness has given way to gloom and moroseness, that equanimity of temper has been replaced by frequent gusts of passion, and that the warm affections, which spring from the relations of parent and child, husband and wife, have been transformed into indifference or hate. These are the cases that confound the wise and defy the scrutiny of the skillful, while they tempt the superficial and conceited to betray their ignorance, under the delusion of superior penetration; which tarnish many a professional reputation and expose even the pretentions of true science to popular mockery and derision" (Ray 1962, 139). In the fourth edition of his *Treatise* (1860) Ray said that the "evidence showed beyond a doubt, he [Hinchman] was violently and dangerously insane" (quoted in Deutsch 1949, 423).

11. In the period from 1850 to 1870 especially, British periodicals show numer-

ous attacks on the insanity plea and on the medical testimony supporting such pleas. See, for example, "Modern State Trials" (Anon, 1850a, 545–72), and "The Plea of Insanity in Trials for Murder" (Anon. 1859, 58–92).

12. See Fox 1971, 147–94. Cresson, the model for Herman Melville's figure of Nathan in *Clarel: A Poem and Pilgrimage in the Holy Land,* died in Jerusalem on 27 October 1860.

WORKS CITED

Collections

Friends Hospital Archives. Frankford, Pennsylvania
   Medical Records

Friends Historical Library. Swarthmore College
   Meeting Records

Library of the Religious Society of Friends. London
   Hodgkin Papers
   Southern Retreat Records

Library of the Retreat. York, England
   Eighteenth & Nineteenth Century Commentaries on Madness

"Minutes of Building Committee Roberts Vaux Clerk Friends Asylum 1813–1817."
   Transcribed by Kathryn W. Jones. Private Collection

Quaker Collection. Haverford College Library
   Archives of Friends Asylum (including managers' minutes, superintendents' jour-
      nals, minutes of contributors, visiting committee minutes, minutes of corpora-
      tion, annual reports)
   Seventeenth and Eighteenth Century Anti-Quakeriana
   Allinson Collection (1832–83) ∫ (Hinchman & Shoemaker Family
   Taylor Collection (1848–71)   (Correspondence)

University of York's Borthwick Institute of Historical Research. York, England
   Archives of York Retreat (including minute books, case books, visitors' records,
      Retreat correspondence, annual reports, records of York Retreat Centenary
      Celebration, Elizabeth Pumphrey's Recollections)
   Tuke Papers (William Tuke's personal correspondence)

Adair, James Makittrick
   1787 *A Philosophical and Medical Sketch of the Natural History of the Human Body
   and Mind.* Bath.
Addison, Joseph, and Richard Steele
   1965 *The Spectator.* Edited by Donald F. Bond. 5 vols. Oxford: Clarendon.
Aikin, M.
   1823 *Memoirs of Religious Impostors from the Seventh to the Nineteenth Century.*
   London.
Alexander, Franz G., and Sheldon T. Selesnick

1966 *The History of Psychiatry: an Evaluation of Psychiatric Thought and Practice from Prehistoric Times to The Present.* New York: Harper.

Anonymous

1661 *Semper Idem: or a Parallel betwixt the Ancient and Modern Phanatics.* London.

1675 *The Sad Effects of Cruelty Detected: Being an Impartial Account of the poor Woman, near Temple-Barr, lately tempted in her distraction to Make away her self.* London.

1806 *A Collection of the Epistles from the Yearly Meeting of Friends in London to the Quarterly and Monthly Meetings in Great Britain, Ireland and Elsewhere, from 1675 to 1805.* Baltimore.

1814 *Account of the Rise and Progress of the Asylum, Proposed to be Established, near Philadelphia, For the Relief of Persons Deprived of the Use of Their Reason, With an Abridged Account of the Retreat, A similar institution near York, in England.* Philadelphia: Kimber & Conrad.

1815 *First Report. Minutes of Evidence taken Before the Select Committee Appointed to Consider of Provision Being Made for the Better Regulation of Madhouses in England. Ordered by the House of Commons, to be Printed, 25 May.*

1824 *Collection de thèses soutenues à la Faculté de Médecine de Paris en 1824.* Vol. 4. Paris: Sorbonne.

1843 *Rules for the Observance of the Attendants upon the Patients at Friends Asylum, near Frankford. Adopted by the Managers Sixth Month 12, 1843.* Philadelphia.

1844–45 *Friends Weekly Intelligencer* 1:20 and 389.

1849. "The Hinchman Case." *The Monthly Law Reporter* 12:169–83.

1849b *The Hinchman Conspiracy Case. In Letters to the New York Home Journal. With an Abstract of the Evidence for the Defence, Furnishing a Complete Explanation of this Most Extraordinary Case.* Philadelphia: Stokes & Brother.

1849c *Speeches of Defendants' Counsel and the Charge of Judge Burnside. In the Case of Hichman vs. Richie et al.* Reported by Oliver Dyer and Dennis F. Murphy. Philadelphia.

1850a "Modern State Trials." *Blackwood's Magazine* 68 (November): 545–72.

1850b *Samuel S. Richie, et al. Plaintiffs in Error, Versus Morgan Hinchman sur Certificate from the Nisi Prius.* Paper Book. Philadelphia: Crissy and Markley.

1859 "The Plea of Insanity in Trials for Murder." *Dublin Review* 46 (March): 58–92.

1868 "A Modern Lettre De Cachet." *The Atlantic Monthly* 21:588–602.

1878a Obituary of Achille-Louis Foville. *Gazette Hebdomadaire de Médecine et de Chirurgie* 15:499–500.

1878b Obituary of Achille-Louis Foville. *The Medical Times and Gazette* 2:232.

1930 *Biographical Sketch of Charles S. Hinchman From Records and Recollections by Lydia S. Hinchman.* For Private Circulation.

1974 "Developments in the Law. Civil Commitment of the Mentally Ill." *Harvard Law Review* 87:1190–1406.

n.d. *Friends' Asylum for the Insane 1813–1913: A Descriptive Account from its Foundation. List of Managers and Officers from the Beginning, Facts and Events in its History with Appendix.* Philadelphia: John C. Winston Company.

Applebaum, Paul S. and Kathleen N. Kemp

1982 "The Evolution of Commitment Law in the Nineteenth Century." *Law and Human Behavior* 6:343–54.

Arnold, Thomas

1782–86 *Observations on the Nature, Kinds, Causes, and Prevention of Insanity, Lunacy, or Madness.* 2 vols. London.

Atkinson, Christopher
    1654 *The Sword of the Lord Drawn and Furbish'd against the Man of Sin.* London.
Bacon, Margaret H.
    1969 *The Quiet Rebels: The Story of the Quakers in America.* New York: Basic Books.
Baltzell, E. Digby
    1979 *Puritan Boston and Quaker Philadelphia: Two Protestant Ethics and the Spirit of Class Authority and Leadership.* New York: Free Press.
Barbour, Hugh
    1964 *The Quakers in Puritan England.* New Haven: Yale University Press.
Barbour, Hugh, and Arthur O. Roberts, eds.
    1973 *Early Quaker Writings 1650–1700.* Grand Rapids, Mich.: Erdmans.
Barclay, Robert.
    1676 *The Anarchy of the Ranters and Other Libertines.* London.
    1967 *Barclay's Apology in Modern English.* Edited by Dean Friday. Elberon, N.J.: Hemlock Press.
Battie, William
    1758 *A Treatise on Madness.* London.
Baxter, Richard
    1655 *The Quakers Catechism.* London.
Beck, William and T. Frederick Ball, eds.
    1869 *The London Friends Meeting: Showing the Rise of the Society of Friends in London: Its Progress, and the Development of Its Discipline; with Accounts of the Various Meeting-houses and Burial Grounds, their History and General Associations.* London.
Bennet, Thomas
    1733 *A Confutation of Quakerism.* London.
Bickford, J. A. R. and M. E. Bickford
    1976 *The Private Lunatic Asylums of the East Riding.* Beverley: East Yorkshire Local History Society.
Blake, William
    1966 *The Complete Writings of William Blake.* Ed. Geoffrey Keynes. London: Oxford University Press.
Blome, Richard
    1660 *The Fanatick History; or, an Exact Relation and Account of the Old Anabaptists, and New Quakers.* London.
Bockoven, J. Sanbourne
    1963 *Moral Treatment in American Psychiatry.* New York: Springer Publishing Company.
Boisen, Anton T.
    1936 *The Exploration of the Inner World: A Study of Mental Disorder and Religious Experience.* Chicago: Willet, Clark.
Bond, Earl
    1947 *Dr. Kirkbride and His Mental Hospital.* Philadelphia: J. B. Lippincott Company.
Bouvier, John
    1857 *A Law Dictionary.* 7th ed. 2 vols. Philadelphia: Child and Peterson.
Braceland, F. J.
    1972 *The Institute of Living: The Hartford Retreat, 1822–1972.* Hartford, Conn.: The Institute of Living.
Braithwaite, William C.
    1955 *The Beginnings of Quakerism.* 2d ed. Revised by Henry J. Cadbury. Cambridge: Cambridge University Press.

Brayshaw, A. Neave
1933   *The Personality of George Fox.* London: Allenson.
Brinton, Howard H.
1972   *Quaker Journals; Varieties of Religious Experience Among Friends.* Wallingford, Pa.: Pendle Hill Publications.
1973.   *The Religious Philosophy of Quakerism: the Beliefs of Fox, Barclay, and Penn as Based on the Gospel of John.* Wallingford, Pa.: Pendle Hill Publications.
Brown, David Paul
1849   *Speech of David Paul Brown in the Case of Hinchman vs. Richie, et al. Delivered on the Sixth of April (Good Friday), 1849.* Philadelphia: King and Baird.
Brown, Theodore M.
1974   "From Mechanism to Vitalism in Eighteenth-Century English Physiology." *Journal of the History of Biology* 7, no. 2: 179–216.
Bucknill, John Charles, and Daniel H. Tuke
1858   *A Manual of Psychological Medicine: Containing the History, Nosology, Description, Statistics, Diagnosis, Pathology, and Treatment of Insanity, With an Appendix of Cases.* London.
Bugg, Francis
1690   *Battering Rams Against New Rome: Contrasting a Farther Discovery of the Grand Hypocrite of the Leaders and Teachers of the People called Quakers.* London.
1696   *The Quakers Set in Their True Light.* London.
1698   *The Pilgrim's Progress from Quakerism to Christianity.* London.
Burrill, Alexander M.
1851a   *A New Law Dictionary and Glossary.* 2 Vols. New York: John S. Voorhees.
Burton, Robert
1927   *The Anatomy of Melancholy.* Ed. Floyd Dell and Paul Jordan-Smith. New York: Tudor.
Bynum, William F., Jr.
1981   "Rationales for Therapy in British Psychiatry, 1780–1835." *Madhouses, Mad-Doctors, and Madmen: The Social History of Psychiatry in the Victorian Era.* Edited by Andrew Scull. Philadelphia: University of Pennsylvania Press, 35–57.
Byrd, Max
1974   *Visits to Bedlam: Madness and Literature in the Eighteenth Century.* Columbia: University of South Carolina Press.
Cadbury, Henry J., ed.
1948   *George Fox's Book of Miracles.* Cambridge: Cambridge University Press.
Cadbury, William W.
1946   "Friends Hospital." *Friends Intelligencer* 103: 68–70.
Caplan, Ruth B. and Gerald Caplan
1969   *Psychiatry and the Community in Nineteenth-Century America.* New York: Basic Books.
Cecil, David
1969   *Melbourne* London: Pan Books.
Chandler, Peleg W., ed.
1864   *The Law Reporter.* 8 vols. Boston: Bradbury, Soden, and Company.
Collier, Howard E.
1944   "Then and Now: Miracles and Healings During the First Period of Quakerism." *Friends' Quarterly Examiner* 78: 280–288.
Coole, Benjamin
1712   *Religion and Reason United: By a Lover of His Country.* 2d ed. London.
Coutes, B. H.
1830   "Notice of the Life of Samuel Powel Griffitts." *The Friend* 3: 281–82.

Cox, Joseph Mason
  1806   *Practical Observations on Insanity.* 2d ed. London.
Crichton, Alexander
  1798   *An Inquiry into the Nature and Origin of Mental Derangement. Comprehend-
  ing a Concise System of the Physiology and Pathology of the Human Mind and a History
  of the Passions and their Effects.* 2 vols. London.
Crowther, Byron
  1811   *Practical Remarks on Insanity: to which is added A Commentary on the Dissection of the Brains of Maniacs; with some account of Diseases incident to the Insane.*
  London.
Crump, C. G., ed.
  1900   *The History of the Life of Thomas Ellwood.* New York: Putnam.
Cullen, William
  1789a   *First Lines of the Practice of Physic.* 4 vols. Edinburgh.
  1789b   *A Treatise of the Materia Medica.* 2 vols. Philadelphia.
  1793   *First Lines of the Practice of Physic.* 2 vols. New York.
Dain, Norman
  1964   *Concepts of Insanity in the United States, 1789–1865.* New Brunswick, N.J.:
  Rutgers University Press.
Dain, Norman, and Eric T. Carlson
  1960   "Milieu Therapy in the Nineteenth Century: Patient Care at the Friend's
  Asylum, Frankford, Pennsylvania 1817–1861." *The Journal of Nervous and Mental
  Disease* 131:277–90.
Davis, Joe Lee
  1943   "Mystical Versus Enthusiastic Sensibility." *Journal of the History of Ideas*
  4:301–19.
DePorte, Michael V.
  1974   *Nightmares and Hobbyhorses: Swift, Sterne, and Augustan Ideas of Madness.*
  San Marino, Calif.: Huntington Library.
Deutsch, Albert
  1949   *The Mentally Ill in America: A History of Their Care and Treatment from
  Colonial Times.* 2d ed. New York: Columbia University Press.
Digby, Anne
  1985   *Madness, Morality and Medicine: A Study of the York Retreat 1796–1914.*
  Cambridge: Cambridge University Press.
Doherty, Robert W.
  1967   *The Hicksite Separation: A Sociological Analysis of Religious Schism in Early
  Nineteenth-Century America.* New Brunswick, N.J.: Rutgers University Press.
Donnelly, Michael
  1983   *Managing the Mind. A Study of Medical Psychology in Early Nineteenth-
  Century Britain.* London: Tavistock Publications.
Doob, Penelope B. R.
  1974   *Nebuchadnezzar's Children: Conventions of Madness in Middle English Literature.* New Haven, Conn.: Yale University Press.
Dove, John
  1756a   *An Eassay on Inspiration: or an Attempt to Shew that the Pretences of the
  ancient and the modern Zamzummin, to that Ray of Divinity, were, and are, Decep-
  tions.* London.
  1756b   *Plain Truth: or, Quakerism Unmask'd.* London.
Earle, Pliny
  1898   *Memoirs of Pliny Earle, M.D., With Extracts from His Diary and Letters*

(1830–92) and Selections from His Professional Writings (1839–91). Edited by F. B. Sanborn. Boston.

Eaton, Leonard K.
1977 *New England Hospitals, 1790–1833.* Ann Arbor: University of Michigan Press.

Elys, Edmund
1695 *Reflections upon a Pamphlet, Entituled, John Elliotts' Saving Grace in all Men Proved to be No Grace and His Increated Being in All a Great Nothing.* N.p..

Emerson, G.
1827 *Biographical Memoir of Dr. Samuel Powel Griffitts.* Philadelphia.

Evans, Charles
1839 *Account of the Asylum for the Relief of Persons Deprived of the Use of their Reason, Near Frankford, Pennsylvania: With the Statistics of the Institution from Its Foundation to the 31st 12th Month, 1838.* Philadelphia.

Evans, Theophilus
1752 *The History of Modern Enthusiasm, from the Reformation to the Present Times.* London.

Falconer, William
1788 *A Dissertation on the Influence of the Passions upon Disorders of the Body.* London.

Farmer, Ralph
1655 *The Great Mysteries of Godliness and Ungodliness.* London.
1657 *Satan Inthron'd in his Chair of Pestilence, or, Quakerism in its Exaltation.* London.

Figlio, Karl M.
1975 "Theories of Perception and the Physiology of Mind in the Late Eighteenth Century." *History of Science* 13 : 177–212.

Flood, James J.
1963 "A Catholic Critique of the Quaker Doctrine of the Inner Light." Ph.D. dissertation. Rome: Pontifical Gregorian University.

Forbush, Bliss
1956. *Elias Hicks: Quaker Liberal.* New York: Columbia University Press.
1968 *Moses Sheppard: Quaker Philanthropist of Baltimore.* Philadelphia: J. P. Lippincott Company.
1971 *The Sheppard & Enoch Pratt Hospital: 1853–1970. A History.* Philadelphia: J. P. Lippincott Company.

Fowler, Thomas
1785 *Medical Reports of the Effects of Tobacco Principally with regard to its Diuretic Quality, in the Cure of Dropsies and Dysuries: together with some observations, on the use of clysters of tobacco, in the treatment of the colic.* London.

Fox, Frank
1971 "Quaker, Shaker, Rabbi: Warder Cresson, The Story of a Philadelphia Mystic." *The Pennsylvania Magazine of History and Biography* 95 April : 147–94.

Fox, George
1659 *The Great Mistery of the Great Whore Unfolded and Antichrist's Kingdom Revealed unto Destruction.* London.
1667 *Something in Answer to Lodowick Muggleton's Book, which he calls the Quakers' Neck Broken.* London.
1825 *Selections from the Epistles, &c. of George Fox.* Edited by Samuel Tuke. York.
1831 *A Collection of Many Select and Christian Epistles, Letters and Testimonies.* 2 vols. Philadelphia.

1911   *The Journal of George Fox.* Edited by Norman Penney. Cambridge: Cambridge University Pres.
1925   *The Short Journal and Itinerary Journals.* Edited by Norman Penney. Cambridge: Cambridge University Press.
1975   *The Journal of George Fox.* Edited by John L. Nickalls. London: London Yearly Meeting of the Religious Society of Friends.
Foucault, Michel
1965   *Madness and Civilization: A History of Insanity in the Age of Reason.* Translated by Richard Howard. New York: Vintage Books.
Frost, J. William
1973   *The Quaker Family in Colonial America: A Portrait of the Society of Friends.* New York: St. Martin's.
Fry, Elizabeth
1847   *Memoirs of the Life of Elizabeth Fry With Extracts from Her Journal and Letters.* Edited by Katharine Fry and Rachel Elizabeth Cresswell. 2 vols. London.
Gilpin, John
1653   *The Quakers Shaken: Or, A Fire-brand snach'd out of the Fire.* London.
Glover, Mary
1984   *The Retreat York: An Early Quaker Experiment in the Treatment of Mental Illness.* Edited by Janet R. Glover. York: William Sessions.
Glueck, Sheldon
1925   *Mental Disorder and the Criminal Law: A Study in Medico-Sociological Jurisprudence with an Appendix of State Legislation and Interpretive Decisions.* Boston: Little, Brown and Company.
1962   *Law and Psychiatry: Cold War or Entente Cordiale?* Baltimore: Johns Hopkins Press.
Goffman, Erving
1961   *Asylums: Essays on the Social Situation of Mental Patients and Other Inmates.* New York: Anchor-Doubleday.
Gould, Stephen Jay
1981   *The Mismeasure of Man.* New York: Norton.
Green, Thomas
1755   *A Dissertation on Enthusiasm; Shewing the Danger of its late Increase, and the great Mischiefs it has occasioned, both in ancient and modern Times.* London.
Grob, Gerald N.
1973   *Mental Institutions in America: Social Policy to 1875.* New York: Free Press.
1978   *Edward Jarvis and the Medical World of Nineteenth-Century America.* Knoxville: University of Tennesseee Press.
1983   *Mental Illness and American Society, 1875–1940.* Princeton, N.J. Princeton University Press.
Hallywell, Henry
1673   *An Account of Familism as it is revived and propagated by the Quakers shewing the Dangerousness of their Tenents, & Their Inconsistency with the Principles of Common Reason & the Delarations of Holy Scripture.* London.
Harper, Andrew
1789   *A Treatise on the Real Cause and Cure of Insanity; in which the Nature and distinctions of this Disease are Fully Explained and the Treatment Established on new Principles.* London.
Hartley, David
1749   *Observations on Man, His Frame, His Duty, and His Expectations.* London.
Haslam, John
1798   *Observations on Insanity.* London.

1809   *Observations on Madness and Melancholy: Including Practical Remarks on those Diseases on Dissection*. 2d ed. London.

Higgins, Catherine
1986   "Out of Mind: The Institutionalized Insane in Nineteenth-Century Philadelphia." Ph.D. dissertation. Bryn Mawr College.

Hill, Christopher
1972   *The World Turned Upside Down: Radical Ideas During the English Revolution*. New York: Viking.
1984   *The Experience of Defeat: Milton and Some Contemporaries*. New York: Viking Penguin.

Hinsie, Leland E. and Robert Jean Campbell
1960   *Psychiatric Dictionary*. 3d ed. New York: Oxford University Press.

Hobbes, Thomas
1651   *Leviathan, or the Matter, Forme, and Power of a Common-Wealth Ecclesiasticall and Civil*. London.

Hodgkin, Thomas
1828   *An Essay on Medical Education, Read Before the Physical Society of Guy's Hospital and at the First Meeting of the Session 1827–28*. London.

Hofstadter, Richard
1944   *Social Darwinism in American Thought*. Philadelphia: University of Pennsylvania Press.

Holmes, Bayard
1911   *The Friends of the Insane: The Soul of Medical Education and Other Essays*. Cincinnati: Lancet-Clinic Publishing Company.

Hughes, John Starrett
1986   *In the Law's Darkness: Isaac Ray and the Medical Jurisprudence of Insanity in Nineteenth-Century America*. New York: Oceans Publications.

Hughson, D.
1814   *The Life of James Nayler, a Phanatic Enthusiast, who profanely and blasphemously personated Jesus Christ, at London, Bristol, &C*. London.

Hume, David
1888 (reprint 1965)   *A Treatise of Human Nature (1739)*. Ed. L. A. Selby-Biggs. Oxford at Clarendon Press.

Hunt, Harold Capper
1937   "The Life of William Tuke." *Journal of the Friends' Historical Society* 34:3–18.
1932   *A Retired Habitation: A History of the Retreat, York*. London: H. K. Lewis and Co.

Hunter, Richard
1966   "Thomas Hodgkin, Samuel Tuke and John Conolly." *Guy's Hospital Reports* 115:263–67.

Hunter, Richard, and Ida Macalpine
1969   *George III and the Mad-Business*. New York: Pantheon Books.
1974   *Psychiatry for the Poor: 1851 Colney Hatch Asylum Friern Hospital 1973. A Medical and Social History*. London: Dawson.

Hunter, Richard, and Ida Macalpine, eds.
1963   *Three Hundred Years of Psychiatry 1535–1860*. London: Oxford University Press.

Huntington, Frank C., Jr.
1982   "Quakerism During the Commonwealth: The Experience of the Light." *Quaker History* 71:69–68.

Ignatieff, Michael
    1978   *A Just Measure of Pain: Penitentiaries in the Industrial Revolution in England.*
    New York: Pantheon.
Jacobi, Maximilian
    1841   *On the Construction and Management of Hospitals for the Insane, With a
    Particular Notice of the Institution at Siegburg.* Translated by John Kitching.
    London.
James, William
    1902   *The Varieties of Religious Experience: A Study in Human Nature.* New York:
    Random.
Jarvis, Edward
    1971   *Insanity and Idiocy in Massachusetts: Report of the Commission on Lunacy,
    1855.* Critical introduction by Gerald N. Grob. Cambridge: Harvard University
    Press.
Jeffrey, Francis
    1807   "Thomas Clarkson's *A Portraiture of Quakerism.*" Review in *Edinburgh
    Review* 10 : 85–102.
Johnson, Samuel
    1958   *The History of Rasselas, Prince of Abissinia.* In *Samuel Johnson's Rasselas, Poems
    and Selected Prose,* edited by Bertrand H. Bronson. New York: Rinehart.
Jones, Kathleen
    1972   *A History of the Mental Health Services.* London: Routledge and Kegan Paul.
Jorns, Auguste
    1931   *The Quakers as Pioneers in Social Work.* Translated by Thomas Kite Brown.
    New York: Macmillan.
Kass, Amalie M. and Edward H.
    1988   *Perfecting the World: The Life and Times of Dr. Thomas Hodgkin, 1798–1866.*
    Boston : Harcourt Brace Jovanovich.
Kass, E. H.
    1966   "Thomas Hodgkin, Physician and Social Scientist." *Guy's Hospital Reports*
    115 : 269–80.
Knapp, Samuel L.
    1834   *The Life of Thomas Eddy, Comprising an Extensive Correspondence with Many
    of the Most Distinguished Philosophers and Philanthropists of This and Other Countries.*
    New York.
Knox, R. A.
    1950   *Enthusiasm: A Chapter in the History of Religion with Special Reference to the
    XVII and XVIII Centuries.* Oxford: Clarendon.
Kuhn, Thomas S.
    1962   *The Structure of Scientific Revolutions.* Chicago: University of Chicago Press.
Laing, R. D.
    1959   *The Divided Self: An Existential Study in Sanity and Madness.* London:
    Tavistock Publications.
    1967   *The Politics of Experience.* New York: Pantheon.
Lawrence, Christopher
    1979   "The Nervous System and Society in the Scottish Enlightenment." In
    Natural Order: Historical Studies of Scientific Culture, edited by Barry Barnes and
    Steven Shapin. Beverly Hills, Calif.: Sage, 19–40.
Leslie, Charles
    1697   *The Snake in the Grass: or, Satan Transformed into an Angel of Light, discover-
    ing the deep and unsuspected Subtility which is Couched under the pretended simplicity, of
    many of the Principal Leaders of those people call'd Quakers.* 2d ed. London.

Levy, Leonard W.
 1957   *The Law of the Commonwealth and Chief Justice Shaw: The Evolution of American Law.* Cambridge: Harvard University Press.
Lewis, John
 1759   *Brief Observations on a Pamphlet Intituled The History of Modern Enthusiam, from the Reformation to the Present times; so far as relates to the People called Quakers.* London.
Locke, John
 1958   *The Reasonableness of Christianity with a Discourse of Miracles and Part of a Third Letter Concerning Toleration.* Edited by I. T. Kamsey. Stanford: Stanford University Press.
 1975   *An Essay Concerning Human Understanding.* Edited by Peter H. Nidditch. Oxford: Clarendon.
Macaulay, Thomas Babington
 n.d.   *The History of England from the Accession of James II.* 5 vols. New York: Literature Club.
MacDonald, Michael
 1982   *Mystical Bedlam: Madness, Anxiety, and Healing in Seventeenth-Century England.* Cambridge: Cambridge University Press.
Maeder, Thomas
 1985   *Crime and Madness: The Origins and Evolution of the Insanity Defense.* New York: Harper and Row.
Marietta, Jack
 1984   *The Reformation of American Quakerism, 1748–83.* Philadelphia: University of Pennsylvania Press.
McGovern, Constance M.
 1985   *Social Origins of the American Psychiatric Profession.* Hanover, N.H.: University Press of New England.
Merrill, John Houston, ed.
 1890   *The American and English Encyclopedia of Law.* Vol. 11. New York: Edward Thomson Company.
Midelfort, H.C. Erik
 1980   "Madness and Civilization in Early Modern Europe: A Reappraisal of Michel Foucault." In *After The Reformation: Essays in Honor of J. H. Hexter,* edited by Barbara C. Malament. Philadelphia: University of Pennsylvania Press, 247–65.
Miller, Perry
 1965   *The Life of the Mind in America: From the Revolution to the Civil War.* New York: Harcourt Brace and World.
Monro, John
 1758   *Remarks on Dr. Battie's Treatise on Madness.* London.
Mullahy, Patrick
 1970   *Psychoanalysis and Interpersonal Psychiatry: The Contributions of Harry Stack Sullivan.* New York: Science House.
Nuttall, Geoffrey F.
 1948   *Studies in Christian Enthusiasm: Illustrated from Early Quakerism.* Wallingford, Pa.: Pendle Hill Publications.
 1952   *Early Quaker Letters from the Swarthmore MSS to 1660.* Calendared, Indexed and Annotated by Geoffrey F. Nuttall. Haverford College Copy.
 1961   *Howel Harris 1717–73: The Last Enthusiast.* Cardiff: University of Wales Press.
 1967   *The Puritan Spirit: Essays and Addresses.* London: Epworth Press.
 n.d.   *James Nayler: A Fresh Approach.* London: Friends Historical Society.

Page, Charles W.
   1912–13 "Dr. Eli Todd and the Hartford Retreat." *The American Journal of Insanity* 69:761–85.
Pagel, Walter
   1982 *Joan Baptista Von Helmont: Reformer of Science and Medicine.* Cambridge: Cambridge University Press.
Pargeter, William
   1792 *Observations on Maniacal Disorders.* Reading, Pa.
Parry-Jones, William Ll.
   1972 *The Trade in Lunacy: A Study of Private Madhouses in England in the Eighteenth and Nineteenth-Centuries.* London: Routledge and Kegan Paul.
Penn, William
   1670 *The Great Case of Liberty of Conscience.* London.
   1694 *Preface to Fox's Journal.* London.
   1957 *The Witness of William Penn.* Edited by Frederick B. Tolles and E. Gordon Alderfer. New York: MacMillan.
Perry, Helen Swick.
   1981 *Psychiatrist of America: The Life of Harry Stack Sullivan.* Cambridge: Harvard University Press, Belknap Press.
Pinel, Philippe
   1806 *A Treatise on Insanity.* Translated by D. D. Davis. London.
Prichard, James Cowles
   1835 *A Treatise on Insanity and Other Disorders Attacking the Mind.* London.
Prynne, William
   1655 *The Quakers Unmasked, and clearly detected to be but the Spawn of Romish Frogs, Jesuites, and Franciscan Freers; sent from Rome to seduce the intoxicated Giddy-headed English Nation.* London.
Rather, L. J.
   1965 *Mind and Body in Eighteenth-Century Medicine: A Study Based on Jerome Gaub's De Regimine Mentis.* Berkeley and Los Angeles: University of California Press.
Ray, Isaac
   1962 *A Treatise on the Medical Jurisprudence of Insanity (1838).* Edited by Winfred Overholser. Cambridge: Harvard University Press.
Reid, Thomas
   1764 *An Inquiry into the Human Mind, on the Principles of Common Sense.* Edinburgh.
   1785 *Essays on the Intellectual Powers of Man.* Edinburgh.
   1788 *Essays on the Active Powers of the Human Mind.* Edinburgh.
Robinson, Nicholas
   1729 *A New System of the Spleen, Vapours, and Hypochondriack Melancholy, Wherein all the Decays of the Nerves, and Lownesses of the Spirits, are Mechanically Accounted For.* London.
Roby, David S.
   1982 "Pioneer of Moral Treatment: Isaac Bonsall & the Early Years of Friends Asylum as Recorded in Bonsall's Diaries 1817–1823." Friends Hospital.
Rothman, David J.
   1971 *The Discovery of the Asylum: Social Order and Disorder in the New Republic.* Boston: Little, Brown.
Rush, Benjamin
   1970 *An Eulogium in Honor of the Late Dr. William Cullen, Professor of the Practice of Physic in the University of Edinburgh; delivered before the College of Physicians of*

Philadelphia, on the 9th of July, agreeably to their vote of the 4th of May, 1970. Published by order of the College of Physicians. Philadelphia.
1827 *Medical Inquiries and Observations Upon the Diseases of the Mind.* 3d ed. Philadelphia.
Ryan, Edward
1793 *The History of the Effects of Religion on Mankind.* 2 vols. London.
Scattergood, Thomas
1845 *Memoirs of Thomas Scattergood, Late of Philadelphia. A Minister of the Gospel of Christ. Compiled for the American Friends Library, Chiefly from his Notes and Letters, by William Evans and Thomas Evans.* London.
1874 *Journal of the Life and Religious Labors of Thomas Scattergood, A Minister of the Gospel in the Society of Friends.* Philadelphia.
Schofield, Robert E.
1969 *Mechanism and Materialism: British Natural Philosophy in an Age of Reason.* Princeton: Princeton University Press.
Scull, Andrew T.
1979 *Museums of Madness: The Social Organization of Insanity in Nineteenth-Century England.* New York: St. Martin's.
1981a "Moral Treatment Reconsidered: Some Sociological Comments on an Episode in the History of British Psychiatry." In *Madhouses, Mad-Doctors, and Madmen: The Social History of Psychiatry in the Victorian Era,* edited by Andrew Scull. Philadelphia: University of Pennsylvania Press, 105–118.
1981b "The Discovery of the Asylum Revisited: Lunacy Reform in the New American Republic." In *Madhouses, Mad-Doctors, and Madmen: The Social History of Psychiatry in the Victorian Era.* Edited by Andrew Scull, Philadelphia: University of Pennsylvania Press, 144–65.
Sessions, William K. and E. Margaret Sessions
1971 *The Tukes of York in the Seventeenth, Eighteenth and Nineteenth Centuries.* York: Ebor Press.
Shaftesbury, Earl of (Anthony Ashley Cooper)
1714 *Characteristicks of Men, Manners, Opinions, and Times.* 2d ed. London.
Sharp, Isaac
1901 "The Society of Friends and Care of the Insane." *The Friend* 41: 714–15.
Sherlock. R.
1654 *The Quakers Wilde Questions Objected Against the Ministers of Gospel, and many Sacred Acts and Offices of Religion with Brief Answers thereunto. Together with a Discourse of the Holy Spirit, his Impressions and workings of the Souls of Men.* London.
Shryock, Richard Harrison
1960 *Medicine and Society in America 1660–1860.* New York: New York University Press.
Skultans, Vieda.
1975 *Madness and Morals: Ideas on Insanity in the Nineteenth Century.* London: Routledge.
1979 *English Madness: Ideas on Insanity, 1580–1890.* London: Routledge.
Smith, Alexander.
1840 "James Douglas' *On the Philosophy of the Mind.*" Review in *Edinburgh Review* 50: 196–205.
Smith, Joseph
1873 *Bibliotheca Anti-Quakeriana.* 5 vols. London.
Smith, Patrick
1740 *A Preservative Against Quakerism, by Way of a Conference between a Minister and his Parishioner.* 2d ed. London.

Smith, Sydney
   1814   "Samuel Tuke's *Description of the Retreat.*" Review in *Edinburgh Review* 23:189–98.
Snell, Beatrice Saxon, ed.
   1937   *The Minute Book of the Monthly Meeting of the Society of Friends for the Upperside of Buckinghamshire 1669–90.* Buckinghamshire: Hague & Gill.
Stewart, Dugald
   1792–1827   *Elements of the Philosophy of the Human Mind.* 3 vols. London.
Swift, Jonathan
   1958   *A Tale of A Tub.* Ed. A. C. Guthkelch and D. Nicol Smith. 2d ed. Oxford: Clarendon.
Szasz, Thomas
   1961   *The Myth of Mental Illness: Foundation of a Theory of Personal Conduct.* New York: Dell.
   1970   *The Manufacture of Madness: A Comparative Study of the Inquisition and Mental Health Movement.* New York: Harper.
Szasz, Thomas S., ed.
   1974   *The Age of Madness: The History of Involuntary Mental Hospitalization Presented in Selected Texts.* New York: Jason Aronson.
Taylor, E. E.
   1946   "The Tukes: Tea Dealers and Reformers." *Friends Quarterly Examiner* 80:3–7.
Thomas, Keith
   1971   *Religion and the Decline of Magic.* New York: Scribner's.
Tolles, Frederick B.
   1960   *Quakers and the Atlantic Culture.* New York: Macmillan.
Tomes, Nancy
   1984   *A Generous Confidence: Thomas Story Kirkbride and the Art of Asylum-Keeping, 1840–83.* Cambridge: Cambridge University Press.
Tucker, Susie I.
   1972   *Enthusiasm: A Study in Semantic Change.* Cambridge: Cambridge University Press.
Tuke, Daniel Hack
   1882   *Chapters in the History of the Insane in the British Isles.* London.
Tuke, Henry
   1823   *The Principles of Religion, As Professed by the Society of Christians, usually called Quakers; Written for the Instruction of their Youth, and for the Information of Strangers.* York.
Tuke, Samuel
   1964   *Description of the Retreat: An Institution Near York for Insane Persons of the Society of Friends. Containing an Account of its Origin and Progress, the Modes of Treatment, and a Statement of Cases (1813).* Edited by Richard Hunter and Ida Macalpine. London: Dawsons of Pall Mall.
   1828   *A Sketch of the Origin, Progress, and Present State of the Retreat, An Institution Near York, For the Reception of Persons Afflicted with Disorders of the Mind, Among the Society of Friends.* York.
   1836   "A Letter to John Wilkinson on some Statements Contained in his letter of resignation of membership in the religious Society of Friends." 2d. ed. London: Darton and Harvey.
   1860   *Memoirs of Samuel Tuke.* 2 vols. York.
Trueblood, D. Elton
   1968   *Robert Barclay.* New York: Harper.

Van Atta, Kim, et al.
1976 "An Account Surrounding the Origin of Friends Hospital and a Brief Description of the Early Years of Friends Asylum, 1817–20." Philadelphia.

Vann, Richard.
1969 *Social Development of English Quakerism 1655–1755*. Cambridge: Harvard University Press.

Von Frankenberg, Abraham.
[1644] 1677 *A Warning Against the Deceit of Setting Up Man's Reason as Judge in Spiritual Matters*. Translated by Stephen Crisp. N.p.

Walker, D. P.
1982 *Unclean Spirits: Possession and Exorcism in France and England in the Late Sixteenth and Early Seventeenth Centuries*. Philadelphia: University of Pennsylvania Press.

Wain, John
1974 *Samuel Johnson*. New York: Viking Press.

Waln, Robert, Jr.
1825 *An Account of the Asylum for the Insane, Established by the Society of Friends, Near Frankford, In the Vicinity of Philadelphia*. Philadelphia.

Watts, Frederick and Henry J. Sergeant.
1867 *Reports of Cases Adjudged in the Supreme Court of Pennsylvania*. Vol. 6. Philadelphia: George T. Bisel Company.

Whitehead, George.
1674 *Enthusiasm Above Atheism: or, Divine Inspiration and Immediate Illumination [by God Himself] Asserted*. N.p.

Whitehead, George and William Penn.
1671 *A Serious Apology for the Principles & Practices of the People call'd Quakers*. London.

Whytt, Robert
1751 *An Essay on the vital and Other Involuntary Motions of Animals*. Edinburgh.

Whytt, Robert
1765 *Observations on the Nature, Causes and Cure of those Disorders which have been called Nervous, Hypochondriac, or Hysteric, to which are prefixed some Remarks on the Sympathy of the Nerves*. Edinburgh.

Wilks, Samuel and G. T. Bettany
1892 *A Biographical History of Guy's Hospital*. London: Ward, Lock, Bowden.

Willey, Basil
1953 *The Seventeenth Century Background: Studies in the Thought of the Age in Relation to Poetry*. New York: Anchor-Doubleday.

Willis, Thomas
[1667] 1681 *An Essay of the Pathology of the Brain and Nervous Stock*. Translated by S. Pordage. London.

Wyeth, Joseph
1699 *Anguis Flagellatus: or A Switch for the Snake, Being an Answer to the Third and Last Edition of the Snake in the Grass*. London.

Zilboorg, Gregory
1941 *A History of Medical Psychology*. New York: Norton.

INDEX